EISENHOWER
VERSUS
MONTGOMERY

EISENHOWER VERSUS MONTGOMERY

The Continuing Debate

G. E. Patrick Murray

PRAEGER

Westport, Connecticut
London

D
756.3
M87
1996

Library of Congress Cataloging-in-Publication Data

Murray, G. E. Patrick.
　　Eisenhower versus Montgomery : the continuing debate / G. E.
　Patrick Murray.
　　　　p.　　cm.
　　Includes bibliographical references and index.
　　ISBN 0–275–94795–5 (alk. paper)
　　1. Eisenhower, Dwight D. (Dwight David), 1890–1969.　2. Montgomery
　of Alamein, Bernard Law Montgomery, Viscount, 1887–1976.　3. World
　War, 1939–1945—Campaigns—Western Front.　4. Generals—United
　States—Biography.　5. Marshals—Great Britain—Biography.
　I. Title.
　D756.3.M87　　　1996
　940.54′21—dc20　　　　　95–42504

British Library Cataloguing in Publication Data is available.

Library of Congress Catalog Card Number: 95–42504
ISBN: 0–275–94795–5

First published in 1996

Praeger Publishers, 88 Post Road West, Westport, CT 06881
An imprint of Greenwood Publishing Group, Inc.

Printed in the United States of America

∞™

The paper used in this book complies with the
Permanent Paper Standard issued by the National
Information Standards Organization (Z39.48–1984).

10 9 8 7 6 5 4 3 2 1

To my two mothers:

Mary Clementine Carter Murray (1918-1950)

Mary Jean Molyneaux Murray (1922-1993)

Contents

Acknowledgments

This book originated from questions raised by Lieutenant Colonel Roger Cirillo, USA, Department of the Army, Center of Military History (CMH), and benefited from his knowledge of both the campaign in northwest Europe, 1944-1945, and the operational art. At Valley Forge Military College I wish to acknowledge the assistance of the late Colonel Harold Fraley, USA (Ret.), Acting Superintendent, Valley Forge Military Academy and College; Mrs. Anna Bullock, Assistant to the Superintendent; Lieutenant Colonel Donald S. Rowe, USA (Ret.), Dean; Lieutenant Colonel Samuel H. Wrightson, USA (Ret.), Assistant Dean; Colonel Victor C. Infortuna, VFMC; Colonel Charles W. Pollock, VFMC; Lieutenant Colonel Philip W. Townsend, Jr., VFMA, Librarian, May H. Baker Memorial Library; Major Jean L. Smith, VFMA; Major Walter R. Johnson, VFMA: Major Maria Brooks, VFMC; and Captain John Hogencamp, VFMC. I would like to thank the following students in History 205: Federico Cubas; Sean Gysen; Chris Matta; Chris Nelson; Alfredo Torres; and Tim Webb.

The following archivists facilitated my research: Herbert Pankratz of the Eisenhower Library, Abilene, Kansas; Will Mahony and the late Ed Reese of the Modern Military Records Division, National Archives and Records Service, Washington, D. C.; Dr. Richard J. Sommers, Archivist-Historian, and David Keogh at the United States Army Military History Institute, Carlisle Barracks, Pennsylvania; Simon Robbins and Phil Reed, the Imperial War Museum, Lambeth, London; Peter Murton, the Royal Air Force Museum, Hendon, London; Richard Taylor, the Liddell Hart Center for Military Archives, King's College, London. I would also like to thank the staff of the Public Record Office, Kew, London, the British Museum, Main Reading Room, and the British Newspaper Library, Collindale, London.

In London my thanks go to the Keeper of the Department of Documents at the Imperial War Museum, Roderick W. A. Suddaby; to the Montgomery Collections Committee of the Imperial War Museum's Trustees, which allowed access to the

Montgomery Papers; and to the present Viscount Montgomery of Alamein, CBE, who permitted me to quote from his father's papers. I must also acknowledge the Trustees of the Liddell Hart Center for Military Archives, King's College, for permission to quote from the Alanbrooke, Gale, Ismay, and Liddell Hart papers. Finally, I acknowledge the permission of Her Majesty's Stationery Office to quote from Crown copyrighted documents housed in the Public Record Office.

The following individuals also played a part in this book and deserve recognition: Jeremy Burke; Deborah Ann Carr; Lieutenant Colonel Carlo D'Este, USA (Ret.); Dr. David Hogan, CMH; Mrs. Jean Anne Linder; Mrs. Kay Murray; Dr. Forrest C. Pogue; Major Dale E. Wilson, Ph.D., USA (Ret.); and Samuel B. Wilson. At Temple University, I want to thank: Dr. James Hilty, Dr. Waldo Heinrichs, Dr. Russell F. Weigley, and Dr. Frank Weber. Dr. Donald Frazier prepared the maps. At Praeger I wish to thank my editors, Dan Eades and Liz Leiba.

My wife, Jacqué, always encouraged me and was a single parent while I worked; someday I may be able to repay her. My daughters Thea and Meg listened while their father talked about Eisenhower and Montgomery. My father, John R. Murray, fostered my research and inspired my effort.

Introduction

Among the more celebrated trials of the Anglo-American coalition leadership of World War II stands the relationship between General Dwight D. Eisenhower and Field Marshal Sir Bernard L. Montgomery. Throughout the campaign in northwest Europe, 1944-1945, Eisenhower and Montgomery disagreed over the invasion of southern France in the summer, opening Antwerp to ship traffic in the fall and leaving Berlin to the Soviets in the spring. However, beginning in August 1944 their most famous argument concerned the direction and command of the Allied advance on the Rhine. Eisenhower favored advancing on the Ruhr, the industrial heart of western Germany, both north and south of the Ardennes plateau, on what came to be called a broad front, while Montgomery favored a single, northern line of attack, the so-called single thrust. *Ike finally got to France*

On 1 September 1944 Eisenhower assumed operational command of the ground forces of the Allied Expeditionary Force from then Field Marshal Montgomery, who had commanded the ground forces in the landing and fighting in Normandy. Two weeks later, on 15 September 1944, Eisenhower assumed command of the Southern Group of Armies, which had landed in southern France in mid-August; Eisenhower was then in operational command of three army groups. For the next four months, Montgomery leveled steady criticism at Eisenhower's command setup, and pursued a campaign to have himself or Lieutenant General Omar N. Bradley, commanding general of the United States 12th Army Group, named ground forces commander.

For fifty years the Anglo-American debate over strategy and command in northwest Europe, 1944-1945, has settled into a nationalistic rut of one-upmanship. Proponents on either side of the Atlantic give short shrift to the legitimacy of logic in the strategic and command arguments of the other side. Too often the nationalistic differences in waging war are dismissed as merely quaint rather than an integral part of any coalition, and questions of national sovereignty have been viewed emotionally.

In an attempt to understand how this argument assumed its present shape this book examines what the postwar memoirs said about the issue in order of publication. It considers the postwar memoirs as primary sources, along with several key official histories that contained many primary sources, and compares them one to another and to the contemporary record as detailed in official documents and headquarters diaries as of 1944-1945. Contemporary opinion will speak for itself, in the form of the books as published, the opinions available in documents but omitted, and the turmoil created among participants. After reading these memoirs, what readers knew was not necessarily the war itself but rather what the books said about the war. Furthermore, most readers did not follow the debate into the more objective official histories; therefore the postwar memoirs dominated what the general public knew about the issue.

Remarkable was the postwar memoir that did not have an ax to grind in the context of the author's wartime experiences, previously published works, and position at the time of publication. Each memoir made an impression like a stone skipped in a lake, sending out concentric circles. Subsequent memoirs had to deal with the allegations made by the previous works, and as time went by the general reader was left with a maze of conflicting opinions.

At the root of the conflict were the two principal commanders themselves. As much as their strategies differed, so too were Montgomery and Eisenhower as unlike as men could be. The American was physically larger, outgoing, and in his spare time liked to play cards with his close friends or headquarters' confidants. A staff officer for most of his career, Eisenhower had a management style that sought consensus and compromise, even on strategic questions. Eisenhower smoked, drank and stayed up late, whereas Montgomery abstained from tobacco and alcohol and went to bed at 9:30 P.M. A troop commander for most of his career, Montgomery was physically smaller and single-minded. Living at a forward tactical head-quarters, he wrote all his directives, which he delivered to his staff officers for them to work out the details. Sending his chief of staff to important meetings, Montgomery gave Americans the impression that he was snubbing Eisenhower. Montgomery justified such behavior by his belief that it was the duty of the senior commander to go forward to his subordinates. In his spare time, Montgomery wrote didactic military pamphlets.[1]

In fact, Montgomery traveled to Eisenhower's headquarters once during the war, on 5 October 1944, because his superior, the Chief of the Imperial General Staff (CIGS), Field Marshal Sir Alan Brooke, was in attendance.[2] Asymmetric contact between SHAEF (Supreme Headquarters Allied Expeditionary Force) and its British and American army groups skewed the conduct of the campaign as well as its historical record. For example, Eisenhower met with Bradley three times more often than he did with Montgomery, which became an issue between governments, following the Yalta Conference of February 1945.

Relations between the two men were never better than strained. Montgomery's repeated questioning of his command led to Eisenhower's threat, during the Battle of the Bulge, to take their differences to the Combined Chiefs of Staff (CCS), made up of the respective service chiefs of both Great Britain and the United

States. Almost certainly, the result would have been Montgomery's dismissal and the embarrassment of the British as the coalition's less powerful partner.

During the war Montgomery's repeated criticism convinced Eisenhower and Bradley, as well as the Chief of Staff of the United States Army General George C. Marshall, that Montgomery was primarily motivated by issues of command and operational control. Moreover, ground forces command or temporary operational control almost always coincided with the main effort, or primary thrust. The supreme commander parceled out supplies and reinforcements according to which army group was conducting the primary thrust. A form of military mercantilism evolved, where headquarters vied for scarce reserves and supplies.

Envy arose over the fact that Montgomery commanded the European theater reserve, the XVIII Airborne Corps during his Operation MARKET-GARDEN, the attempted crossing of the Rhine in mid-September 1944. During the Battle of the Bulge, Eisenhower placed the Englishman in command of two American armies. After the war, Montgomery's most influential proponent, Chester Wilmot, highlighted the field marshal's arguments over strategy almost to the exclusion of command, and a generation of readers concluded that the debate between Montgomery and Eisenhower had been primarily over strategy rather than command. That was not how it appeared to American generals during the campaign of 1944-1945.

As Supreme Commander Allied Expeditionary Force (SCAEF), General Eisenhower became the most famous soldier in the Western world, went on to hold the post of chief of staff of the United States Army, and served two terms as president of the United States. Yet, within a year of the war's end, Ralph Ingersoll's 1946 *Top Secret* charged that Eisenhower did not deserve credit for winning the war, and if anything he had prolonged it. *Top Secret* began a process of charge and countercharge that took twenty years to play itself out counting the contemporary participants, such as the supreme commander, army group commanders, army commanders, members of the British Chiefs of Staff Committee, highly placed headquarters aides, and a head of state.[3]

Eisenhower's headquarters diary at SHAEF was kept by his aide, Captain Harry C. Butcher, USNR (United States Naval Reserve). Butcher's 1946 published diary, *My Three Years with Eisenhower: The Personal Diary of Captain Harry C. Butcher, USNR, Naval Aide to General Eisenhower, 1942 to 1945*, needs to be read with care, not just because of its impact on British sensibilities, but because for much of the period under discussion Butcher was absent from Eisenhower's headquarters on detached duty. Another memoir emerged from SHAEF headquarters in 1948; it was by Eisenhower's driver and later receptionist, Mrs. (later Lieutenant) Kay Summersby. Summersby's *Eisenhower Was My Boss* appeared in 1948 and was quickly forgotten, but neither diary had been authorized to speak publicly for Eisenhower, and both created problems for him.[4]

The public first learned of Eisenhower's discontent with Montgomery and how close their differences came to being discussed by the Combined Chiefs of Staff in Montgomery's 1946 biography by the former war correspondent of the London *Daily Express*, Alan Moorehead.[5] Moorehead assisted Montgomery's chief of staff,

Major General Sir Francis de Guingand, in the proofreading of de Guingand's 1947 wartime memoir, *Operation Victory*, thereby repeating chronological errors concerning the command controversy during the German Ardennes counteroffensive. De Guingand's book contained the most concise refutation of Montgomery's single thrust in print, and was written following a bitter humiliation at Montgomery's hands. While agreeing with Eisenhower's strategy and without mentioning Ingersoll's criticism, Eisenhower's chief of staff, Lieutenant General (later General) Walter Bedell Smith, wrote a series of articles in 1946 for *The Saturday Evening Post*, entitled "Eisenhower's Six Great Decisions."[6]

Within three years after the war, Eisenhower issued his official report and wrote a best-selling memoir.[7] Eisenhower signed his report on 13 July 1945; however, it was not released to the public until 23 June 1946. Eisenhower's report is cited in a report by General of the Army George C. Marshall, chief of staff, dated 1 September 1945. Several contemporaries believed that for the sake of good relations with Montgomery, Eisenhower delayed its release to change his discussion of the campaign in Normandy prior to the breakout on 25 July 1944. Eisenhower's 1948 memoir, *Crusade in Europe*, became a best-seller, making him a wealthy man.[8] Written in response to what Eisenhower called "crack pot" theories that the war could have ended in September 1944, it offended Montgomery who took personally Eisenhower's public comments regarding single thrust.

Field Marshal the Viscount Montgomery of Alamein--he received his peerage on 1 January 1946--went on to hold the top post in the British armed forces, CIGS, to head up the European Defense Union, and later to serve as deputy supreme commander of the North Atlantic Treaty Organization (NATO). His position as Eisenhower's deputy must have accentuated his regrets over not serving in an analogous position during the war. Over the next several years Montgomery published two reports, ghosted by his Operations officer, Brigadier David Belchem; but these created little controversy. Originally privately printed for the veterans of the British 21st Army Group and Eighth Army, *Normandy to the Baltic* and *El Alamein to the River Sangro* proved so popular they earned a commercial market.[9] Because he had deliberately avoided controversial issues in *Normandy to the Baltic*, Eisenhower's *Crusade in Europe* struck Montgomery as a low blow.

Three memoirs critical of Montgomery and his command of two American armies during the Battle of the Bulge appeared over the next several years. General George S. Patton, Jr.'s *War As I Knew It*, and Colonel Robert S. Allen's study of Third Army headquarters, *Lucky Forward*, both argued in 1947 that Eisenhower had prolonged the war by opting for Montgomery's Operation MARKET-GARDEN in September 1944. General Omar Bradley published his war memoir, *A Soldier's Story*, while serving in 1951 as chairman of the Joint Chiefs of Staff. Bradley's book was critical of Eisenhower but reserved its ire for Montgomery.[10]

In 1952 Chester Wilmot's *The Struggle for Europe* seemingly broke new ground by accusing Eisenhower of prolonging the war through his failure to adopt a single, concentrated assault into Germany in September 1944, which allegedly forfeited central Europe to the Russians. Wilmot actually restated an argument made earlier by P. J. Grigg, Great Britain's secretary of state for war, in his 1948 memoir, *Prejudice and Judgment*. The publication of Montgomery's *Memoirs* in 1958 and Sir Arthur Bryant's second volume in his edition of Field Marshal Alanbrooke's diaries, *Triumph in the West*, marked the completion of the British counterattack on Eisenhower's command and strategy and led to the break between Eisenhower and Montgomery.[11]

Prime Minister Winston Leonard Spencer Churchill published the sixth volume of his memoirs of World War II, *Triumph and Tragedy*, in 1953. Churchill omitted his wartime reservations regarding Eisenhower's command from *Triumph and Tragedy* because each man currently held his country's highest political office.[12] The American official historian, Forrest C. Pogue, published in 1954 *The Supreme Command* in the official history of the *United States Army in World War II*. Pogue's measured treatment of Montgomery's single thrust varied widely from the opinions voiced by staff officers at SHAEF, but Pogue considered he was writing a history of an Anglo-American undertaking and had to be fair to both sides.[13]

The present study seeks to approach the sources chronologically as much as possible. Therefore, the American official histories on logistics by Roland G. Ruppenthal are grouped with the Canadian official history by Colonel Charles P. Stacey and the British official history by Major Lionel F. Ellis. Also in the chapter dealing with the final works produced by participants in the debate are the memoirs of General Hastings Lionel Lord Ismay, Churchill's chief of staff during the war, and the memoirs of Eisenhower's deputy supreme commander, Marshal of the Royal Air Force Lord Arthur Tedder.[14]

A distinct ethnocentrism attached to the writing of both British and Americans on the last eleven months of the Second World War on the western front.[15] It was as if nothing else in the war against Hitler mattered but the disposition of forty Anglo-American divisions. For example, the British official history *Grand Strategy*, Volume 5, *August 1943-September 1944*, by John Ehrman, described the German army's defeat in Normandy as "its worst defeat since Stalingrad."[16] It has become a matter of faith that in August-September 1944 a concentrated single thrust in northwest Europe alone would have ended the entire war against Nazi Germany. When Montgomery in mid-August 1944 made his first call for forty divisions to advance on the Rhine, Eisenhower did not yet have that many divisions under his command and would not until sometime in September, so Montgomery's forty-division request rings false as to timing. This ethnocentric notion was based on proximity to the Ruhr, the industrial heart of Germany, without which Germany's war effort would collapse. Geographic proximity to the Ruhr would determine the strategic compromises of coalition warfare, which suffered from a shortage of transportation. The shortest route to the Ruhr nearly always received priority from SHAEF.

Revisionists came to regard September 1944 as marking the moment that Eisenhower failed to win the war in northwest Europe by failing to concentrate his attack along only one axis of advance upon the Rhine, that is, Montgomery through Holland or Patton through Lorraine. By choosing to advance to the Rhine on two separate avenues of approach, that is, a broad front, critics argued that Eisenhower lost the chance to end the war. This belief was reflected in the headquarters of the

British 21st Army Group; it was in evidence at the 12th Army Group as well as the Third United States Army. Blame for the war continuing beyond September 1944 neglected the fact that there was insufficient transportation available to the Anglo-American forces in the late summer of 1944 to turn the dislocation of the German army in the West into a strategic victory that would have ended the war. This operational criticism of Eisenhower and SHAEF broadened in the postwar period, especially following the Berlin crisis of 1948, and took on a political dimension.

For most of the eleven-month campaign in northwest Europe, two-thirds of the German *Wehrmacht* was fighting the Soviet Red Army, and the Anglo-Americans were engaging approximately one-third of the German army except during the Battle of the Bulge when about half the German army faced west. In the summer of 1944 the Soviets held down some 160 German divisions, and their Operation BAGRATION wrote off the entire German Army Group Center, over twenty-five divisions, and they moved to the Vistula some 300 miles nearer to Germany. According to David M. Glantz and Jonathan M. House in their recent *When Titans Clashed: How the Red Army Stopped Hitler* (1995), German losses in Army Group Center were over 400,000, easily the equivalent of their losses in Normandy. John Erickson states in his *The Road to Berlin* (1983): "When Soviet armies shattered Army Group Centre, they achieved their greatest single military success on the Eastern Front. For the German army in the east it was a catastrophe of unbelievable proportions, greater than that of Stalingrad, obliterating between twenty-five and twenty-eight divisions, 350,000 men in all."[17] British military historian John Ellis points out in his *Brute Force: Allied Strategy and Tactics in the Second World War* that the Russians were responsible for nearly 90 percent of all German soldiers killed or wounded in the Second World War, almost 5 million on the eastern front compared to 580,000 in North Africa, Italy, and northwest Europe.[18]

By May 1945 Eisenhower's broad front, in conjunction with the Red Army, had destroyed the German army and the regime it kept in power. Whether implied or intended, Eisenhower's broad-front strategy was the counterpart to President Franklin D. Roosevelt's policy of unconditional surrender. Combined with unconditional surrender, the broad-front strategy ensured that there would be no armistice with the German army as there had been in November 1918. No armistice was possible with the nation that had twice in a quarter century plunged the world into war, and it was unlikely that either government of the Western Allies would have survived an armistice with Hitler. The broad-front strategy had guaranteed victory at the least political cost to the Allied coalition.

NOTES

1. During his overseas assignments Montgomery published the following: *Some Notes on High Command in War* (Italy: September, 1943); *Some Notes on the Conduct of War and the Infantry Division in Battle* (Belgium: November, 1944); *21st (British) Army Group in the Campaign in North West Europe, 1944-1945* (Berlin: October, 1945); *Lecture on*

Military Leadership (Germany: November, 1945), Dwight D. Eisenhower, Pre-Presidential Papers, 1916-1952, Principal File, Box 83, Bernard Montgomery, Eisenhower Library [hereafter EL], Abilene, Kansas.

2. Alfred D. Chandler, Jr., ed., and Stephen E. Ambrose, assoc. ed., *The Papers of Dwight David Eisenhower: The War Years*, 5 vols. (Baltimore and London: Johns Hopkins University Press, 1970), 5:164-89.

3. Ralph Ingersoll, *Top Secret* (New York: Harcourt, Brace, 1946).

4. Harry C. Butcher, *My Three Years with Eisenhower: The Personal Diary of Captain Harry C. Butcher, USNR, Naval Aide to General Eisenhower, 1942 to 1945* (New York: Simon and Schuster, 1946); Kay Summersby, *Eisenhower Was My Boss*, ed. Michael Kearns (New York: Prentice-Hall, 1948).

5. Alan Moorehead, *Montgomery* (London: Hamish Hamilton, 1946; New York: Coward-McCann, 1947).

6. Francis de Guingand, *Operation Victory* (London: Hodder and Stoughton, 1947); Walter Bedell Smith, *Eisenhower's Six Great Decisions: Europe, 1944-1945* (New York and London: Longmans, Green, 1956); *The Saturday Evening Post* ran the articles from 8 June to 13 July 1946.

7. *Report by the Supreme Commander to the Combined Chiefs of Staff on the Operations in Europe of the Allied Expeditionary Force, 6 June 1944 to 8 May 1945* (Washington, D.C.: Government Printing Office, 1945; reprint, New York: Arco, 1946).

8. George C. Marshall, *Biennial Report of the Chief of Staff of the United States Army to the Secretary of War, July 1, 1943 to June 30, 1945* (Washington, D.C.: The War Department, 1945; reprint, New York: Simon and Schuster in Cooperation with the Council on Books in Wartime, 1945); Dwight D. Eisenhower, *Crusade in Europe* (Garden City, N. Y.: Doubleday, 1948).

9. Field Marshal the Viscount Montgomery of Alamein, *Normandy to the Baltic* (London: Hutchinson, 1947) and *El Alamein to the River Sangro* (London: Hutchinson, 1948).

10. George S. Patton, Jr., *War As I Knew It*, Annotated by Colonel Paul D. Harkins (Boston: Houghton Mifflin, 1947); Robert S. Allen, *Lucky Forward* (New York: Vanguard Press, 1947; reprint, New York: MacFadden-Bartell, 1965); Omar N. Bradley, *A Soldier's Story* (New York: Holt, 1951).

11. Chester Wilmot, *The Struggle for Europe* (London: Collins; New York: Harper and Brothers, 1952); P.J. Grigg, *Prejudice and Judgment* (London: Jonathan Cape, 1948); *The Memoirs of Field-Marshal the Viscount Montgomery of Alamein* (London: Collins, 1958); Arthur Bryant, *Triumph in the West: A History of the War Years Based on the Diaries of Field-Marshal Lord Alanbrooke, Chief of the Imperial General Staff* (Garden City, N. Y.: Doubleday, 1959).

12. Winston S. Churchill, *The Second World War*, vol. 6, *Triumph and Tragedy* (Boston: Houghton Mifflin Company; Cambridge, Mass.: Riverside Press, 1948-1953).

13. Forrest C. Pogue, *The Supreme Command (United States Army in World War II: The European Theater of Operations*, Washington, D.C.: Office of the Chief of Military History, Department of the Army, 1954).

14. Roland G. Ruppenthal, *Logistical Support of the Armies*, vol. 1, *May 1941-September 1944 (United States Army in World War II: The European Theater of Operations*, Washington, D.C.: Office of the Chief of Military History, Department of the Army, 1953); *Logistical Support of the Armies*, vol. 2, *September 1944-May 1945 (United States Army in World War II: The European Theater of Operations*, Washington, D.C.: Office of the Chief of Military History, Department of the Army, 1959); Charles P. Stacey, *The Victory Campaign (Official History of the Canadian Army in the Second World War*, vol 3, *The Op-*

erations in North-West Europe, 1944-1945, Ottawa: Queen's Printer and Controller of Stationery, 1960); Major Lionel F. Ellis with Lieutenant Colonel Arthur Warhurst, *Victory in the West,* vol. 2, *The Defeat of Germany (History of the Second World War. United Kingdom Military Series,* London: Her Majesty's Stationery Office, 1968); *The Memoirs of General Lord Ismay* (New York: Viking Press, 1960); Arthur Tedder, *With Prejudice: The War Memoirs of Marshal of the Royal Air Force Lord Tedder* (Boston: Little, Brown, 1966).

15. H.P. Willmott, *The Great Crusade: A New Complete History of the Second World War* (New York: Free Press, 1991), 363-64.

16. John Ehrman, *Grand Strategy: August 1943-September 1944,* vol. 5 *(History of the Second World War, United Kingdom Military Series,* London: Her Majesty's Stationery Office, 1956), 378.

17. Glantz and House state: "Army Group Center lost almost 450,000 men," see David M. Glantz and Jonathan M. House, *When Titans Clashed: How the Red Army Stopped Hitler* (Lawrence, Kan.: University Press of Kansas, 1995), 214; for the Erickson quotation, see John Erickson, *The Road to Berlin: Continuing the History of Stalin's War with Germany* (Boulder, Colo.: Westview Press, 1983), 228.

18. John Ellis, *Brute Force: Allied Strategy and Tactics in the Second World War* (New York: Viking Press, 1990), 129-30. Ellis notes that when German prisoners of war taken by the Western Allies are factored into the equation, the Russian percentage drops to about 80.

1

The Journalists Fire First: Butcher, Moorehead, and Ingersoll

Let us have no part in the profitless quarrels in which other men will inevitably engage as to what country, what service, won the European war.
--General Dwight D. Eisenhower
Victory Order of the Day, 8 May 1945[1]

General of the Army Dwight Eisenhower's order of the day was a vain hope. Within a year the veneer of amity that he had attempted to apply to the Anglo-American coalition worked loose at its edges. Several journalists, two of them Americans in uniform, Harry Butcher and Ralph Ingersoll, and Alan Moorehead, of the London *Daily Express*, began exposing the coalition's wartime disagreements. In retrospect, the British press had publicized most of these controversies during the war, and the earliest works closely mirrored wartime press accounts. Thus began the process of charge and countercharge based on national and personal prestige that threatened to overshadow the Allied achievement, much to Eisenhower's dismay.

BUTCHER'S *MY THREE YEARS WITH EISENHOWER*

By May 1945 few soldiers knew better the value of public relations than did Eisenhower. He had spent nearly every waking moment of the last three years forging the Anglo-American military coalition, which along with the Soviet Union defeated Hitlerism. The care and nurturing of the good relationship between the United States and Great Britain, which he considered his adopted home, became a concern during the years following the war.[2] Given the effort Eisenhower put into developing both personal relationships in Great Britain and goodwill between the two nations, he had reason to worry over the publication of a memoir by his former naval aide, Captain Harry C. Butcher, USNR.

The general must have realized that publication of frank opinions arrived at under wartime stress would potentially diminish the luster of his guiding the more fractious actors within the coalition. The single greatest controversy from an American point of view occurred during the Battle of the Bulge, the German Ardennes counteroffensive of December 1944. Eisenhower's decision to give Field Marshal Bernard Law Montgomery operational command of the American First and Ninth Armies, which had been under the command of Lieutenant General Omar N. Bradley's United States 12th Army Group, fueled the initial postwar American memoirs. Although Montgomery's operational control of the First Army ceased in mid-January 1945, he continued to control the Ninth Army until early April 1945. This chapter examines how Montgomery's enlarged command appeared to the contemporary authors who were the first to publish in 1946.

Before he was the aide of the man who became the world's best-known soldier, Harry C. Butcher studied journalism at Iowa State University. In 1928 while editing *Fertilizer Review* in Washington, D.C., Butcher met Dr. Milton Eisenhower of the Department of Agriculture, who introduced him to his older brother, Major Dwight Eisenhower, then a student at the Army War College. On a visit to the War Department in 1942 as a vice president for public relations at the Columbia Broadcasting System (CBS), Butcher, an officer in the naval reserve, encountered then Brigadier General Eisenhower who was at the time chief of the Operations Division. Shortly afterward, Chief of Staff of the United States Army General George C. Marshall named Eisenhower the commanding general of the European theater of operations (ETO). Realizing the public relations demands of his new position, Eisenhower looked for a man with Butcher's experience and received permission from Chief of Naval Operations Admiral Ernest J. King to name Butcher his aide.[3] "Captain Butcher had," Eisenhower wrote in 1946, "as his duty in my office, the keeping of a diary in which he placed both personal and official matters . . . for my ultimate use and possibly for use of War Department historians." Eisenhower's headquarters diary, known as the Butcher diary, began in London on 8 July 1942 and ended in Washington on 10 July 1945, and contained over one million words; the published version was 640,000 words and 876 pages. For the best part of eight months, from 25 August 1944 to 15 April 1945, however, Butcher was on detached duty to the Public Relations Division (PRD) at Supreme Headquarters Allied Expeditionary Force (SHAEF).[4]

When the war was over, Eisenhower permitted Butcher to use the diary "to refresh his memory in writing up the story of his experiences as my confidential aide."[5] Eisenhower expected a short, informal narrative, which did not cite from the official memoranda that accounted for much of the diary's pages. Fearing that publication of confidential memoranda might damage the ongoing Anglo-American alliance, on 22 December 1945 Eisenhower and Butcher reviewed Butcher's manuscript.[6] Subsequently, the general asked Butcher to tone down his treatment of General Charles de Gaulle and Field Marshal Montgomery in order to avoid "bad feeling [that] would . . . defeat the very purposes that I strove so hard to advance during the war." The general took his former aide to task: "My feeling is that you were admitted into a circle where every individual had a right to believe that the matters discussed were to remain secret. Your admission into that circle was by reason of the fact that as my Aide I was responsible for bringing you into the secret."[7]

Public criticism of his command during the war taught Eisenhower the value of public relations. His first experience with public criticism came in North Africa when he made a deal with the anti-Semitic Vichy French admiral, Jean Darlan, recognizing the admiral as the head of state of French North Africa in return for turning over the French fleet and agreeing to fight the Germans.[8] The subsequent press outcry in Britain and the United States took Eisenhower by surprise. Eisenhower learned that military success by itself did not always guarantee favorable public opinion. Moreover, the episode sounded a warning against accepting conditional surrender of fascists.

During the final days of the Normandy campaign, Eisenhower experienced a second public relations flap. On 15 August 1944 Butcher told his old friend Wes Gallagher, an Associated Press correspondent, that General Bradley was in command of 12th Army Group. Gallagher bypassed the censors at both SHAEF and the British Ministry of Information and announced the Allied change of command in France. Formerly First United States Army commander and Montgomery's subordinate, Bradley rose to army group command on 1 August 1944 when the Third United States Army, under Lieutenant General George S. Patton, Jr., became operational; the United States thus had two armies in Normandy. Command of the First United States Army passed to Bradley's former deputy, Lieutenant General Courtney H. Hodges. The American forces' newspaper, *Stars and Stripes*, printed Gallagher's story from the Associated Press wire. To make matters worse, SHAEF's PRD denied the change in command.[9]

Any change in command involving allies is apt to be controversial, and in this case the changeover diminished the prestige of Britain's premier soldier of the Second World War. Until 1 August 1944 Montgomery, the victor of El Alamein, commander in chief of the British 21st Army Group, and temporary ground forces commander, had exercised operational control of both British and American ground forces. With the formation of an American army group, however, Montgomery retained only the right to "coordinate" operations with Bradley's 12th Army Group. To the British public, Bradley's promotion amounted to Montgomery's demotion.

In a military alliance between nations, command takes on political ramifications. By prior agreement between Prime Minister Winston S. Churchill and President Franklin D. Roosevelt, the position of supreme commander went to an American because the United States would eventually provide the bulk of troops and supplies. Originally, Washington opinion for the supreme command favored General Marshall, but Roosevelt concluded that his chief of staff's considerable organizational talents and skill in dealing with Congress were too important to trade for what was essentially a theater command in northwest Europe.[10] If Marshall was not to be the supreme commander, then it had to be Eisenhower, who was commander in chief of the Allied Force Headquarters in the Mediterranean.

As a result of his victory at El Alamein, Montgomery was Britain's most famous general by 1943, which promised to complicate his relationship with an American supreme commander. In the planning stages for OVERLORD, Eisenhower wanted to keep secret Montgomery's command of the ground forces.

Asked at his press conference on 17 January 1944 whether Montgomery would be ground forces commander, Eisenhower cautioned correspondents not to go out on a limb. The correspondents knew that the day before Montgomery had said as much to the United States 29th Division: "'I came home the other day from Italy to take command of the British Army and the American Army of which General Eisenhower is the Supreme Commander, and he has put one army, the First American Army, under me for the battle. We are going to fight and this is a very great honor for me.'"[11]

Two months later a SHAEF directive of 10 March 1944 gave Montgomery, as commander in chief of the British 21st Army Group, "responsibility for the command of all ground troops engaged in the operation until some time as the Supreme Commander allocates an area of responsibility to the Commanding General, First [later 12th] (US) Army Group."[12] The directive also laid down as a guiding principle that American forces were to be on the right flank, while the British and Canadian forces were to be on the left. There was no fixed date on which the American army group would become operational; it would depend on the supreme commander's opinion when "the number of American divisions in Normandy warranted control by "the First (US) Army Group Commander."

Butcher noted in the headquarters diary that a second American army was expected to become operational about two months after D-Day, which would be the first week of August. Until Eisenhower could set up an advance headquarters on the continent and take over personal control of the land battle, Montgomery would retain the duties of ground forces commander.[13]

Because Eisenhower had refused to announce Montgomery as his ground forces commander in January, he also refused to announce the change in command in August. SHAEF again denied a story that all the correspondents knew and would become public knowledge in weeks, if not days. On 16 August 1944 SHAEF's PRD issued the following, "It is officially stated at Supreme Headquarters that announcement of General Bradley's Command of the Twelfth Army Group in no way affects the position of General Montgomery as overall commander of all Allied ground forces under General Eisenhower." The Associated Press story and subsequent SHAEF denial infuriated the London *Daily Mirror*, which produced in its 17 August edition an editorial and an editorial cartoon that Butcher termed "scathing." Titled "That's S.H.A.E.F.--That was!", Philip Zec's cartoon pictured double images of Eisenhower and Montgomery turning from side to side. The left side read "Pessimism," "There's Still a Long Way to Go," "Monty Is Demoted," and "Nazi Resistance Stiffening," while the right side stated "Optimism," "Terrific Advances--Anything May Happen," "Monty Is Not Demoted," and "It's in the Bag." "In general," the *Daily Mirror* editorial concluded, "the handling of war news has been amateurish, inconsistent and confusing." This time it was Montgomery who suffered from "this latest exhibition of official ineptitude," and the paper asked, "When is he going to get his apology?"[14]

General Marshall and Secretary of War Henry L. Stimson cabled Eisenhower on 17 August in response to that morning's *New York Times*. Hanson Baldwin, the paper's correspondent, pointed out that many Americans suspected the British of ulterior motives and if the current command setup continued the number would

The *Daily Mirror* (London), Thursday, 17 August 1944. Editorial page cartoon by ZEC, page 3, with the caption, "That's S.H.A.E.F.—That was!" Reprinted by permission of Mirror Syndication International.

grow. "Each army in France should have its own commander," Baldwin argued, "operating under one supreme command. This is a principle--one which Gen. John J. Pershing fought--that is as old as the first World War. It should be honored today." Marshall and Stimson called Eisenhower's attention to American public opinion, which wondered why American soldiers remained under Montgomery's command when they constituted the bulk of the forces and casualties. Eisenhower was directed to assume command of the "American contingent."[15]

The chief of staff and secretary of war wanted to head off congressional debate on the subject, which they were afraid would occur by the next day. On 18 August the anti-Roosevelt, anti-British Washington *Times-Herald* confirmed Marshall's fears. While referring to the London *Daily Mirror* editorial charging SHAEF incompetence, the *Times-Herald* noted:

It is generally recognized in congressional circles and common gossip in military circles that General Eisenhower is merely a figurehead and that actual command of the invasion is in the hands of the British General Staff and the British dominate the American War Department and army.

All of Eisenhower's immediate chief subordinates are Britishers. The deputy commander in chief is Air Chief Marshal Tedder. Montgomery is deputy commander in the field. Admiral Bertram Ramsay is leader of the Allied naval forces and Air Chief Marshal Trafford L. Leigh-Mallory is in command of the Allied air forces. Eisenhower's chief of intelligence is Maj. Gen. K.W.D. Strong, Britisher.[16]

On the continent Eisenhower remained concerned that the Germans not know that there were now two Allied army group commanders owing to their different styles of command. But the Germans had to have known of the existence of Bradley's new command, if only from radio signals emanating from an additional headquarters. Through an elaborate Allied deception, known as FORTITUDE SOUTH, Patton had recently been replaced as the fictitious commander of the fictitious FUSAG, First United States Army Group, about to invade the Pas de Calais region of France.[17]

Butcher termed the command issue a "first-class problem." As *My Three Years with Eisenhower* spelled out, Eisenhower was "peeved" that the press and the public could not simply accept a victory as such; they had to squabble over how it was won and by whom. On the issue of command Butcher wrote: "Ike feels that the development of command arrangements in this campaign was as carefully planned as the operation itself."[18]

Once again, as in the Darlan affair, Eisenhower received a valuable lesson in the power of the press and its impact on public opinion, and given the cable from the War Department this issue now lay beyond his personal preference to let events dictate when he would assume ground command. Therefore, on 1 September 1944 with SHAEF's forward headquarters operational at Jullouville, just south of Granville on the shore of the Cotentin not far from Mont St. Michel, Eisenhower assumed command of the ground forces from Montgomery.

MOOREHEAD'S *MONTGOMERY*

Field Marshal Montgomery, promoted on 1 September 1944 by King George VI, could not step aside without comment when, according to Alan McCrae Moorehead, "he was entirely master of the battlefield." Moorehead, an Australian-born journalist and war correspondent for the London *Daily Express*, covered the 21st Army Group during the campaign in northwest Europe; his biography of the field marshal appeared in England in 1946 and in the United States in 1947. *Collier's* magazine, a competitor of *The Saturday Evening Post*, published a selection on 5 October 1946, entitled "Montgomery's Quarrel with Eisenhower." Both the biography and the article divulged sharp disagreements between the general and the field marshal.[19]

Moorehead pointed out that in August 1944 Montgomery believed the supreme commander ought to stick to the political side of the war and parcel out the supplies and reinforcements, but as for battlefield command it was "inefficient and dangerous to swap horses in midstream." "As for the American Press, Montgomery argued, this point was of no account. *Victories were the only thing that mattered, not public opinion.* Victories moulded public opinion. Give the people victories and the public opinion would follow."[20]

For *the* national hero of Great Britain to maintain that public opinion did not matter must have seemed rather strange to his American superior. Montgomery had come out of the desert a national monument to good public relations. He was on record as stating that he regarded his war correspondents as part of his staff.[21] It was facetious for a soldier who wore corduroy pants, sweaters, and a tanker's black beret to say he did not hold with public opinion. Montgomery did not hold with Eisenhower's citing American public opinion as a valid reason for preventing him from winning the war using American troops.

When Eisenhower assumed command of the ground forces, Moorehead described Montgomery as "bitterly" disappointed. Further upset followed when Eisenhower turned down Montgomery's plan to wipe out Germany "with one bold and decisive stroke." Montgomery asked for "forty divisions, or about a million men, and the cream of the Air Force." With these he was certain he "could make one major thrust along the northern coast of Europe, enter the Ruhr and bring Germany to surrender."[22]

Moorehead had less to say on this latter subject than Butcher, but both authors would confuse their readers by making important chronological errors. *My Three Years* on page 642 dated Montgomery's plan 14 August 1944, when it correctly pertained to 14 September 1944: "General [sic] Montgomery feels that if his Army Group is given practically all the maintenance available to both Americans and British, his 21st Army Group could rush right on into Berlin."[23] Eisenhower refused because Montgomery's plan meant immobilizing Patton's Third Army and two corps of Hodges' First Army, at a minimum. Believing Montgomery's proposed push on Berlin would be on too narrow a front to prevent German flanking attacks, Eisenhower feared that immobilizing the remainder of his command would render it incapable of coming to Montgomery's defense.

Butcher's published diary of 13 September described Eisenhower's plan to advance "on a wide front to take advantage of all existing lines of communication." The supreme commander expected to use the Aachen gap in the north and the Metz gap in the south, while bringing Lieutenant General Jacob L. Devers' 6th Army Group up to the Rhine at Coblenz. *My Three Years* summarized Eisenhower's broad front as follows: "Ike intends to hustle all his forces up against the Rhine, including those coming in from southern France. He will build up maintenance and reserves as rapidly as possible and then put on one sustained and unremitting advance against the long-coveted heart of the enemy country--the Ruhr industrial area."[24] Eisenhower discussed his options with Butcher on 24 September; Butcher titled the entry, "I Get Brought Up to Date."[25] One was to concentrate all of his resources behind a "knifelike and narrow thrust" into the heart of Germany, hoping it would bring about a German surrender. The second was to drive through Germany's forward defenses, regroup, and prepare for an attack into Germany using all of his forces, "which definitely would force capitulation." Eisenhower's strategy assumed that the Germans were worse off for manpower than the Allies, and that they were spread out on a huge eastern front, the width of Italy as well as the 300-mile western front; given sufficient pressure, eventually the German line would break.

Moorehead benefited indirectly from *My Three Years with Eisenhower*, which appeared in the London *Sunday Dispatch* of 27 January 1946. The *Sunday Dispatch* serialization detailed Eisenhower's frustration with the pace of Montgomery's assault on Caen during the Normandy campaign, and the headline read, "General's Aide Says: Eisenhower Nearly Sacked Montgomery." Montgomery immediately wrote Eisenhower: "This is a terrible pity. And the repercussion is bound to be that some British author will retaliate by getting at you."[26] As a result of the serialization of Butcher's diary, the field marshal gave Moorehead use of his papers, which he had previously refused. Following Moorehead's *Collier's* article, Montgomery sent Eisenhower a handwritten letter, marked "Private":

It seems to be assumed that Moorehead (the writer) had access to my official correspondence and diaries. Indeed, he quotes verbatim some sentences in the private correspondence that passed between us from time to time.

I want to assure you that no one has at any time seen the correspondence that used to pass between us privately. The more private letters were not even seen by Freddie de Guingand.

Is it possible that Moorehead got a sight of some of these letters at SHAEF; or was told about them by someone there? These newspaper chaps are complete artists at finding things out.[27]

The command controversy that would dominate the memoirs grew out of Eisenhower's decision on 20 December 1944, during the German counteroffensive, to split command within the salient. He placed Montgomery in charge of the northern half, and Bradley retained command over the southern half. As a result Montgomery commanded four Allied armies: the British Second; the Canadian First; the American Ninth; the American First.

On 28 December 1944 Eisenhower met Montgomery at Hasselt, Belgium. The next day Montgomery wrote Eisenhower suggesting that he give him power to control and coordinate operations of Bradley's army group, but Moorehead mistakenly placed Montgomery's letter in the first week of January, following the Montgomery press conference of 7 January 1945. Noting pressure from Washington to resist British demands for a ground forces commander, Moorehead described Eisenhower's dilemma as follows: "Again he reasoned: could not the Field-Marshal see how impossible it was to fly against public opinion in the United States? Doggedly Montgomery replied: 'Victories make public opinion. Give me the Ninth Army and I will take the Ruhr.'"[28] The issue was not about the Ninth Army at this point, Moorehead was mistaken, and Montgomery's actual message to Eisenhower did not mention the Ruhr.

Moorehead got most of the story from Montgomery's chief of staff, Major General Sir Francis de Guingand, who was at SHAEF's Versailles headquarters on 30 December and saw that the field marshal's letter had touched a nerve. "Very well," Moorehead described Eisenhower thumping the table, "if Montgomery wanted a showdown he should have it. Let the matter go back to Washington and London. Let them decide. It was either he or Montgomery. One of them would have to go."[29] De Guingand set off for Montgomery's tactical headquarters with Eisenhower's draft ultimatum in his pocket, arriving later that night. Moorehead believed that had Eisenhower carried out his threat not even Churchill could have saved Montgomery's job; only the field marshal's prompt acceptance of Eisenhower's authority on the issue of command sufficed. At this point, Moorehead claimed Eisenhower made a magnanimous gesture; having established his authority, he gave Montgomery the Ninth United States Army. Actually, Eisenhower had always intended Montgomery to employ the Ninth Army in crossing the Roer and the Rhine.[30]

A public command crisis followed Montgomery's press conference of 7 January 1945. Ostensibly called for the field marshal to express displeasure with the criticism of Eisenhower in the British press, it became a public relations fiasco. The Bulge battle made the American high command look as though the German commander, Field Marshal Gerd von Rundstedt, had outwitted them, and on top of this came Montgomery, sporting a red airborne beret for the occasion. Alan Moorehead caught the feeling evoked by the press conference: "To rival Americans it sounded as if he were saying: 'There you are. Look what happened in the Ardennes. You had to call on me for assistance. I had to get you out of the mess.'"[31]

INGERSOLL'S *TOP SECRET*

The postwar American memoirs emerging from headquarters south of the Givet-Houffalize-Prüm line shed more heat than light on the crisis in command during the Battle of the Bulge. Givet-Houffalize-Prüm was the boundary line Eisenhower used to divide Montgomery's and Bradley's command responsibility during the battle: Prüm was at the east end in Germany; Houffalize in the center in Belgium;

Givet in France at the western end.[32] Ralph Ingersoll's *Top Secret* grew out of his wartime experiences in Bradley's 12th Army Group headquarters. During the Ardennes counteroffensive Bradley's tactical headquarters was located in Luxembourg City, forty miles south of Houffalize.

According to the *New York Times*, *Top Secret* was written at such "blood-bursting heat . . . that an ex-sergeant must have been needed to pour buckets of ice water on [Ingersoll's] typewriter's smoking keys as he wrote."[33] Employing three secretaries, Ingersoll dictated 10,000 words a day by the side of Lake Tahoe, Nevada.

Ralph McAlister Ingersoll was a prodigious lover and drinker, and he had returned from Europe with several Bronze Stars and seven campaign stars, a Legion of Merit, an Arrowhead, and another man's wife; but above all Ingersoll was a prodigious writer. Graduated from Yale in 1921, Ingersoll went to work editing at *Fortune* and *Time* magazines, but he was famous for founding and editing *PM*, the New York tabloid known for its left-wing political editorials. He had resigned his army reserve commission in 1935, so his divorced status caused him to be drafted in 1942, at age forty-one. After writing a 6,000-word front-page editorial that argued he was more valuable to the war effort as editor of *PM* than as a private, he enlisted in the army.[34] Commissioned a second lieutenant in 1943, Ingersoll finished the war as a lieutenant colonel. He turned his service in North Africa, where he saw combat briefly, into the 1943 best-seller, *The Battle Is the Pay-Off*, published by Harcourt, Brace, and Company.

Assignment to the Operations Section, G-3, of 12th Army Group as its Special Operations officer gave him regular access to British officers and cables, including the ULTRA secret. Accustomed to thinking in terms of plots, Ingersoll believed that the British, from the prime minister and chiefs of staff down to Montgomery and his supporters in Fleet Street, schemed to use American troops, gained at Bradley's expense, to their ultimate advantage, that is, Britain's position in the postwar world. The British army was a wasting asset, and in order to be entitled to a "50-50 partnership" at the peace settlement while contributing "20 to 25 per cent of the actual effort" the British reasoned that Montgomery was entitled to additional American troops.[35]

This was not the first time that Ingersoll had smelled a British rat. He was certain that Eisenhower was a political general whom the British had "popped into the job of Supreme Command" because he was pliable. He believed that Eisenhower's incompetence allowed the British to dominate strategy from the second rank, and they had all the power they needed behind the scenes in the persons of his British deputy supreme commander, his three British service deputies, and his "British-dominated" staff. When the reader compares this contention of Ingersoll's to the trouble that General Walter Bedell Smith, Eisenhower's chief of staff, encountered in dealing with the CIGS, Field Marshal Brooke, over taking British staff officers from the Mediterranean to the European theater, Ingersoll's accusations appear without merit in this instance. Smith spent weeks fighting with Brooke to allow Eisenhower to take several British staff officers (particularly Major General Sir Kenneth Strong, Eisenhower's British Intelligence officer) from the Mediterranean to SHAEF, but Brooke complained about Smith to Eisenhower because he worried about denuding the Mediterranean of competent staff officers.[36]

Surely, if Brooke had planned to dominate Eisenhower by dominating his staff, he would have gladly transferred all the British officers "with sand in their shoes" to northwest Europe. Brooke's position was entirely within bounds as a matter of national sovereignty because Eisenhower had no claims on British staff officers other than those assigned willingly by Whitehall.

Always alert to backstage influence, Ingersoll claimed that in dividing Bradley's command in December, Eisenhower succumbed to his "British advisors" and the prime minister. Ingersoll inaccurately stated that despite Bradley's having already taken steps to fight the battle, and the "entire British Army [being] in retreat," Eisenhower panicked and put the cautious Montgomery in command. Moreover, Ingersoll believed that Montgomery's hidden agenda was to embarrass Bradley and to be renamed ground forces commander.[37] "Within an hour after the command of the American First and Ninth Armies had been put under Montgomery's temporary command, the British press was howling in headlines and arguing in editorials for the appointment of Montgomery as 'Ground Forces Commander'--over all Allied forces on the Continent, permanently."[38]

Ingersoll misled his readers. The entire British army was not in retreat. Furthermore, neither nation's press would know for over two weeks that Montgomery had taken over for Bradley in the northern Bulge, not until James Shepley of *Time* magazine got the story past a censor in New York. Shepley had literally flown home with the story, and *Time* broke it on 5 January 1945.[39] The Anglo-American public learned of the command change the next day. The facts were that prior to 20 December, Montgomery ordered Lieutenant General Brian Horrocks' British XXX Corps behind the Meuse River near Namur, and contrary to what Ingersoll said, Bradley did not order Hodges to take Major General J. Lawton Collins' VII Corps out of the line to form a reserve; Montgomery did that.

At this point Secretary of War Henry Stimson cabled Eisenhower to name the man responsible for the Ardennes debacle, and directed him to remove that man from his command regardless of rank. "The whole Allied world which had been so complacent was scared now--and mad," Ingersoll wrote and "it was open season for goat hunting."[40] Considering that the commander ultimately responsible for the failure to credit the Germans with any offensive capability was General Bradley, and none other than Ralph Ingersoll himself wrote the intelligence estimate that dismissed First Army's fears of an attack, there was reason to fear goat hunters at 12th Army Group.

On 6 January 1945, the president of the United States and the chief of staff of the United States Army spoke to the ramifications of the command shift. The *New York Times* printed Sidney Shalett's "Roosevelt Explains Shift" on page three. The president informed Americans that Montgomery's enlarged command, which he refused to call a promotion, was no slap at Eisenhower's command, and Marshall called it a "normal" step to take in such an emergency. Shalett wrote: "There was a strong implication in War Department circles that, in all probability, the reduction of General Bradley's command would be temporary rather than permanent. . . . There was reassertion of the War Department attitude that any British effort to lessen General Eisenhower's command would meet strong opposition."[41] Roosevelt went on the record pointing out that Montgomery's increased command "does not mean that Marshal Montgomery has become Deputy Commander to Eisenhower." Shalett's story also mentioned that there had been discussion in Britain of bringing in Field Marshal Harold Sir R.L.G. Alexander from the Mediterranean to be third man in the triumvirate of Eisenhower-Tedder-Alexander. General Marshall confused the issue slightly by stating that the changeover had occurred on the night of 17 December rather than 20 December. Both the president and the chief of staff emphasized that the transfer was not a slap at Bradley. Clearly, Roosevelt's and Marshall's on-the-record remarks were meant to signal their ally that there would be no chance of Montgomery becoming ground forces commander, following the emergency.

The subsequent imbroglio over the Montgomery press conference probably saved Bradley from a potentially embarrassing investigation such as accompanied the Pearl Harbor debacle. Alan Moorehead was in attendance, and he believed that the field marshal's press conferences "were never very successful" because of his penchant to talk down to reporters, to repeat himself, and to deal in simplicities. Moorehead believed that Montgomery's conferences "spread the already popular belief that the Field-Marshal . . . was no ball of mental fire." The problem sprang from his conception of correspondents as transmitters of simplified accounts, instead of sophisticated people who made complicated stories readily understood. Moorehead said of Montgomery's 7 January 1945 press performance: "There was a slight flavour of patronage in his references to the part played by Bradley and the other American generals."[42]

Given the highly volatile subject of British command of American troops and the inflamed passions in 12th Army Group, it is likely that anything Montgomery said would have upset the Americans. Two years later when Dr. Forrest C. Pogue, the American official historian, interviewed Moorehead in London in January 1947, Moorehead told him that Monty's "professionalism" caused him to look on Americans as citizen-generals at war; it was no good telling him that they were using their own men and material. Moorehead told Pogue that the field marshal failed to realize that "political considerations of satisfying home opinion entered into the picture."[43]

Moorehead believed that Montgomery meant well by his performance; he certainly never dreamed that his remarks might prove hurtful to the Allied cause. The Germans picked up Chester Wilmot's depiction of the field marshal's remarks broadcast over the BBC. Broadcasting a bogus summary on the German propaganda service, "Arnhem Calling," over a frequency adjacent to the BBC's had its desired effect on Bradley's nationalistic American headquarters. When Bradley read the transcription of the phony broadcast, he was apoplectic, and the 12th Army Group did not notice until the next day that it had been hoodwinked. On 11 January the *Daily Telegraph* printed the German version of Wilmot's original broadcast of 7 January:

Field-Marshal Montgomery came into the fight at the strategic moment. He scored a major success across the Laroche road, which American tanks cut on Saturday.

Many tanks, as well as British and American infantry, are coming up. Gains of from 1,000 to 3,000 yards were made yesterday. Our forces are not more than 12 miles apart on opposite sides of the salient. The American Third Army from the south made two and a half miles at one point.

To the south of the line at a point two miles north of Strasbourg the Germans have about 500 to 600 men and some tanks across the Rhine river. In the three weeks since Montgomery tackled the German Ardennes offensive he has transformed it into a headache for Rundstedt. It is the most brilliant and difficult task he has yet managed. He found no defence lines, the Americans somewhat bewildered, few reserves on hand and supply lines cut.

The American First Army had been completely out of contact with Gen. Bradley. He quickly studied maps and started to "tidy up" the front. He took over scattered American forces, planned his action and stopped the German drive.

His staff, which has been with him since Alamein, deserves high praise and credit. The Battle of the Ardennes can now be written off, thanks to Field-Marshal Montgomery.[44]

Top Secret testified to the extent of American Anglophobia: "You will find American officers who still believe that this famous broadcast actually originated in the BBC studios. They are certain that BBC blamed it on the Germans only after it had become too hot to handle."[45] Many of the officers who still believed the story had been broadcast by the BBC were probably south of the Givet-Houffalize-Prüm line. Anglophobia was alive and well at Bradley's headquarters where its *bête noire* was the London *Daily Mail*, London's most popular morning tabloid, which Bradley's aide, Major Chester A. Hansen, labeled "anti-American." Twelfth Army Group was put off by the nationalism in the British press that heralded the changeover in command. Hansen called it a "cataclysmic 'Roman Holiday'" and was certain that something had to be done to address what he regarded as an overreaction on the part of Fleet Street.[46]

Once *Time* announced that Montgomery was in command of two American armies, the British papers referred to the First United States Army as "Monty's troops," whereas they had previously referred to "Hodges' troops." On 6 January 1945, Alexander Clifford, the *Daily Mail*'s military correspondent and one of Montgomery's coterie, noted: "Montgomery with four armies under his command now commands the biggest single army group on either the Western or Eastern Fronts." Clifford also referred to the changeover as a "promotion" for Montgomery.[47] The *Daily Mail*'s editorial on 6 January was pleased by the increase in the field marshal's command, noting that lately he "had been relegated to a comparatively minor role." The paper also praised Eisenhower "for the moral courage he has shown in making such a far reaching change in field commands at this time."[48] On 8 January the *Daily Mail*'s political correspondent, Wilson Broadbent, claimed: "Montgomery Foresaw Attack." Citing the usually reliable political sources, Broadbent said that the situation in the Ardennes was desperate until Montgomery "asserted his leadership," and the field marshal was ready when the attack occurred because "he had felt some forebodings about German intentions."[49]

Broadbent's story was not a complete misconception. The field marshal did bring leadership to a chaotic situation, but his headquarters had been as much in the dark about German intentions as any. For example, on 16 December Montgomery had gone golfing, and on the previous night's report to the CIGS, Montgomery declared, "I do not propose to send any more evening situation reports until the war becomes more exciting. Therefore, if no report is received from me it means there is nothing to report."[50]

Once the war became "more exciting" the *Daily Express* printed Moorehead's story: "A 1914 General Asks Me How Rundstedt Did It." The unnamed, retired British general had written to him asking why the Germans could move forty miles in ten days while the Allies could gain only five, if that. Moorehead traced the situation to Eisenhower's decisions on strategy and command: One, he took over field command; two, he brought all his armies up to the Rhine in tandem. Army commanders found that even if they caused a breach in the German line, they did not have sufficient troops to exploit it. Secrecy, terrain, and forward basing of divisions all played a part in the German surprise attack. Moorehead concluded that the Allied grand strategy had "temporarily gone astray." The war correspondent believed that there was simply no subtlety to Allied command. Finally, Moorehead recommended the appointment of either an American or a British ground forces commander, and second, concentration on one "definite spearhead to pierce the German front."[51]

The strongest statement in support of Montgomery in the London papers came from A. J. Cummings of the *News Chronicle*. The headlines of Cummings' "Spotlight" column on 6 January announced "Monty Should Be Deputy C.-in-C.," but Cummings doubted that would happen. "The Americans profess their full confidence in Eisenhower and have let it be understood that Washington would 'frown upon' any proposals for 'lessening or splitting Eisenhower's command.'" The problem as Cummings saw it was that Eisenhower did not have enough time to devote to running the ground war, but a deputy ground commander would be able to do the thinking required for that task. Montgomery was the obvious man for the job, but as Cummings noted, "Eisenhower probably knows that neither his own generals nor the Washington War Department nor the American public would acquiesce in the appointment of Montgomery to a vital position on the Supreme Staff."[52] Cummings concluded that even if Montgomery should not be chosen for the job, there had to be changes in personnel and method in the Allied "Brains Trust in the West."

All of this British press campaign to get Montgomery named permanent ground forces commander, or deputy supreme commander, took place in public. At 12th Army Group, Ingersoll and others concluded that the British government had instigated it. As a result of the fear that the loss of the First and Ninth Armies might become permanent, Bradley held his own press conference on 9 January 1945. The two principal instigators were Ingersoll and Hansen. Ingersoll convinced Bradley that someone had to speak up for the American army because Eisenhower did not have the "guts to tell the truth." Furthermore, Ingersoll did not believe that Roosevelt or Marshall would let the supreme commander speak out.[53]

Eisenhower was the ranking American, and he chose not to speak to the command issue. Indeed, he preferred to keep the command alteration secret until the "salient was under full control and the two armies [American First and Third] are approaching one another."[54] Contrary to Ingersoll's view, Eisenhower understood perfectly what was about to take place over the press leak. Notes taken at the time by Air Marshal James Robb, SHAEF's air officer, recalled Eisenhower describing censorship as a two-edged sword. Since the changeover was secret, it automatically acquired news value, and the press inevitably got around censorship. The supreme commander said that the American press would now overreact to the British press. "For two and a half years I have been trying to get the press to talk of 'ALLIED' operations," Eisenhower said, "but look what happened."[55] Eisenhower refused to address the issue publicly, believing that the British government and army would act responsibly.

On 9 January 1945 General Bradley held his own press conference, which he did not clear in advance with SHAEF. In a statement prepared by Hansen and Ingersoll, Bradley gave birth to the myth that in leaving the Ardennes lightly manned, he had taken a "calculated risk." He further bent the truth by stating that no large supply dumps in the area were attacked, whereas the First Army had to destroy its huge gasoline dump near Spa to prevent the Germans from capturing it. Bradley recognized Montgomery's "notable contribution" in stationing British troops to protect Antwerp (in case of a breakthrough) and in fighting Germans at the tip of the salient. He pointed out that the relief of Bastogne by Patton's Third Army was the key to the battle; in fact the Germans had to rush their best troops to face Patton. Concerning Montgomery's newly enlarged command, the Hansen-Ingersoll press release overstated the case: "This was a temporary measure only and when the lines are rejoined Twelfth Army Group will resume command of all Allied troops in this area."[56] The First Army would return to Bradley's command when the emergency passed, but Montgomery would retain the Ninth Army until April.

Characteristically, the London *Daily Mail* objected to Bradley's press conference, and its 11 January editorial called Bradley's statement "A Slur on Monty." Taking Bradley's headquarters to task for believing all too quickly the phony German BBC report, the *Daily Mail* criticized SHAEF for under utilizing Montgomery's talents in the weeks preceding the Bulge. After all, the editorial claimed, Montgomery was "one of the very few commanders on either side who have made no mistakes." The *Daily Mail* regretted that the private disputes of the generals were now breaking out into public. "It is unusual, to say the least, for one commander in the field to tell the world what is to be the future professional status of another officer of equal rank." Such a statement should not have come from Bradley, the paper concluded, but from the supreme commander.[57]

The supreme commander, always careful of his public relations, refused to comment on command as he had previously refrained in January and August 1944. His silence infuriated Bradley's headquarters, but unlike Bradley, Eisenhower knew that steps were being taken to control the press outbreak. At 21st Army Group main headquarters, General de Guingand called in the British correspondents who proved that they had filed balanced stories; their editors were responsible for the "flaming headlines which told the British public that 'Monty' had defeated the enemy in the salient." The British minister of information, Brendan Bracken, signaled SHAEF that recent broadcasts praising Montgomery and disparaging the First

Army had been made on a German station, and the BBC explained the German scheme to its listeners, including American headquarters.[58]

The army group commanders' battle of the press conferences reached into the highest level of the British government. On 11 January 1945, the minister of information informed the War Cabinet that he had spoken to the editor of the *Daily Mail*, who agreed that the paper would "discontinue articles on this matter unless some new circumstances supervened."[59] None did. Ingersoll and Hansen credited Bradley's press conference as halting the press campaign to have Montgomery named ground forces commander; the reality was that the same British government that they blamed for the press flap stopped the command snipping in the *Daily Mail*.[60]

The War Cabinet's discussion of the *Daily Mail* editorial of 11 January focused on the "risk that public statements made by High Allied Commanders during the conduct of the campaign might well lead to some embarrassment, and possibly even to some impairment of friendly relations between the Allies."[61] Indeed the field marshal's press conference had been on the War Cabinet's agenda since 8 January, when Minister of Labor and National Service Ernest Bevin wondered why Montgomery needed to make public speeches. Churchill admitted that Montgomery had informed him that he intended to hold a press conference.[62] On 12 January the prime minister said he would have the CIGS again draw the commanders' attention to existing instructions on press conferences, especially the provision that the government clear the complete text before making any public statement. When pressed by the Cabinet to disavow Montgomery's remarks, Churchill declined, saying that would be "extremely hard" on the field marshal who had so distinguished himself in his recent command.[63]

CONCLUSION

Of the books discussed at length in this chapter, Butcher's *My Three Years with Eisenhower* best stood the test of time. Butcher's book provided the most intimate portrayal of Eisenhower in print, but it suffered from the author's extended absence from SHAEF. Of the 331 days of the campaign across France and Germany, the general's aide was out of the headquarters on public relations duty in Paris for 229 days, nearly 70 percent of the time. In terms of the diary, 271 pages of *My Three Years with Eisenhower* covered the period 6 June 1944 to 7 May 1945, while Butcher's tenure as a public relations officer coincided with 152 pages. Butcher devoted thirty pages of the 152 to press conferences (two by Eisenhower and one by Bedell Smith), his trip to forward press camps, and Eisenhower's instructions for press coverage and censorship.

While Butcher was away from the headquarters, Eisenhower's British military assistant, Colonel James Gault, kept the diary, and Gault's entries were concerned exclusively with operations, which was the standard. Gault's entries read like an after-action report, with no anecdote, opinion, or insight. Throughout his hiatus, Butcher saw Eisenhower nearly once a week and kept up with the diary, but the entries lost the intimate flavor that they enjoyed in North Africa or Telegraph Cottage, Eisenhower's getaway south of London. "History's eyes to the hour-by-hour record of the critical months ahead," David Eisenhower wrote, were closed by Butcher's exile.[64]

My Three Years does not show how Eisenhower conducted operations as Supreme Commander Allied Expeditionary Force (SCAEF), but it portrays a large man, possessed of immense patience, as well as a temper, and blessed with enough common sense to perform a crushing job. It is difficult to imagine any of his contemporaries handling the entire range of Eisenhower's responsibilities as gracefully as he did.

Rushed into print to capitalize on the postwar demand, Moorehead's biography of Montgomery displayed the same problems of accuracy affecting Butcher's and Ingersoll's works. Moorehead laid the cornerstone to Montgomery's postwar myth that everything went according to plan throughout his command. Furthermore, Moorehead revealed to Forrest Pogue that his subject could be devious at times, although his biography announced that Montgomery never intrigued. The *Daily Express* correspondent claimed that he attempted unsuccessfully to get the field marshal's chief of staff to prevent Montgomery's January press conference. When de Guingand said that was an odd position for a newsman to take, Moorehead responded that he wanted to win the war.[65] In effect, Moorehead portrayed Montgomery acting as his own press agent, a dangerous combination. Moorehead's reader learned that there had been serious disagreements between Eisenhower and Montgomery in December 1944. Indeed, the description of de Guingand's delivering the Eisenhower ultimatum over the issue of ground forces command broke new ground.

Top Secret was a mean-spirited diatribe against a crumbling empire. Employing a plot theory of history, it discounted Stalinism and warned against the likelihood of a third world war in Europe fought by the United States for Britain's imperial and continental aims. Because it was so critical of the British and sympathetic to the Russians, the book enjoyed a meteoric career and a short shelf-life.

However much it failed to persuade the public that Dwight Eisenhower was not a hero, *Top Secret*'s criticism of Eisenhower reads like Chester Wilmot's *The Struggle for Europe* in 1952 or Montgomery's memoirs in 1958. "I believe that in August of 1944," Ingersoll wrote, "a Supreme Commander . . . could have ended the war by Christmas by decisively backing *either* Montgomery of Bradley. But there was no such Supreme Allied Commander. There was no strong hand at the helm, no man in command. There was only a conference, presided over by a chairman."[66] Ingersoll argued that Eisenhower should never have attempted to take over command of the ground armies because SHAEF was not designed for active command, and his staff was not a field staff. SHAEF was built to coordinate the Anglo-American war effort, not to run battles. "It was constructed to be informed of decisions not to make them."[67]

Top Secret and subsequent works arguing that SHAEF prolonged the war were to have a major impact on Eisenhower's decision to write his own memoir. In July 1946 Eisenhower wrote to General Sir Hastings Lionel Ismay, who had been Churchill's wartime chief of staff, and was "Pug" to his friends. Ismay would be

Eisenhower's British confidant by mail for the rest of their days. Disturbed by Ingersoll's book, Eisenhower reflected:

I refuse to give up hope . . . of promoting a mutual understanding that we so often discussed during the war. . . . Extremists on both sides of the water can indulge in all the backbiting and name-calling that they please--they can never get away from the historical truth that the United States and the British Empire, working together, did a job that looked almost impossible at the time it was undertaken.[68]

NOTES

1. Alfred D. Chandler, Jr., and Louis Galambos, eds., et al., *The Papers of Dwight David Eisenhower: The Occupation*, 9 vols. (Baltimore and London: Johns Hopkins University Press, 1978), 6:17.

2. See Eisenhower's letter to Field Marshal Sir Alan Brooke, Chief Imperial General Staff (CIGS), of 16 December 1944 in Alfred D. Chandler, Jr., ed., and Stephen E. Ambrose, associate ed., et al., *The Papers of Dwight David Eisenhower: The War Years*, 5 vols. (Baltimore and London: Johns Hopkins University Press, 1970), 4:2350-51.

3. Harry C. Butcher, *My Three Years with Eisenhower: The Personal Diary of Captain Harry C. Butcher, USNR, Naval Aide to General Eisenhower, 1942 to 1945* (New York: Simon and Schuster, 1946), xii-xiii; David Eisenhower, *Eisenhower: At War, 1943-1945* (New York: Random House, 1986), 7; the Harry C. Butcher Papers, Correspondence File, (undated), Eisenhower Library [hereafter EL], Abilene, Kansas.

4. For the Eisenhower quotation see Chandler and Galambos, eds., *The Papers of Dwight David Eisenhower: The Occupation*, 6:327-28; Butcher, *My Three Years with Eisenhower*, 651-802.

5. Chandler and Galambos, eds., *The Papers of Dwight David Eisenhower: The Occupation*, 6:327-28.

6. Louis Galambos, ed., et al., *The Papers of Dwight David Eisenhower: The Chief of Staff*, 9 vols. (Baltimore and London: Johns Hopkins University Press, 1978), 7:685, n.1.

7. Ibid., 7:685.

8. Butcher, *My Three Years with Eisenhower*, 191.

9. Eisenhower, *Eisenhower: At War*, 413-14.

10. Winston S. Churchill, *The Second World War*, vol. 5, *Closing the Ring*, 6 vols. (Boston: Houghton Mifflin; Cambridge, Mass.: Riverside Press, 1948-1953), 85; Robert Sherwood, *Roosevelt and Hopkins: An Intimate History* (New York: Harper and Brothers, 1948), 802-803.

11. As quoted in Butcher, *My Three Years with Eisenhower*, 479; Nigel Hamilton, *Master of the Battlefield: Monty's War Years, 1942-1944* (New York: McGraw-Hill, 1983), 511.

12. For the SHAEF Directive, see the Papers of Field Marshal Viscount Alanbrooke, 14/4, Memorandum Prepared by DMO [Director Military Operations] for CIGS, 4 December 1944, Liddell Hart Center for Military Archives [hereafter LHCMA], King's College, London; the First United States Army Group (FUSAG) was later named the United States 12th Army Group to avoid confusion with the First United States Army (FUSA), see Omar N. Bradley, *A Soldier's Story* (New York: Holt, 1951), 180; *My Three Years with Eisenhower*, 649 provides the timetable.

13. Bradley, *A Soldier's Story*, 352.

14. Butcher, *My Three Years with Eisenhower*, 648-49. provides background; *New York Times*, 31 August 1944, p. 6 summarizes the story including SHAEF's denial; *Daily Mirror* (London), 17 August 1944, p. 3.

15. Forrest C. Pogue, *George C. Marshall: Organizer of Victory, 1943-1945* (New York: Viking Press, 1973), 425.

16. Washington *Times-Herald*, 18 August 1944, p. 2; Butcher, *My Three Years with Eisenhower*, 647-48.

17. Anthony Cave Brown, *Bodyguard of Lies* (New York: Harper and Row, 1975), 473-99, 736-38.

18. Butcher, *My Three Years with Eisenhower*, 648-49.

19. Alan Moorehead, *Montgomery* (London: Hamish Hamilton, 1946; New York: Coward-McCann, 1947).

20. Ibid., 205, italics in the original.

21. Phillip Knightley, *The First Casualty: From the Crimea to Vietnam: The War Correspondent As Hero, Propagandist, and Myth Maker* (New York: Harcourt Brace Jovanovich, 1975), 305.

22. Moorehead, *Montgomery*, 206.

23. Montgomery had been a field marshal since 1 September when Butcher made this entry on 14 September 1944; Butcher, *My Three Years with Eisenhower*, 642, for Eisenhower's opinion; see Chandler and Ambrose, eds., *The Papers of Dwight David Eisenhower: The War Years*, 4:2143-45. Forrest Pogue pointed out the error in his official history, *The Supreme Command (United States Army in World War II: The European Theater of Operations*, Washington, D.C.: Office of the Chief of Military History, Department of the Army, 1954), 560. For an example of the misdating creeping into the debate see Martin van Creveld, *Supplying War: Logistics from Wallenstein to Patton* (Cambridge: Cambridge University Press, 1977), 223.

24. Butcher added a footnote: "When the Ruhr industries are mentioned, those of the Saar Valley generally are implied as well." *My Three Years with Eisenhower*, 642n.

25. Butcher, *My Three Years with Eisenhower*, 671-73.

26. Dwight D. Eisenhower, Pre-Presidential Papers, 1916-1952, Principal File, Box 82, Montgomery (7), 28 January 1946, EL.

27. Dwight D. Eisenhower, Pre-Presidential Papers, 1916-1952, Principal File, Box 82, Montgomery (6), 29 October 1946, EL; for Montgomery allowing Moorehead use of his papers see Nigel Hamilton, *Monty: Final Years of the Field-Marshal, 1944-1976* (New York: McGraw-Hill, 1986), 606.

28. For Montgomery's powers of coordination, see *The Memoirs of the Field-Marshal the Viscount Montgomery of Alamein* (London: Collins, 1958), 318; for the pressure from Washington, Eisenhower's dilemma and Montgomery's message see Moorehead, *Montgomery*, 217-18.

29. Moorehead, *Montgomery*, 218.

30. For Eisenhower's intentions concerning the United States Ninth Army, see the Kay Summersby Diary, 9 December 1944: "Monty is going to be given the 9th Army for his attack North of the Rhur [sic]." Dwight D. Eisenhower, Pre-Presidential Papers, 1916-1952, Principal File, Box 140, Summersby Diary [hereafter SD], EL.

31. Moorehead, *Montgomery*, 217.

32. Vincent J. Esposito, ed., *The West Point Atlas of American Wars*, vol. II: *1900-1953* (New York: Frederick A. Praeger, 1959), Map 61.

33. Charles Poore, "Books of the Times," *New York Times*, 18 April 1946, p. 25; for details on Ingersoll, see Roy Hoopes, *Ralph Ingersoll: A Biography* (New York: Atheneum, 1985), 306. The woman, Elaine Cobb, was the wife of Captain Mortimer H. Cobb, USN.

34. Hoopes, *Ralph Ingersoll*, 261-62.

35. Ingersoll, *Top Secret*, 282.

36. For Eisenhower's selection, see Ingersoll, *Top Secret*, 77 78; for British "domination," see *Top Secret*, 47; for Smith's problems with Brooke, see Interview with Lieutenant General Walter Bedell Smith, Ambassador to Russia, 8 May 1947, OCMH Collection, *Supreme Command*, Pogue Interviews, USAMHI; for the Brooke-Smith confrontation see D.K.R. Crosswell, *The Chief of Staff: The Military Career of General Walter Bedell Smith* (Westport, Conn.: Greenwood Press, 1991), 213.

37. Ingersoll, *Top Secret*, 263-64; Hoopes, *Ralph Ingersoll*, 304.

38. Ingersoll, *Top Secret*, 276.

39. *Time* 45, (8 January 1945): 21.

40. Ingersoll, *Top Secret*, 278; for Ingersoll's role in the G-2 Estimate, see Hoopes, *Ralph Ingersoll*, 303.

41. *New York Times*, 6 January 1945, p. 3.

42. Moorehead, *Montgomery*, 215-16.

43. Interview with Alan Moorehead, 21 January 1947, OCMH Collection, *Supreme Command*, Pogue Interviews, USAMHI.

44. Richard Lamb, *Montgomery in Europe, 1943-1945: Success or Failure?* (London: Buchan and Enright, 1984), 331-32.

45. Ingersoll, *Top Secret*, 279n.

46. "Monty Takes Command," 1, Hansen Diary [hereafter HD], 6 January 1945, Chester B. Hansen Papers [hereafter CBHP], USAMHI.

47. The *Daily Mail* (London), 6 January 1945, p. 1.

48. Ibid., p. 2.

49. Ibid., 8 January 1945, p. 8.

50. The Papers of Field Marshal Viscount Montgomery of Alamein, 15 December 1944, Reel 10, BLM 111/69, Imperial War Museum [hereafter IWM], Lambeth, London.

51. The *Daily Express* (London), 4 January 1945, p. 3.

52. The *News Chronicle* (London), 6 January 1945, p. 2.

53. Hoopes, *Ralph Ingersoll*, 306. Bradley's fear of losing both American armies was unwarranted as Eisenhower's directive of 31 December 1944 made clear that Montgomery's command was temporary; see Chandler and Ambrose, eds., *The Papers of Dwight David Eisenhower: The War Years*, 4:2388-89.

54. Diary of Air Marshal Robb, Meeting in Supreme Commander's Office, 5 January 1945, Papers of Air Chief Marshal Sir James Robb, AC 71/9/26, Royal Air Force Museum [hereafter RAFM], Hendon, London.

55. Diary of Air Marshal Robb, Meeting in Supreme Commander's Office, 9 January 1945, Papers of Air Chief Marshal Sir James Robb, AC 71/9/26, RAFM.

56. Twelfth Army Group Advance Headquarters, 9 January 1945, Press Releases by Omar N. Bradley, 9 January 1945-1 May 1945, Hansen World War II Documents and Reports, CBHP, USAMHI.

57. The *Daily Mail* (London), 11 January 1945, p. 2.

58. Diary of Air Marshal Robb, Meeting in Supreme Commander's Office, 10 January 1945, for comment on war correspondents; for Brendan Bracken's signal, 11 January 1945, Papers of Air Chief Marshal Sir James Robb, AC 71/9/26, RAFM.

59. Public Record Office [hereafter PRO]: CAB 65/49, War Cabinet Conclusions, 11 January 1945, PRO, Kew, London.

60. HD, 12 January 1945, CBHP, USAMHI; Ingersoll, *Top Secret*, 281-82.

61. PRO: CAB 65/49, War Cabinet Conclusions, 11 January 1945.

62. Ibid., 8 January 1945.

63. PRO: CAB 65/51, War Cabinet, Confidential Annex, 12 January 1945.

64. Eisenhower, *Eisenhower: At War*, 413-14.

65. Interview with Alan Moorehead, 21 January 1947, OCMH Collection, *Supreme Command*, Pogue Interviews, USAMHI.

66. Ingersoll, *Top Secret*, 219, italics in the original.

67. Ibid., 166.

68. Galambos, ed., et al., *The Papers of Dwight David Eisenhower: The Chief of Staff*, 7:1192.

2

The Dichotomy of Postwar Memoirs: Patton, Allen, Smith, de Guingand, Montgomery, and Summersby

> In every case, practically throughout the campaign, I was under wraps from the Higher Command. . . . and [I] feel that had I been permitted to go all out, the war would have ended sooner and more lives would have been saved. Particularly . . . in the early days of September, we were halted, owing to the desire, or necessity, on the part of General Eisenhower in backing Montgomery's move to the north. At that time there was no question of doubt but that we could have gone through and on across the Rhine within ten days.
>
> --General George S. Patton, Jr.[1]

Either infuriating or bland, the postwar memoirs contained a dichotomy of opinion over command and strategy that continues to the present day. Beginning in 1946 with Ralph Ingersoll's *Top Secret*, it was alleged that Eisenhower or SHAEF (often used as a euphemism for Eisenhower) prolonged the war in September 1944. In 1947 two American authors, Colonel Robert S. Allen and General George S. Patton, Jr., blamed Eisenhower for lengthening the war by opting for Montgomery's northern drive in September 1944 rather than a Third Army attack through the Siegfried Line east of Metz.[2] Less controversial authors, such as General Smith in 1946, and in 1947 both General de Guingand and Field Marshal Montgomery himself, played up the importance of Allied unity, which Eisenhower stressed, as the essential factor in the eventual Allied victory. In 1948 Kay Summersby, Eisenhower's driver and receptionist, published the strongest praise to date of Eisenhower's role in forging amity in the high command of northwest Europe. According to this school of thought, even a perfect strategy would have been futile without Allied unity, which Montgomery's chief of staff believed would have been jeopardized by the field marshal's proposed single thrust.

Each side of the debate emphasized a different aspect of Eisenhower's command: One stressed victories won, the other opportunities lost. From 1946 onward accounts critical of SHAEF's handling of the ground campaign in northwest Europe threw Eisenhower and his supporters on the defensive. Immediately after the war, extreme viewpoints expressed in hastily written books set the tone for the writing on strategy and command, broad front and single thrust, for the next generation. For the purpose of this study the misconceptions are as significant as the facts, and various misconceptions have stood the test of time.

As time went on and critics came to view the cold war's geographical division of Europe as a byproduct of an incomplete Allied victory brought about by SHAEF and Eisenhower, the memoirs would become more critical, particularly on the British side of the Atlantic. In the immediate postwar era, however, there were only occasional hints of the depth of the criticism to come. More germane to this study was the extent to which even Montgomery was prepared in 1946-1947 to maintain Anglo-American unity by glossing over his differences with Eisenhower's conduct of ground operations.

SMITH'S "EISENHOWER'S SIX GREAT DECISIONS"

Britain's wartime prime minister also realized that the writing of the recent past would affect the present. In January 1946 Churchill dropped by the Pentagon to visit Lieutenant General Smith, Eisenhower's former chief of staff and recently appointed ambassador to the Soviet Union. Churchill believed that it was of paramount importance for Britain and America to maintain their wartime sense of common purpose, which extended to personal accounts of the history of the wartime alliance. According to Smith, Churchill encouraged him to lend his pen in the effort: "He felt that accounts would be written by participants of both nationalities from a less impartial viewpoint, and that as a result there might, during the critical postwar years, be some loss of that feeling of common purpose and ability to work together which we developed during the period of crisis and hazard."[3] Judging by Churchill's "Iron Curtain" speech at Fulton, Missouri, later in that trip, the Anglo-American alliance had to continue to work together in a new era of "crisis and hazard."[4]

Conversation with Churchill led to Smith's "Eisenhower's Six Great Decisions," which ran in *The Saturday Evening Post* from 8 June to 13 July 1946. Smith's articles countered the notion popularized by Ingersoll's *Top Secret* that SHAEF had prolonged the war and that Eisenhower was a figurehead. The former SHAEF chief of staff described at length in his article, "Eisenhower's Six Great Decisions: 5, Encirclement of the Ruhr," how Eisenhower had settled on his strategy. At a high-level SHAEF conference in May 1944, Eisenhower agreed with his staff's contention that Germany had two hearts, the Ruhr and Berlin. Without the Ruhr, its industrial heart, Eisenhower and his planners reasoned, Germany could no longer make war. Therefore, based on its importance to the German war effort, the Ruhr was the key objective inside Germany.

During the course of the meeting, Eisenhower drew three avenues of advance on the staff map. Beginning in Normandy, Eisenhower penciled in two lines. One crossed northern France and Belgium and reached the Rhine north of the Ruhr. The second began in southern Normandy and followed the Loire, crossed the Seine below Paris, and paralleled the northern axis of advance until it met the Rhine south of the first. Eisenhower sketched a third line branching off from the southerly advance in eastern France and moving in a southeasterly direction, avoiding the Ardennes, until it met the Rhine in the area of Coblenz. SHAEF expected this assault to drive into Germany through the so-called Frankfurt corridor. Smith concluded:

There, penciled on the map, was the draft of our grand strategy. In the months that followed, subsidiary plans were changed as the enemy revealed his own strategy--or lack of it--for countering our designs. But our broad advance across France and into Germany followed the original pattern. I doubt that there has ever been a campaign in history where actual operations fitted so closely the initial plan of a commander, adopted so far in advance. Long before we stepped foot in Europe and tested the enemy's strength in battle, we had decided on the blueprint for his defeat.[5]

Eisenhower concurred with the recommendation of SHAEF'S Planning Staff. A draft planning paper had pointed toward the subsequent strategic design of the campaign in northwest Europe as early as 25 April 1944. The planners argued that it would be necessary for the Allies to advance "on as broad a front as possible." Advancing on a broad front had the advantage of allowing for "deception, surprise and manoeuvre" and would force the Germans to divide their forces, opening them to defeat in detail.[6] By 3 May 1944 the Planning Staff finished the paper that formed the basis of the discussion outlined by Smith. The staff paper assumed that the Allies would not possess a strong numerical advantage over the Germans until February 1945, some eight months after D-Day. Accordingly, the planners advised:

We must, therefore, avoid a line of advance which leads us to a head-on collision with the main GERMAN forces without opportunity for manoeuvre. . . . As operations progress and our superiority becomes more marked, we must advance on a front sufficiently broad to threaten an advance by more than one of the "gaps" into GERMANY. By doing so we should be able to keep the GERMANS guessing as to the direction of our main thrust, cause them to extend their forces, and lay the GERMAN forces open to defeat in detail.[7]

SHAEF's Planning Staff consisted, in this instance, of three British officers: Captain P. N. Walter, Royal Navy, Allied naval expeditionary force; Brigadier Kenneth G. McLean, General Staff; and Group Captain H. P. Broad, Royal Air Force, Allied expeditionary air force.[8] SHAEF'S planners rejected the notion of a single line of advance north of the Ardennes because the area's many rivers negated the use of armor. A single front north of the Ardennes would restrict the Allied advance to too narrow a front, which grew progressively narrower as it approached the Rhine, allowing the Allies insufficient room to maneuver, surprise, or outflank the Germans. Since no vital German interest could be threatened by an attack toward Dijon and Lyons in southeastern France, it was ruled out. An advance eastward toward Metz enjoyed favorable tank country until it drew even with Chalons, where the terrain presented difficulties for both armored operations and airfield construction. The easterly Metz axis suffered in comparison by being beyond the range of light and medium bombers based in the United Kingdom and because it did not directly threaten the Ruhr. Consequently, SHAEF planners concluded that the best possible course of action was an advance on two mutually supporting axes: one, on a line Amiens-Maubeuge-Liege-the Ruhr, which would be the main advance; two, on the line Verdun-Metz, which would be the subsidiary advance.[9]

DE GUINGAND'S *OPERATION VICTORY*

Early in 1947, Eisenhower's strategy received a prominent endorsement from Major General Sir Francis de Guingand. De Guingand's 1947 *Operation Victory* was the first postwar memoir out of the British camp bearing on the debate over strategy and command. Known to his contemporaries as "Freddie," de Guingand served as Montgomery's chief of staff for three years, beginning in the desert in August 1942 with the British Eighth Army and ending in May 1945 in northwest Europe with the 21st Army Group. De Guingand's memoir maintained the same independence of mind and ability to get on with his American counterparts that he had shown throughout the war.

Perhaps the manner in which Montgomery treated him over the last months of their service together accounted for de Guingand's willingness to disagree in public with Britain's most famous soldier and current CIGS. Following the German surrender, Montgomery commanded the British Army of the Rhine until mid-1946, when he was scheduled to become CIGS. Montgomery arranged for de Guingand to assume the office of Director of Military Intelligence (DMI) at Whitehall on the expectation of his later becoming Montgomery's vice chief of the imperial general staff. By January 1946, then Lord Alanbrooke had observed de Guingand's performance as DMI and told Montgomery that he was unacceptable for promotion to vice chief.[10] In truth, de Guingand had never fully recovered from nervous exhaustion suffered while serving as Montgomery's chief of staff. Having heard Alanbrooke on the matter, Montgomery walked to de Guingand's office and told him that he would not have him as his vice chief. When de Guingand asked why, Montgomery said, "Because it would not do me any good."[11]

Rejected by his superior, Major General de Guingand then faced retirement at his substantive rank of colonel because Whitehall had never promoted him permanently to the rank he had held for three years. Only appeals from Eisenhower and Bedell Smith on behalf of de Guingand's promotion stirred Whitehall to action; Montgomery had refused to lobby on behalf of his former chief of staff. De Guingand took his accumulated leave and went to Cannes to write his memoir in a villa provided by his friend Aly Khan.[12] Written quickly, it was a commercial success and attracted great notice in Britain. Unfortunately, de Guingand, fearing the book would be a commercial failure, elected to take a lump sum payment from his British publisher. Thus he lost the royalties due him when the book sold through seven hardback and one paperback edition.[13]

Operation Victory was no "My Three Years with Montgomery." De Guingand wrote that it would be easy for him to write sensational stories about Montgomery's relations with his famous contemporaries. Obviously, there were times "when men in high appointments possessing great strength of character" found it impossible to agree. At such times, when nerves were frayed, men sometimes made comments they did not wish repeated. "They are forgotten," wrote de Guingand, "unless people in my position wish to remember them merely for personal gain and sensation." The problem with such sensational writing, according to de Guingand, was that it allowed the parts to distract attention from the whole. Freddie pronounced his former superior "difficult" at times, especially when he did not get his way. Concerning Montgomery's relationship with Eisenhower, de Guingand admitted to a "measure of disagreement," but concluded that the two men had always resolved their difficulties, and their relationship stood up to the "stress and strain of war." Overall, he concluded: "Eisenhower's handling of Montgomery was a fine achievement."[14]

The book was controversial in Britain because of its dismissal of Montgomery's single-thrust scheme. Sir Francis stated that "this was the only major issue over which I did not agree with my Chief. I have always held the contrary view, and . . . I am more than ever convinced that I was right."[15] His objections to Montgomery's strategy were based on logistics, lines of communications, engineering difficulties, and Nazi fanaticism. Without the Belgian port of Antwerp and its railroads, it would have been impossible to maintain a sizable force east of the Rhine. Adding truck transport from Patton's Third Army was merely a stopgap measure, and the road and bridge network from Normandy to the Rhine was not up to the additional strain. It was doubtful that the British would have found any intact bridges over the Rhine. Moreover, their bridging equipment was still in England. To those who believed that by crossing the Rhine Montgomery could have compelled a German surrender, the former 21st Army Group chief of staff argued, "It took a Russian offensive using about 160 divisions, massive offensives on our part, as well as eight more months of devastating air attack, to force the Germans to capitulate. And even then Hitler and his gang never gave up."[16]

De Guingand believed that the Germans would have wiped out any Allied force that crossed the Rhine in the fall of 1944. Besides, there was nothing wrong with Eisenhower's insistence on joining up with the Allied forces coming up the Rhone River Valley from the south. No one could blame Eisenhower if "he felt it necessary to tidy up the whole front."[17] De Guingand also argued against Montgomery's notion that Patton could have been stopped in his tracks without cost to the Allies; the Germans would have been free to redeploy the divisions that had been deployed against Patton. Lastly, de Guingand asked what the American people would have thought and said if Eisenhower had opted for Montgomery's plan and it failed. What would American commanders who had been sat down have said about Montgomery then? Denying American troops an offensive role would have had a devastating impact on their morale. More than likely, de Guingand concluded, Montgomery's single-thrust strategy would have produced a crisis between the Allies.

Therefore, de Guingand agreed with Eisenhower's conclusion that a single line of advance on Germany in August 1944 was militarily unsafe and by inference politically impossible. Commenting on "the only major issue" in which he had disagreed with the field marshal, de Guingand declared overoptimism the culprit. Owing to the devastating victory that they had won in Normandy, the Allies underestimated Germany's powers of recuperation. "Just as the enemy managed to produce forces to organize a defence at Arnhem," de Guingand wrote, "so do I believe he would have produced an answer to a single thrust into Westphalia as favoured by Montgomery."[18]

Operation Victory repeated Alan Moorehead's chronological error of placing Montgomery's press conference before Eisenhower's ultimatum over the ground forces command. Moorehead proofread his manuscript, and since both men wrote at high speed it is speculation as to which author originated the chronological error. Each man had been present at only one of the two events during the Battle of the Bulge. While de Guingand had carried Eisenhower's ultimatum to Montgomery, he had not attended Montgomery's press conference, which Moorehead had witnessed. De Guingand believed that the British press campaign to name Montgomery ground forces commander was dangerous because it potentially restricted Eisenhower as to future command changes. When the British press undermined Bradley's self-image, American public opinion might have prevented Eisenhower from placing American troops under British command in the future. "If this happened," de Guingand concluded, "Eisenhower's hands might have become tied, in that he would not have been allowed to group his forces with complete freedom, irrespective of nationality."[19] The equipoise of the alliance was in question.

At this point, de Guingand said he flew to SHAEF to spend the night with General Smith because he sensed that a moment of crisis had arrived. The next day he spoke to Eisenhower, whom he described as "more worried than I had ever seen him."[20] Montgomery's chief of staff flew next to his superior's headquarters at Zonhoven, north of Hasselt. De Guingand's 1947 memoir chose not to mention that he carried Eisenhower's ultimatum on the subject of command, nor did de Guingand mention that Montgomery had brought up the issue in conference with Eisenhower on 28 December and by letter on 29 December 1944. In 1947 de Guingand described Montgomery writing the conciliatory message to Eisenhower that prevented a showdown over the command issue.

De Guingand did not have to wait long for Montgomery's reaction to his comments on single thrust. On 26 February 1947, Montgomery informed him that he had just finished reading *Operation Victory*, calling it "quite first rate." The field marshal added, however, that he could not remember de Guingand's disagreeing with his plan for a single thrust on the Ruhr. Montgomery stated what he believed were Eisenhower's real reasons for rejecting his strategy, adding his brief explanation of why Eisenhower and now de Guingand were wrong:

The real reason that Ike wouldn't do it was that it meant halting the right, i.e. the bulk of the Americans. He said that public opinion in America wouldn't stand it; I told him that victories won wars and not public opinion. . . . The broad front strategy finally led us into the most frightful mess, involved a great waste of life, and meant that the war had to go on to the summer of 1945. My plan involved a bold move; but the prize was terrific. Ike wouldn't face adverse American opinion, and told me so; admin reasons were brought up afterwards.[21]

When *The Times* serialized *Operation Victory*, the paper of record revealed de Guingand's criticism of Montgomery's strategic conception of the late campaign. Sir Charles Richardson, de Guingand's biographer, has pointed out that this public debate threatened to diminish Montgomery's standing with the other services, with the British government, and with Eisenhower and the Pentagon.[22] All of this was taking place while Montgomery, according to his official biographer, Nigel Hamilton, was "determined to drag Britain backwards into a transatlantic alliance by his own personal effort."[23]

Montgomery had reason to be upset with de Guingand. A year earlier Montgomery had written concerning his forthcoming *Normandy to the Baltic*, mentioning how he had instructed his former Operations officer at 21st Army Group, Brigadier David Belchem, who was preparing the manuscript, to "keep entirely off all political arguments and international background, inter-service arguments, and so on." Montgomery wanted exactly what he got: "A plain tale of facts, unembellished by any controversial or unsavoury details." Appalled by Butcher's serializations in the London *Sunday Dispatch*, Montgomery predicted the future while he explained his current innocuous approach to the past: "It is possible that later on, in my evening of life, I may give the true facts to the world; but not yet and not until I have retired from Active Army Life. Butcher is doing enough harm. . . . Tedder seems to have said some very indiscreet things to him in Normandy, and very probably was even more indiscreet later on: and it will all come out."[24]

MONTGOMERY'S *NORMANDY TO THE BALTIC*

In early May 1946 the CIGS wrote the War Office for permission to find a commercial publisher for both of his privately printed books, *El Alamein to the River Sangro* and *Normandy to the Baltic*. Montgomery advocated commercial publication to combat the growing number of misinformed books and articles. *Normandy to the Baltic*, a history of the 21st Army Group, appeared in 1947; *El Alamein to the River Sangro*, a history of the British Eighth Army, appeared commercially in 1948. Both were written to foster professional study and battlefield tours by soldiers.[25]

Hanson Baldwin, the military correspondent of the *New York Times*, called *Normandy to the Baltic* "dry-as-dust," noting that it read as though pieced together from an after-action report.[26] For the purposes of the present study, however, it is necessary to point out what *Normandy to the Baltic* omitted. It avoided all controversies, mentioned men by name only in praise, and singled out General Eisenhower as the leader of the Allied team that won the war. A far cry from

Ingersoll, Allen, and Patton, the following selection from the foreword set the tone
of the book:

A great Allied team went into battle in North-West Europe in June 1944 under the supreme
command of General Eisenhower. The efficiency of the team to which we all belonged can
best be judged by the results it achieved. When Allies work together there are bound to be
different points of view, and when these occur it is essential that they are thrashed out fully
and frankly; but once a final decision is given, it is the duty of all members of the team to
carry out that decision loyally. The Allied team worked in this spirit, and by its team work
achieved overwhelming victory.[27]

As far as command was concerned, Montgomery ventured an opinion that a
weakness in the OVERLORD command structure was a lack of an American-style
task force commander on the level of an army group. Such a commander could
have coordinated all of the combat arms. However, Montgomery noted that this
would have meant changes in the naval and air commands as well. As it was, the
lack of a single commander meant much time was wasted in multiple briefings and
conferences for senior officers of several services.[28]

From 23 August to 12 September, the field marshal argued, the Allies enjoyed
the period of maximum strategic opportunity. Citing an intelligence report that
showed the Germans deploying, at the time, two weak Panzer divisions and nine
infantry divisions north of the Ardennes, Montgomery informed the supreme commander that the time was ripe for "one powerful full-blooded thrust across the
Rhine and into the heart of Germany."[29] Naturally, a "full-blooded" assault aimed
at achieving a truly "decisive result" required the "whole resources of the Allied
armies." The 21st Army Group commander acknowledged that this "would have
entailed reverting sectors of the Allied front to a purely static role."[30] *Normandy
to the Baltic* talked of bouncing the Rhine, or crossing without pause, before winter
and before the Germans could turn that river into a massive barrier. In arguing for
a single thrust and priority on all supplies, Montgomery said that a bridgehead over
the Rhine would have served as "a springboard from which to develop operations
into the heart of Germany." *Normandy to the Baltic* cited a British estimate that
predicted that without the Ruhr, "the German capacity for waging war would peter
out within six months."[31]

Then came the setback at Arnhem during Operation MARKET-GARDEN, in
which only 2,400 paratroopers of the British 1st Airborne Division made it back
into Allied lines. Unfortunately, Montgomery chose to classify this operation as
"ninety per cent successful."[32] The Germans recovered, there was no Allied bridgehead over the Rhine to outflank the Siegfried Line, and the Allies experienced a
long winter campaign. *Normandy to the Baltic* summarized the situation by mid-
October this way: "The Allied drive to the Rhine had now virtually come to a halt.
We had won a great victory in Normandy and had advanced north of the Seine on
a broad front. Great successes had been achieved, but we had nowhere been strong
enough to secure decisive results quickly."[33]

Normandy to the Baltic demonstrated a high degree of similarity between Montgomery's and Eisenhower's conception of Germany's eventual defeat. Montgomery stated during a conference on 18 October 1944 with Eisenhower and Bradley that the present circumstances were analogous to Normandy before the breakout. "It seemed to me that the decisive battle for Germany might well be fought west of the Rhine," Montgomery wrote, "just as the battle for France was fought south of the Seine."[34] General Smith's article, "Eisenhower's Six Great Decisions: 4, Victory West of the Rhine," referred to Eisenhower's constant objective to defeat the German army west of the Rhine. Through a series of "interlocking campaigns," Smith said, Eisenhower intended to turn the German reluctance to give ground into an Allied advantage.[35]

Montgomery called Germany's decision to fight in the Reichswald, a forest on the Dutch-German border near Cleve, rather than withdraw over the Rhine, their third great mistake of the campaign. The previous two mistakes also demonstrated a reluctance to withdraw--for example, their counterattack on Mortain in Normandy and their Ardennes counteroffensive. The supreme commander saw the fruition of his broad-front strategy in the Germans' repeated willingness to see their forces destroyed rather than withdraw to fight again. The Germans would lose a war of attrition, and Eisenhower saw the Ardennes counteroffensive as a blessing in disguise. General Smith's article, "Eisenhower's Six Great Decisions: 3, The Battle of the Bulge," makes this point with the following quote from the supreme commander's order of the day of 22 December 1944: "By rushing out from his fixed defenses the enemy may give us the chance to turn his great gamble into his worst defeat. . . . Let everyone hold before him a single thought--to destroy the enemy on the ground, in the air, everywhere--to destroy him!"[36]

Following their defeat in the Ardennes, Montgomery believed that the Germans should have withdrawn across the Rhine and attempted to delay the Allies at that river barrier. When the Germans decided to fight in the Reichswald, however, Montgomery knew that their losses would bring about the end of the war in "a matter of weeks."[37] The Germans would be defeated west of the Rhine, just as they had been defeated south of the Seine. "General Eisenhower's belief that the Germans would choose the fatal course of fighting till it was too late to withdraw proved correct," General Smith wrote, "in every instance except one. At Cologne the enemy retreated across the river with forces intact."[38]

There was very little in Montgomery's *Normandy to the Baltic* that would have upset Dwight Eisenhower. Montgomery wrote de Guingand in mid-April 1947, informing him that no one's feelings would be hurt by the book because "we have been extremely tactful."[39]

PATTON'S *WAR AS I KNEW IT*

General Patton's *War As I Knew It* appeared posthumously in mid-November 1947 and immediately added fuel to Ingersoll's fire. Patton died in December 1945 of complications following a traffic accident in which he suffered a broken neck. Included in his papers was the manuscript of his wartime memoir, which he had written utilizing his extensive wartime diary. In order to publish it, Patton's widow, Beatrice Ayer Patton, and Colonel Paul Harkins, his deputy chief of staff, deleted many of the personal references and added an introduction to each chapter.[40] To speculate on the book that Patton might have written after the Berlin Airlift or during the Korean War at the height of the cold war, had he lived to see it, is to imply that it would have been even more critical of Eisenhower than the edition released in 1947.

In late October 1947, then Chief of Staff of the United States Army General Eisenhower complained to then Ambassador Smith about Patton's upcoming memoir. Eisenhower alluded to a serialization that had recently appeared in *The Saturday Evening Post*, alleging that SHAEF had prevented Patton from winning the war in September 1944. "I am beginning to think," Eisenhower wrote, "that crackpot history is going to guide the future student in his study of the late conflict."[41]

George Patton had been America's greatest practitioner of armored warfare, certainly its most publicized. As commanding general of the Third United States Army, he had emphasized speed and audacity. He was also a Russophobe. He was given a role in the postwar occupation of Germany and was expected to crack down on former Nazis, but his anti-Semitism and political conservatism led to his final humiliation. Privately, he had called the treatment of the Germans needlessly severe and politically counterproductive, for he believed the Americans would need the Germans on their side when the time came to fight the Russians.[42] In October 1945, following a Patton press interview likening the Nazis to Republicans and Democrats, Eisenhower felt compelled to relieve him of command of the Third Army.[43] Patton went off to command the Fifteenth United States Army, which was a headquarters preparing historical studies of the war.

War As I Knew It stated that SHAEF prolonged the war. On 22 August 1944, Patton believed that the Third Army could have advanced with three corps, two up and one back, on a line Metz-Nancy-Epinal: "We could have crossed the German border in ten days."[44] A week later the war reached a crucial stage, according to the Third Army commander: "It was evident at this time that there was no real threat against us as long as we did not allow ourselves to be stopped by imaginary enemies."[45] Patton's plan was to drive east and cut the Siegfried Line before the Germans could man it; however, SHAEF did not concur. On 2 September, Patton attended a meeting with Eisenhower at Bradley's headquarters at Chartres, during which Eisenhower quoted Clausewitz to his subordinates in a didactic fashion and spoke of the upcoming battle of Germany, which Patton believed audacity would have obviated. *War As I Knew It* omitted what Patton confided to his diary: "Ike is all for caution since he has never been to the front and has no feel of actual fighting. Bradley, Hodges, and I are all for a prompt advance."[46]

ALLEN'S *LUCKY FORWARD*

Colonel Robert S. Allen's *Lucky Forward* (1947) was even more critical of SHAEF and Eisenhower than his superior's edited memoir. Allen, another journalist in uniform, was, along with Drew Pearson, coauthor of the "Washington Merry Go Round." Allen recalled a meeting at Chartres on 30 August 1944 among Bradley, Patton, and Major General Harold R. "Pinky" Bull, SHAEF's G-3 Operations officer. Patton told Bull that the only Germans in front of him were retreating; however, with gasoline deliveries of 33,000 gallons of a requested 450,000, there was no way the Third Army could maintain contact. Allen believed that only SHAEF stood between the Germans and their complete defeat at the hands of the Third Army.[47] The Third Army's gasoline shortages stemmed from Eisenhower's decision to have Montgomery make the main attack and to use what gasoline he could rush to the front for Montgomery's northern advance.

Deprived of needed fuel, Patton resorted to the "Rock Soup" method of attack, and he told the following parable: "A tramp once went to a house and asked for some boiling water to make rock soup. The lady was interested and gave him the water, in which he placed two polished white stones. He then asked if he might have some potatoes and carrots to put in the soup to flavor it a little, and finally ended up with some meat."[48] The point was that Patton continued to attack by reconnaissance in force until he had made contact with enough Germans to demand resupply. As a result of Patton's continued offensive, on 12 September 1944, Montgomery complained to Eisenhower that the First Army's promised support for his northern offensive was jeopardized through lack of fuel. Learning of Montgomery's allegation during a meeting at 12th Army Group an infuriated Patton responded, "That's a goddamned lie." Of the Third Army's requested gasoline delivery of 300,000 gallons, Communications Zone (COMZ), the American army's logistical command linking the Normandy bases with frontline units, was able to deliver on 11-12 September only 70,250 and 65,000 gallons, respectively. Patton asked: "How the hell are these small quantities holding up him or First Army? That claim is absurd."[49]

Three days later Patton met Bradley at Verdun, along with General Bull, and found Bradley depressed. It seemed that Montgomery had talked SHAEF into moving all supplies to the First Army and sitting down the Third Army. In addition, SHAEF directed Bradley to provide a corps of two divisions to Lieutenant General Alexander Patch's Seventh Army, which had only one corps of its own.[50] Patton's diary for 15 September noted Bradley's full apprehensions regarding American formations: "Brad told Ike that if Monty takes control of the XIX Corps and VII Corps of the First Army, as he wants to, he, Bradley, will ask to be relieved."[51] By 18 September Bradley knew he would retain the First Army's VII Corps and he had regained his sense of humor when he called Patton to tell him of Montgomery's latest demand. According to Bradley, Montgomery wanted all American troops to halt in place so that he could make a "'dagger thrust with the Twenty-First Army Group at the heart of Germany.'" Waxing sarcastic, Bradley said it would be more like a "'butter knife thrust,'" and told Patton that he should attack at once to prevent being assigned a static role.[52]

Earlier in that week, Bradley and Patton had discussed either a showdown with SHAEF, resignation, or both. Patton's diary summarized the state of command in northwest Europe: "Ike feels that we think he is selling us out but he has to, as

Monty will not take orders, so we have to."[53] Butcher's unpublished diary entry of 2 August 1944 shed light on Eisenhower's reluctance to command Montgomery. Butcher noted at the time that Eisenhower had been "distraught" over Montgomery's performance in Normandy: "After all, Monty has issued directives as lofty as the Ten Commandments but has so far not carried through on them except as performed by Bradley and then only by Ike "pushing on the reins" with Bradley for whom Ike feels not only responsibility but authority to press."[54]

Bradley and Patton understood that Eisenhower did not command Montgomery in the same manner as he commanded them, and Butcher noted that Eisenhower was far more comfortable commanding Bradley. Both had graduated from West Point in 1915, both were from the Middle West, neither had fought in World War I, and they had shared the fraternal deprivations of the American army in the 1920s and 1930s. On the other hand, Montgomery had become a legend in his own time as a result of El Alamein, and he was an unparalleled hero to the British populace. The British general was Eisenhower's superior in terms of combat experience, having been wounded in World War I, and in command experience, having commanded every unit from company to army group. Eisenhower had never heard a shot fired in anger before World War II and had never commanded so much as a division; however, he had commanded a base and a tank battalion. Furthermore, as the ranking British officer in the European theater, Montgomery had responsibilities to his own government; he was superior to Bradley in that regard. There is little wonder that Eisenhower treated his British subordinate differently from his American colleagues, and they not only noticed it, they resented it.

With Patton's gasoline and transport going to Hodges' First Army to support Montgomery's northern attack on Arnhem, there were bitter feelings at Third Army headquarters when Montgomery came a cropper at Arnhem. "It was a double defeat," Robert Allen wrote. "In the north, it was a defeat for Montgomery at the hands of the enemy. In the south, it was a defeat for Third Army at the hands of SHAEF." Montgomery's victory over SHAEF, Allen contended, had given Hitler "a new lease on life."[55] As far as Allen was concerned, halting Patton made SHAEF ultimately responsible for "the tragic and costly Battle of the Bulge," which "enabled the Nazis to continue the war until the following May."[56] To demonstrate SHAEF's culpability in prolonging the war, Allen quoted Major General Richard Schimpf, commanding officer of the German 3rd Parachute Division: "There is no question that if your Third Army had not been halted before Metz in September, it could have penetrated the Siegfried Line very quickly and been on the Rhine in a short time."[57]

Allen and Patton agreed that it had been unnecessary to put Montgomery in command of two American armies during the Battle of the Bulge. Neither believed Bradley's communications problems had warranted the move. *War As I Knew It* said that it appeared that Bradley was being "sidetracked," either because of Eisenhower's lack of confidence in him or because it was the only way to prevent Montgomery from "regrouping." Patton's unpublished diary explained the regrouping term: "It is either a case of having lost confidence in Bradley or having been forced to put Montgomery in through the machinations of the Prime Minister or with the hope that if he gives Monty operational control, he will get some of the British divisions in. Eisenhower is unwilling or unable to command Montgomery."[58] Despite what they said about Montgomery following orders, Bradley and Patton did everything possible to diminish the effects of Eisenhower standing down the Third Army on the Moselle.

War As I Knew It quoted Bradley as telling Patton at dinner on Christmas Day, 1944, that Montgomery had told him that the First Army was in such a bad way it would be unable to attack for three months.[59] *Lucky Forward* maintained that the Third Army was slugging it out with the Germans, while the northern armies under Montgomery did virtually nothing. Allen quoted a Third Army G-2 officer's comment after reading a First Army report that said the Third Army was doing most of the fighting: "Well at least he's frank. . . . He admits that we are the only Army that's fighting. That's quite a concession coming from them. But you can tell them this. If First Army will stay put, we'll run the Krauts up their ass. And then if Monty will stay put for a few days, we'll run both the Krauts and First Army up his ass, trains first."[60]

Emotions ran high during the Bulge, based on wounds both real and imaginary. Coverage in the British press, which attributed the victory to Montgomery, whom Patton described as "God's gift to war," served more to highlight the national differences in command rather than the Allied successes. Allen cited the complaint of the *Daily Mail's* correspondent attached to the Third Army during the Bulge: "I'm having a bit of a go with the office about my stories. It seems the *Mail* has gone all anti-American and has been tossing out some of my stories which have given honest praise to the Yanks for the magnificent fight they are making in the Bulge."[61] Had Patton lived, his memoir might have been closer to his diary entry of 27 December 1944: "I wish Ike were more of a gambler, but he is certainly a lion compared to Montgomery, and Bradley is better than Ike as far as nerve is concerned. . . . Monty is a tired little fart. War requires the taking of risks and he won't take them"[62]

SUMMERSBY'S *EISENHOWER WAS MY BOSS*

In mid-October 1948 Montgomery wrote Eisenhower: "Your late lady driver and secretary has written a book in the States. I am being asked questions about it. Can you send me a copy, it is not obtainable in this country."[63] Eisenhower, then president of Columbia University in New York City, replied disingenuously, "So far as Mrs. Summersby's book is concerned, I have not read it and do not know where it can be obtained. If I happen to run into a copy somewhere I will forward it to you. . . . I do not see why you should be called upon to answer inquiries arising from inconsequential, personal accounts of anything as big as the war was."[64] Kay Summersby had sent Eisenhower a copy, but he was not thrilled. Moreover, as Mrs. Summersby was also in New York, Eisenhower curtly ended their personal relationship.[65]

Born Kathleen McCarthy-Morrogh on the island of Iniss Beg, off County Cork, Ireland, Kay married an Englishman, Gordon Summersby, who in 1942 was serving in India. When she met Eisenhower, she was a driver in the British Women's Motor Transport Corps. Separated from her husband, she intended to marry an American officer, Colonel Richard Allen, as soon as their divorces became final; however, Allen was killed by a landmine in North Africa. One of Eisenhower's several drivers, the general promoted Summersby to office work. Usually referred to as a secretary, she served primarily as a receptionist, and Eisenhower had her answer his "fan mail" and keep a record of his thoughts in Butcher's absence.[66] Commissioned a lieutenant in the Women's Army Corps (WAC), she became an American citizen following the war.

At the end of June and early in July 1944, Summersby traveled on leave to Washington, D.C., where she met Mamie Eisenhower, the general's wife.[67] Addressing the rumors concerning her, Summersby wrote, "In addition to being a woman overseas, I was a *foreign* woman--and I traveled with the High Brass. Therefore, I was a Bad Woman."[68] With the publication of Merle Miller's 1974 *Plain Speaking: An Oral Biography of Harry S. Truman*, the story of the love affair between Eisenhower and Summersby received further notoriety. According to Miller, President Truman said that Eisenhower had written General Marshall after the war expressing a desire to divorce Mamie to marry Summersby. Thereupon, Marshall wrote a blistering letter telling Eisenhower that if he followed through on his wish, he, Marshall, would ruin Eisenhower's career. Truman told Miller that before he left office he had the Marshall letters destroyed.[69] Miller's uncorroborated story led Summersby, then terminally ill, to arrange for a second memoir, *Past Forgetting: My Love Affair with Dwight D. Eisenhower*; ghostwritten, it appeared posthumously in 1976 and confirmed there had been an affair, contradicting her earlier memoir. Writing in *American Heritage* in 1995, Robert H. Ferrell and Francis H. Heller demolished the credibility of Miller's oral history, pointing out that there was nothing to corroborate Miller's story regarding Eisenhower, Summersby, and Truman. "In the Miller tapes in the Truman Library," Ferrell wrote, "there is no Truman conversation, nothing about Kay Summersby."[70] Ferrell concluded that Miller made up the Truman story concerning Marshall, Eisenhower, and Summersby out of whole cloth.

In December 1948, Harry Butcher wrote Eisenhower: "From Kay's visits with us in Santa Barbara it was obvious to me that she was intent upon writing her story partly from need of money and, also, from pique."[71] Butcher put Summersby in touch with the literary agent George Bye, and Bye assured Eisenhower that the resulting book would be dignified. When Eisenhower objected to the working title of Summersby's book, "Eisenhower's Girl Friday," Bye saw that the title was changed. It was too late, however, to prevent *Look* magazine from using that title in its serialization.[72] Butcher told Eisenhower that Summersby's book surpassed his expectations and that its favorable portrayal from a woman's point of view could only help the general. The inference drawn from Butcher's remarks was that Eisenhower had to be thinking about a presidential campaign.

Eisenhower Was My Boss grew out of Summersby's office diary that she kept concerning Eisenhower's visitors, trips to the front, and matters of concern. As Eisenhower's receptionist she saw all his important guests, and she often accompanied him on visits to American headquarters. Therefore, *Eisenhower Was My Boss*, based as it was on her unpublished diary, was in some respects more valuable than Butcher's more famous published diary. First, because she was around Eisenhower, rode with him for hours at a time, and he obviously discussed important topics in her presence, Summersby's memoir is valuable for Eisenhower's opinions concerning strategy and command. Second, because of her perspective as an Irishwoman living in wartime Britain, Summersby captured the distinct Anglo-American tone of SHAEF headquarters better than any of the postwar memoirs. Eisenhower imbued an Allied spirit into SHAEF. "Historians probably will agree," Summersby wrote, "that this was General Eisenhower's greatest achievement in World War II--this ability to submerge national pride into an international determination to win the war."[73] SHAEF developed an Allied family atmosphere; the headquarters had a morning coffee break and afternoon tea.

Reflecting the impact of the British press, Summersby rejected its caricature of Eisenhower as the "Chairman of the Board," referring to him as a supreme commander in the fullest sense of the term.[74] British papers were portrayed as troublesome during the Battle of the Bulge when some called for "a unified ground command." Summersby incorrectly wrote that Eisenhower explained that Montgomery's command of two American armies was temporary when, in fact, it was General Marshall who had first done so. She described Bradley's demeanor upon being informed by Eisenhower that Montgomery would maintain Lieutenant General William Simpson's Ninth Army, following the Bulge, as the only time she saw Bradley display "real anger." Accompanying Eisenhower to 12th Army Group, she described the situation as follows: "[Bradley] also indicated an unhealthy state of mind among his staff, who complained not only at losing the Ninth Army but at the flood of publicity on Field Marshal Montgomery." The 12th Army Group staff asked, "Whose side are you on, Monty's or Bradley's, or just whose?"[75]

Summersby admitted to a lack of objectivity, saying she "grew to dislike the very name of Montgomery." Her antipathy grew out of Montgomery's ban on women in the 21st Army Group area; whenever Eisenhower went to see Montgomery she had to stay behind. Despite her bias, Summersby noted that Montgomery was clearly Britain's "most glamorous and successful general to date," and therefore it was virtually impossible for Eisenhower to sack him. Any move by Eisenhower against the field marshal would have created such protest in Britain that Allied unity would have been jeopardized.[76]

When Montgomery renewed his call for the appointment of a ground forces commander during the Battle of the Bulge, Summersby portrayed her boss as struggling to prevent the alliance from going off into separate nationalistic camps. On the one hand Eisenhower sent Montgomery a stiff note telling him that a ground forces commander was out of the question. On the other hand Eisenhower commented to her, "If I can keep the team together, anything's worth it."[77] Eisenhower's management of the crisis was successful, and she cited Montgomery's reply that he was sorry to have upset Eisenhower and promised his full support to make the new directive work. *Eisenhower Was My Boss* described how General Marshall and Eisenhower met in January 1945 prior to the Malta Conference, and quoted Marshall as saying, "As long as I'm Chief of Staff, I'll never let them saddle you with the burden of an overall ground commander."[78]

Summersby broke new ground by describing General Smith's confrontation with Field Marshal Brooke at the Malta Conference, which Smith attended representing Eisenhower. When Brooke stated that Eisenhower listened too much to his army group commanders, Smith said diplomacy held together the Anglo-American alliance, and if the British Chiefs of Staff doubted Eisenhower's ability, they should put the issue to the Combined Chiefs of Staff. At that point, Summersby noted, Brooke conceded that "the Allies had no other man who could take or hold down the Supreme Commander's job anywhere near as competently as General Eisenhower."[79]

CONCLUSION

Montgomery's 1947 book was more significant for what it did not say. There was no mention of Berlin as the ultimate goal of Montgomery's single thrust in either *Normandy to the Baltic* or *Operation Victory*, only the Ruhr. Nearly all of the debate over command was absent from *Normandy to the Baltic*, giving the impression that strategy was the sole issue of contention. The omission of Berlin as the stated objective of the single thrust, as we shall see in the next chapter, had caused the single thrust to appear more realistic to the postwar reader than it did to Eisenhower in late August and early September 1944.

Normandy to the Baltic made the point that the heart of Germany was the Ruhr, and Montgomery predicted that without the Ruhr, Germany would lose its capacity to continue the war within six months. Let us assume for the sake of argument that Eisenhower went along with Montgomery's plan to assault the Ruhr, and that the 21st Army Group crossed the Rhine in late September and then seized the Ruhr by the end of October. According to *Normandy to the Baltic*, German resistance would have "petered out" within six months or sometime between the end of March and the beginning of April 1945, approximately one month before the war actually ended. This was a far more reasonable hypothesis than the one that argues that if Eisenhower had given Montgomery or Patton everything that one called for, to the exclusion of the other, then either Montgomery or Patton would have ended the war in the West, and by implication in the East as well, in 1944.

Normandy to the Baltic was part of the dichotomy of postwar writing; however bland, it was exactly what the CIGS had ordered. Montgomery had not changed his mind about Eisenhower's handling of the ground forces, but now that he carried the ultimate responsibility for advising his government on military policy he was restrained. The same could not be said of *War As I Knew It*. Patton's memoir was critical of SHAEF and, along with *Lucky Forward*, reached a wide audience.

Moreover, Patton's posthumous criticism of SHAEF carried a certain imprimatur. Only de Guingand's *Operation Victory* managed some reflection on the popular thought of the day when it speculated that the most Montgomery might have achieved before winter set in was a bridgehead over the Rhine. Montgomery had the good sense to request an attack by an army group reinforced by another army, as opposed to Patton, who wanted his readers to believe that the attack of a single army into Germany in September 1944 was a serious plan.

Yet, fifty years after the campaign in northwest Europe ended, the hurried catch phrases of the participants reappear annually in the work of journalists or biographers. Ingersoll originated the argument that SHAEF prolonged the war, but he trusted the Russians while fearing Albion. Writing while the cold war with the Soviets was coagulating, *Lucky Forward* and *War As I Knew It* would provide grist for the mill of future critics who saw a political argument rising out of the debate over strategy and command. Memoirs written in 1947 had very different final chapters from memoirs written in 1948. After 1948 the last chapter of every memoir would focus on Berlin.

NOTES

1. George S. Patton, Jr., *War As I Knew It*, annotated by Colonel Paul D. Harkins, (Boston: Houghton Mifflin, 1947), 331.

2. Robert S. Allen, *Lucky Forward: The History of General Patton's Third U.S. Army* (New York: Vanguard Press, 1947; reprint, New York: MacFadden-Bartell, 1965) refers to SHAEF when he means Eisenhower; Patton's *War As I Knew It* refers to the "High Command" or the "top brass" in lieu of criticizing Eisenhower.

3. Walter Bedell Smith, *Eisenhower's Six Great Decisions: Europe, 1944-1945* (New York and London: Longmans, Green, 1956), v-vi. Smith's book added an acknowledgment, five "Situation Reports" as introductions to each chapter, and the first and last chapters, "Prelude to Invasion," and "Epilogue to Victory." He changed the title of Chapter 1 to "The Invasion Tide," from the original "The Invasion Gamble," and "The Battle of the Bulge" became "The Ardennes Counteroffensive." The present study considers only what Smith wrote in 1946 and was available to the readers of *The Saturday Evening Post*.

4. John Lewis Gaddis, *The United States and the Origins of the Cold War, 1941-1947* (New York and London: Columbia University Press, 1972), 306-308.

5. Walter Bedell Smith, "Eisenhower's Six Great Decisions: 5, Encirclement of the Ruhr," *The Saturday Evening Post* 219 (6 July 1946): 20, 68; Smith, *Eisenhower's Six Great Decisions*, 157.

6. SHAEF G-3 Division, "Post-'NEPTUNE,' Courses of Action after Capture of Lodgement Area, Section I-Main Objective and Axis of Advance," 25 April 1944, National Archives [hereafter NA], Record Group [hereafter RG] 331, Box 74, SHAEF, General Staff, Post-OVERLORD Planning, vol. 1:3.

7. SHAEF Planning Staff, "Post-'NEPTUNE,' Courses of Action after Capture of Lodgement Area, Section I-Main Objective and Axis of Advance," 3 May 1944, NA, RG 331, Box 77, SHAEF, Secretariat General Staff [SGS], Post-OVERLORD Planning, vol. 1: 4.

8. Ibid., 7.

9. Ibid., 6-7. The argument against Patton's proposed single thrust was that it would have to swing northward on the far bank of the Rhine in country that favored the defense before it could mount an attack on the Ruhr.

10. For Alanbrooke on de Guingand, see Charles Richardson, *Send for Freddie: The Story of Monty's Chief of Staff Major-General Sir Francis de Guingand* (London: William Kimber, 1987), 180-81. Field Marshal Sir Alan Brooke became Baron Alanbrooke of Brookeborough in September 1945 and viscount in January 1946.

11. Francis de Guingand, *From Brass Hat to Bowler Hat* (London: Hamish Hamilton, 1979), 114.

12. Richardson, *Send for Freddie*, 187-206.

13. De Guingand, *From Brass Hat to Bowler Hat*, 20-24.

14. Francis de Guingand, *Operation Victory* (London: Hodder and Stoughton, 1947), 185-86.

15. Ibid., 411.

16. Ibid., 412.

17. Ibid., 413.

18. Ibid., 419.

19. Ibid., 434.

20. Ibid.; de Guingand would go into the issue in depth seventeen years later in his *Generals at War* (London: Hodder and Stoughton, 1964) in Chapter Six, "Europe 1944--A Signal that Saved the Team," 99-117.

21. Richardson, *Send for Freddie*, 194-95.

22. Ibid., 196.

23. Nigel Hamilton, *Monty: Final Years of the Field-Marshal, 1944-1976* (New York: McGraw-Hill, 1986), 654.

24. Richardson, *Send for Freddie*, 189-90.

25. Hamilton, *Monty: Final Years of the Field-Marshal*, 634; for details on publication, see M-601, Montgomery to Permanent Under Secretary (PUS), War Office, 6 May 1946, Papers of Field Marshal Viscount Montgomery of Alamein, Reel 11, BLM 126/99, IWM.

26. Hanson W. Baldwin, "Marshal Montgomery's Own Story," *New York Times Book Review*, 28 March 1948, p. 26.

27. Field Marshal the Viscount Montgomery of Alamein, *Normandy to the Baltic* (London: Hutchinson, 1947), v.

28. Ibid., 33-34.

29. Ibid., 118.

30. Ibid., 119.

31. Ibid., 120.

32. Ibid., 143.

33. Ibid., 160.

34. Ibid., 167.

35. Walter Bedell Smith, "Eisenhower's Six Great Decisions: 4, Victory West of the Rhine," *The Saturday Evening Post* 218 (29 June 1946): 26; Smith, *Eisenhower's Six Great Decisions*, 122-23.

36. Walter Bedell Smith, ""Eisenhower's Six Great Decisions: 3, The Battle of the Bulge," *The Saturday Evening Post* 218 (22 June 1946): 46; Smith, *Eisenhower's Six Great Decisions*, 117.

37. Montgomery, *Normandy to the Baltic*, 196.

38. Smith, "Eisenhower's Six Great Decisions: 4, Victory West of the Rhine," *The Saturday Evening Post*, 48; Smith, *Eisenhower's Six Great Decisions*, 146.

39. Montgomery to de Guingand, 14 April 1947, Papers of Major-General Sir Francis de Guingand, IWM.

40. Martin Blumenson, ed., *The Patton Papers*, 2 vols. (Boston: Houghton Mifflin, 1972-1974), 2:747-48 describes the manuscript and book; see 818-31 for Patton's traffic accident and death. Harkins went on to write *The Army Officers Guide* and to serve as the commandant of cadets at West Point and to command Military Assistance to Vietnam in 1961-1962. See George Herring's biography in Roger J. Spiller, ed., *Dictionary of American Military Biography*, vol. 2 (Westport, Conn.: Greenwood Press, 1984), 444-47.

41. Louis Galambos, ed., et al., *The Papers of Dwight David Eisenhower: The Chief of Staff*, 9 vols. (Baltimore and London: Johns Hopkins University Press, 1978), 9:2014-15.

42. Ladislas Farago, *Patton: Ordeal and Triumph* (New York: Ivan Obolensky, 1964), 806-807.

43. Martin Blumenson, *Patton: The Man Behind the Legend, 1885-1945* (New York: William Morrow, 1985; reprint, New York: Berkley Books, 1987), 287-88.

44. Patton, *War As I Knew It*, 114.

45. Ibid., 119.

46. Blumenson, *The Patton Papers*, 2: 537; Patton, *War As I Knew It*, 124.

47. Allen, *Lucky Forward*, 105.

48. Patton, *War As I Knew It*, 125.

49. Allen, *Lucky Forward*, 110.

50. Patton, *War As I Knew It*, 131.

51. Blumenson, *The Patton Papers*, 2:548.

52. Patton, *War As I Knew It*, 133. Patton thought nothing of insulting Field Marshal Montgomery in a press conference held about this time. Describing how Montgomery told SHAEF to halt the Third Army, Patton said that once the field marshal had regrouped he would make a "lightning dagger-thrust at the heart of Germany." Mimicking Montgomery, Patton said the Germans would be off guard, and "I shall pop out at them like an angry rabbit." See Charles R. Codman, *Drive* (Boston: Little, Brown, 1957), 182.

53. Blumenson, *The Patton Papers*, 2:548.

54. Dwight D. Eisenhower, Pre-Presidential Papers, 1916-1952, Principal File, Butcher Diary, 2 August 1944, Box 169 (July-August 1944), (2), 1561-62, EL.

55. Allen, *Lucky Forward*, 117-18.

56. Ibid., 105.

57. Ibid., 31-32.

58. Blumenson, *The Patton Papers*, 2:601.

59. Patton, *War As I Knew It*, 203.

60. Allen, *Lucky Forward*, 193.

61. Ibid., 203n.

62. Blumenson, *The Patton Papers*, 2: 608.

63. Montgomery to Eisenhower, 14 October 1948, Dwight D. Eisenhower, Pre-Presidential Papers, 1916-1952, Principal File, Box 82, Bernard Montgomery (5), EL; Kay Summersby, *Eisenhower Was My Boss*, ed. Michael Kearns (New York: Prentice-Hall, 1948).

64. Eisenhower to Montgomery, 3 November 1948, in Louis Galambos, ed., et al., *The Papers of Dwight David Eisenhower: Columbia University*, 11 vols. (Baltimore and London: Johns Hopkins University Press, 1984), 10:277.

65. Eisenhower did not send Summersby a copy of *Crusade in Europe*; at least her name does not appear on any of the lists at the Eisenhower Library. Dwight D. Eisenhower, Pre-

Presidential Papers, 1916-1952, Principal File, Box 138, Crusade in Europe, Presentation Copies (1), EL.

66. Lester David and Irene David, *Ike and Mamie: The General and His Lady* (New York: G. P. Putnam's Sons, 1981), 151. For the potential for scandal during the war in the Eisenhower-Summersby relationship see Anthony Cave Brown, *Bodyguard of Lies* (New York: Harper and Row, 1975), 535-36.

67. Summersby, *Eisenhower Was My Boss*, 155-56.

68. Ibid., 162. Summersby wrote: "Next war, My Girl, you may as well do all those things of which you're accused; they'll *say* you did, anyhow" (italics in the original), 162.

69. Miller, *Plain Speaking: An Oral Biography of Harry S. Truman* (New York: Berkley Publishing, 1974), 339-40. Dr. Forrest Pogue, Marshall's official biographer, doubted Miller's story. Pogue points out that hundreds of men divorced their wives without affecting their careers. Furthermore, the letters that Marshall wrote to men in these cases commonly expressed regret, not anger. Pogue Interview, 17 March 1991. See the comments of Miller's researcher, Daniel K.R. Crosswell, in the preface to his *The Chief of Staff: The Military Career of General Walter Bedell Smith* (Westport, Conn.: Greenwood Press, 1991), xiii. Crosswell said he found no evidence of an affair between Summersby and Eisenhower while working on Miller's *Ike the Soldier: As They Knew Him* (New York: G. P. Putnam's Sons, 1987); Robert H. Ferrell and Francis H. Heller, "Plain Faking?," *American Heritage* 46 (May/June 1995): 16.

70. Kay Summersby Morgan, *Past Forgetting: My Love Affair with Dwight D. Eisenhower* (New York: Simon and Schuster, 1976), 251, notes that she had never heard of the letter Eisenhower was supposed to have written until Miller's book appeared. Her name was changed because of her six-year second marriage to a New York stockbroker, Reginald Morgan.

71. Butcher to Eisenhower, 13 December 1948, Dwight D. Eisenhower, Pre-Presidential Papers, 1916-1952, Principal File, Box 16, Harry C. Butcher (3), EL.

72. Galambos, ed., et al., *The Papers of Dwight David Eisenhower: Columbia University*, 10: 159-60.

73. Summersby, *Eisenhower Was My Boss*, 78.

74. Ibid., 220.

75. Ibid., 211.

76. Ibid., for her lack of objectivity; 168, for Montgomery's status in Britain.

77. Ibid., 207.

78. Ibid., 216.

79. Ibid., 218-19.

3

Eisenhower's *Crusade in Europe* and *The Sunday Times*

I explained to Montgomery the condition of our supply system and our need for early use of Antwerp. I pointed out that, without railway bridges over the Rhine and ample . . . supplies on hand, there was no possibility of maintaining a force in Germany capable of penetrating to its capital. There was still a considerable reserve in the middle of the enemy country and I knew that any pencillike thrust into the heart of Germany such as he proposed would meet nothing but certain destruction.

--General Dwight D. Eisenhower[1]

Published in November 1948, Dwight Eisenhower's *Crusade in Europe* set the tone for the historic debate over strategy and command. Eisenhower's "pencillike" depiction of Montgomery's proposed single thrust sparked a literary and military controversy that continues to the present. While Eisenhower's memoir was extraordinarily successful in terms of sales and received mainly glowing reviews, it began the break between Eisenhower and Montgomery that became final a decade later following publication of the field marshal's memoir. In response, Montgomery began a private attack on Eisenhower's interpretation of the campaign. On 21 November 1948, *The Sunday Times'* negative review showed signs of prompting from Montgomery.

EISENHOWER'S *CRUSADE IN EUROPE*

Since 1948 and *Crusade in Europe*, historians have revisited broad front versus single thrust using the language of Eisenhower's memoir, while also attempting to put the debate into the context of the war, where it does not always belong. Historians have failed to place Eisenhower's "pencillike" phrase into the context of the earlier memoirs of Ingersoll, Allen, and Patton. In fact, the general had been worried for over a year that a "crackpot" history of the war might prevail.

Correspondence between Eisenhower and Bedell Smith shows that the allegations that SHAEF had prolonged the war had struck a nerve, and that Eisenhower's memoir was intended to respond to published criticism of SHAEF by American authors. By failing to name Patton in regard to the single-thrust strategy, Eisenhower's memoir created the perception in Montgomery's camp that the criticism was aimed entirely at the British field marshal.

Contrary to the wartime image of a man who read only western novels, Eisenhower was a student of military history. Therefore, as SCAEF, Eisenhower had to know that he would write his memoir. Throughout his career, Eisenhower had been an able rather than a facile writer; primarily, he was an inveterate reviser of drafts. Years as a staff officer and attendance at both the Command and General Staff School and the Army War College provided an opportunity for writing and for publishing in professional journals. Eisenhower published signed and unsigned articles in the *Infantry Journal* and a signed article in the *Cavalry Journal*. Following the First World War, then Chief of Staff of the United States Army General John J. Pershing selected Eisenhower to produce a guidebook to American battle monuments in France; subsequently, Eisenhower lived in France for eighteen months while revising the guidebook. Back at the War Department working for another chief of staff, Eisenhower wrote speeches for General Douglas MacArthur, and he continued to write MacArthur's speeches while serving under him in the Philippines.[2] As supreme commander, Eisenhower was responsible for writing and dictating correspondence that filled volumes.

Eisenhower's postwar correspondence to wartime associates explained both the motivation and timing of his memoir. In August 1945 the general confided to his brother Milton that he had begun an outline to aid him in future writing on the war. Moreover, as one of the world's most famous men, Eisenhower, along with his wife, Mamie Doud Eisenhower, was increasingly in the company of the country's elite. Assured by President Truman that he would have to serve only two years as chief of staff, Eisenhower faced retirement on $15,000 a year. His memoir had to earn enough money for him and his wife to retire on, and he believed that he would have to be retired in order to publish it.[3]

Throughout the spring and summer of 1946, Eisenhower had Ingersoll's *Top Secret* on his mind. For example, he cabled Montgomery that, "If you are worrying about a trashy book by a man named Ingersoll and called "Top Secret" I am told that I am second only to you in his disapprobation."[4] To Lord Arthur Tedder, Eisenhower called the book a "libel," a vilification of "all things British," and noted that it demonstrated how prejudice and distortion sold books.[5] Writing to Ambassador Smith in Moscow, Eisenhower admitted that he refused to read Ingersoll. His letter was in response to Smith's description of his recent trip to Great Britain, where Smith had refused requests from the British press to comment on *Top Secret*. Soviet papers, Smith wrote, played up *Top Secret* to highlight wartime contention between the Anglo-Americans.[6]

Following the serialization of Patton's memoir in *The Saturday Evening Post*, Smith wrote from Moscow in November 1947 venting his irritation with those who argued that "SHAEF prevented people from winning the war." Eisenhower responded by saying that too many of the books on the market, and he mentioned by name Ingersoll, Allen, Patton, and Moorehead, were flawed by errors and prejudice. The general credited Smith's articles in *The Saturday Evening Post* with beginning the correction of false perceptions, and he recommended their expansion into a book. According to Eisenhower, a book based on SHAEF documents might not sell as well as an argumentative work, but it would refute "some of the arguments made by partisans" and it would stand the test of time.[7]

In April 1948 Smith wrote Eisenhower expressing his regret that Omar Bradley never publicly repudiated "Ingersoll's drivel." Bradley's silence, Smith concluded, probably meant that he shared Ingersoll's opinions. "To some extent," Eisenhower responded, "I also share your wonder that Bradley never found it appropriate to say anything about the Ingersoll tripe." Editorially, Smith urged Eisenhower to strike back: "I really feel very strongly, Ike, that in these matters you should not pull a single punch, but state frankly and fully not only what you did and what you ordered, but also your own estimate of the tools with which you were working . . . like Patton, Montgomery, and Bradley." Smith reserved his harshest criticism for Montgomery's "intransigent attitude and behind the scenes conniving to get his own way with regard to military operations, to enhance his own prestige and to obtain a major measure of command."[8]

Years later Eisenhower's informal memoir *At Ease: Stories I Tell to Friends* credited two New York publishers with convincing him to write *Crusade in Europe*. Douglas M. Black, of Doubleday, and William Edward Robinson, of the New York *Herald Tribune*, argued that in the interest of historical accuracy Eisenhower had to write sooner rather than later. Pointing out that the books by Butcher, Ingersoll, Moorehead, Allen, and Patton were hurriedly written, Black and Robinson warned Eisenhower that unless he addressed their misconceptions future generations might regard them as factual. Black and Robinson argued that it was Eisenhower's duty to the American people to answer them.[9]

The publishers were preaching to the converted. As chief of staff of the army, Eisenhower had already taken steps to see that the army's official histories of the Second World War would be among the most objective and thorough works of their kind ever published. On 26 July 1946 to a former combat historian of the First United States Army, and current official historian of SHAEF, Dr. Forrest C. Pogue, Eisenhower wrote, "In order to insure a complete and factual account, all records relating to your subject which are within the custody of the War Department . . . will be open for your use." Following the Patton articles in *The Saturday Evening Post*, Eisenhower directed the opening of War Department records to outside historians. Eisenhower believed that the army's records were public property, and he said that the "right of the citizens to the full story is unquestioned."[10]

Black and Robinson also made Eisenhower an offer he could not refuse. They offered a lump-sum payment of $635,000 for the rights to his memoirs in book and syndication, which the Internal Revenue Service agreed to tax as a capital gain, as the onetime sale of property. Thus Eisenhower paid $158,750 in taxes. As a result of his book deal, Eisenhower became independently wealthy. By 1966 *Crusade in Europe* had sold 1,170,000 copies, and it is still in print. The book sold so well that the general would have been better advised in the long run to have paid the taxes on the royalties as a professional author while retaining the copyright.[11]

In early February 1948, Eisenhower turned over the chief of staff's office to General Bradley and immediately began the writing process during his terminal leave from the army. Working up to sixteen hours a day throughout the remainder of February, March, and April, Eisenhower completed his first draft by 24 March and finished the manuscript by early May.[12] While Eisenhower dictated, Kenneth McCormick, his editor at Doubleday, Joseph Barnes of the *Herald-Tribune*, and Major Kevin McCann, his aide and speech writer, turned his dictation into a first draft. Eisenhower checked the first drafts for accuracy, assuring himself that his editors had not changed the meaning of what he had said. It was a "blitz" requiring three secretaries and a staff of researchers. Later, Barnes recalled one session in which Eisenhower dictated five thousand words that needed almost no editing; Barnes said he had never seen the like of it in a lifetime career in newspaper and book publishing. Doubleday hired retired Brigadier General Arthur S. Nevins, formerly a member of the Operations Section, G-3 Division, SHAEF, to lead the team of researchers verifying the factual statements made in *Crusade in Europe*. Through Eisenhower's records and personal correspondence, Nevins and his team supplied the footnotes to Eisenhower's dictation, and when they could not substantiate a specific comment, Eisenhower personally revised that section.[13] What emerged was a cautious, relatively well-researched, hurriedly written personal account of the war in Europe.

Eisenhower admitted to Colonel James Gault, his wartime British military assistant, that writing his memoir proved more difficult than he had imagined. His greatest difficulty came from having to discuss frankly his differences of opinion with Churchill, Brooke, and Montgomery. Nor was Patton spared, but Eisenhower maintained that he never said anything "belittling or hurtful," to anyone, British or American.[14] *Crusade in Europe* would be a far cry from Eisenhower's official report, which said that in "matters of command . . . all relationships between American and British forces were smooth and effective."[15] Writing to Gault, he commented on his hopes for the book:

I feel that it would be completely dishonest if I should pretend that at all times and on every occasion we were in complete . . . agreement; but in spite of the necessity for telling the truth about these specific instances, I am desperately attempting to make the true story of the book that of allied cooperation and subordination of national to allied interests. If I should fail in this, then I shall always be sorry that I ever attempted to write the thing.[16]

Eisenhower's first chapter placed Allied disagreements into historical perspective. "Differences there were," Eisenhower wrote, "differences among strong men representing strong and proud peoples, but these paled into insignificance alongside the miracle of achievement represented in the shoulder-to-shoulder march of the Allies to complete victory in the West."[17] History had demonstrated the difficulties of coalition warfare, and Eisenhower noted that staff studies always pointed out that Napoleon had been successful partially because he was continually fighting coalitions. Eisenhower quoted the advice of his mentor, Major General Fox Conner, Pershing's Operations officer in World War I, on coalition command given while they were serving in the Panama Canal Zone in the early 1920s: "'We cannot escape another great war. When we go into that war it will be in company with allies. Systems of single command will have to be worked out. We must not accept the 'coordination' concept under which Foch was compelled to work. We must insist on individual and single responsibility--leaders will have to learn how to overcome nationalistic considerations in the conduct of campaigns.'"[18]

Nevertheless, "nationalistic considerations" were to have incalculable impact on both strategy and command. Indeed, Eisenhower realized the overriding importance of nationalism as it affected command of the armies of his allies, Britain and France: "No written agreement for the establishment of an allied command can hold up against nationalistic considerations should any of the contracting powers face disaster through support of the supreme commander's decisions."[19] Nationalism, Eisenhower realized, militated against bold strategy. If a supreme commander's strategy caused the loss of several British divisions, or the loss of French territory, then his job would certainly have been in jeopardy, if not the coalition itself.

Further complicating a supreme commander's job, Eisenhower noted that sovereign states did not give disciplinary power to foreign generals; armies in the Allied coalition reserved for themselves the promotion and relief of officers. Eisenhower, as SCAEF, could not command British or French generals in the same fashion he did Americans. How then was a supreme commander able to maintain discipline and control? "Only trust and confidence," Eisenhower said, "can establish the authority of an allied commander in chief so firmly that he need never fear the absence of this legal power." Success was predicated on the commander's getting others to follow his example through persuasion rather than what Eisenhower called "fixed notions of arbitrary command practices," that is, the absence of orders.[20]

Military success rested on the personalities of the supreme commander and his staff officers. Without mentioning their names, Eisenhower noted that far too often the professionalism and strength of character required of generals led either to grandstanding for the press or "arrogant and even insufferable deportment."[21] A coalition commander could not get by with grandstanding (Patton) or insufferable deportment (Montgomery); the commander of a coalition had to have the trust of his subordinates. In 1953 Eisenhower explained to speech writer Emmet John Hughes his method for maintaining loyal subordinates during the war: "In the hurley burley of a military campaign--or a political effort--loyal, effective subordinates are mandatory. To tie them to the leader with unbreakable bonds one rule must always be observed--take full responsibility, promptly, for everything that remotely resembles failure--give extravagant and public praise to all subordinates for every success."[22]

As SCAEF, Eisenhower received his orders from the Combined Chiefs of Staff, the British and American Chiefs acting in concert. Eisenhower quoted their directive to him: "You will enter the continent of Europe and, in conjunction with the other Allied Nations, undertake operations aimed at the heart of Germany and the destruction of her Armed Forces."[23]

Eisenhower provided an outline of his plan for the campaign. Following the landing in Normandy, Eisenhower planned to pursue the Germans to their border on a "broad front" using two army groups with the emphasis in the north, while linking up with troops coming up from southern France. A buildup on the German border would take place while the Allies maintained "an unrelenting offensive" to kill as many of the enemy as possible. Eisenhower intended to destroy the German army west of the Rhine at the same time the Allies attempted to grab bridges over the river. After crossing the Rhine, his plans called for an envelopment of the Ruhr, again emphasizing the northern flank, after which the final attack through Germany would be determined. Echoing Bedell Smith's *Saturday Evening Post* analysis, Eisenhower concluded, "This general plan, carefully outlined at staff meetings before D-Day, was never abandoned, even momentarily, throughout the campaign."[24]

Despite criticism and attempts by the British Chiefs of Staff to dissuade him from it, Eisenhower stuck to his strategy of destroying the German army west of the Rhine by first gaining the line of the Rhine River. "Our objective was the destruction of the German armed forces," wrote Eisenhower. If the Allies "could overwhelmingly defeat the enemy *west* of the river," then Eisenhower was certain that the Germans would have little left to defend the Rhine; especially since the Red Army had entered Poland, and the bulk of the German army was on the eastern front.[25] The Allies could not afford to let the Germans retreat behind the Rhine, where they would have gained the advantage of shorter lines of communication and supply--what military men refer to as the advantage of interior lines.

The supreme commander's press conference of 15 August 1944 attempted to warn the home fronts of Britain and America of the upcoming battle for Germany. Eisenhower was afraid that the euphoria over the victory in Normandy would produce a sense that the war was over followed by a slackening of war production. In the optimism of August and September, Eisenhower said the fanaticism of large parts of the German army went almost unnoticed, as well as the desperate measures taken by the Gestapo and Storm Troopers to maintain loyalty to Hitler. While he pointed out these factors to his superiors at the time, he also tried to use the press to alert the public to the coming battle for the Siegfried Line and Germany.[26] Butcher's *My Three Years with Eisenhower* referred to Eisenhower's remarks of 15 August: "At a press conference this morning Ike vehemently castigated those who think they can measure the end of the war 'in a matter of weeks.'"[27]

Battlefield commanders, however, were "obsessed" in September 1944 with the idea "that with only a few more tons of supply" they could have ended the war. While commending their offensive spirit, Eisenhower refused in 1948 to acknowledge the possibility of a successful single thrust in September 1944 that did anything more than cross the Rhine. The following passage is Eisenhower's generic rejection of single thrust, but more to the point it is a refutation of Ingersoll, Allen, and Patton: "In the late summer days of 1944 it was known to us that the German still had disposable reserves within his own country. Any idea of attempting to thrust forward a small force [one army], bridge the Rhine, and continue on into the heart of Germany was completely fantastic."[28] Any such force, and Eisenhower kept its commander nameless, would have started out with no more than ten or twelve divisions and would have had to drop off flank guards to protect itself from German counterattack. The Germans would have defeated such a force, which meant the strategy would have played into the hands of the enemy. Since this passage precedes more specific criticism, which mentioned Montgomery by name, it is safe to infer that this passage referred as much to Patton as to Montgomery.

From a generic criticism of single thrust, Eisenhower launched into specific criticism of Montgomery's plan. On 4 September 1944, 21st Army Group electrified the world by capturing Antwerp, one of Europe's great ports. Eisenhower wrote that while SHAEF was planning on how to take best advantage of this lucky happenstance, "Montgomery suddenly presented the proposition that, if we would support his Twenty-first Army Group with all supply facilities available, he could rush right on into Berlin and, he said, end the war."[29] At a time in which speed was of the utmost importance, Eisenhower and Montgomery did not meet to discuss the field marshal's plan until 10 September, nearly one week later. The two met inside the supreme commander's B-25 on an airfield outside Brussels because the temporarily crippled Eisenhower had to be carried aboard the plane for the flight from Granville with his knee in a cast. He had wrenched his knee while pushing his small plane out of the sand, following an emergency landing on the beach near Granville. Montgomery had refused to come to Granville. Eisenhower's 1948 language shaped the debate in the books that followed, and the current writer has italicized parts of Eisenhower's account:

I explained to Montgomery the condition of our supply system and our need for early use of Antwerp. I pointed out that, without railway bridges over the Rhine and ample . . . supplies on hand, there was no possibility of maintaining a force in Germany capable of penetrating to its capital. There was still a considerable reserve in the middle of the enemy country and I knew that any *pencillike thrust* into the heart of Germany such as he proposed would meet nothing but certain destruction. *This was true, no matter on what part of the front it might be attempted.* I would not consider it.[30]

The reader should note that *Crusade in Europe's* specific criticism of Montgomery's single thrust cast aspersion on Patton's proposal. Eisenhower pulled his punches by omitting Patton's name in connection with the single-thrust strategy, but there can be no doubt that Eisenhower's reference to "no matter . . . what part of the front" pertained to southern single-thrust notions advanced by Ingersoll, Allen, and Patton.

Eisenhower also pulled his punches regarding Montgomery, whom he described as commanding detached from his main staff, surrounded only by a few aides, which meant that dealing with the field marshal required additional time and staff work. Eisenhower claimed that the field marshal refused to deal with staff officers except his own and continued to debate strategy up to the moment of execution.[31]

On the other hand, Eisenhower called Montgomery's ability to inspire "devotion and admiration" among his troops the greatest asset any commander could possess. The Englishman's penchant for taking infinite pains made him, according to Eisenhower, the master of "the set-piece attack."[32] Eisenhower's 1948 comments were a far cry from the secret appraisal of Montgomery that he sent to Marshall in early April 1943:

He is unquestionably able, but very conceited. For your most secret and confidential information, I will give you my opinion which is that he is so proud of his successes to date that he will never willingly make a single move until he is absolutely certain of success--in other words, until he has concentrated enough resources as that anybody could practically guarantee the outcome. This may be somewhat unfair to him, but it is the definite impression I received.[33]

Whereas Ingersoll, Allen, and Patton had criticized SHAEF for prolonging the war, only Montgomery had called for a ground forces commander. Eisenhower informed American readers that it was British practice to designate three separate commanders for the air, ground, and naval forces. Describing Montgomery's proposal that he retain command of all the ground forces, including his own 21st Army Group, Eisenhower concluded, "To my mind and that of my staff the proposition was fantastic." As Eisenhower explained, an army commander exists to provide day-to-day control of a specific section of the front; the campaign was no longer a beachhead of 80 to 100 miles where one man could command the entirety. There was no way Montgomery could exercise command over his own army group while commanding two others. "The only effect of such a scheme," Eisenhower wrote, "would have been to place Montgomery in a position to draw at will, in support of his own ideas [single thrust], upon the strength of the entire command."[34] Dismissing Montgomery's calls for concentration, the supreme commander saw the field marshal's insistence on ground forces command as nothing less than *de facto* command of virtually the entire expeditionary force, which from the standpoint of an American officer would have been truly "fantastic," but hardly "pencillike."

No single ground forces commander could possibly control the ground battle along the 300-mile-long European front, according to Eisenhower. Furthermore, it was SHAEF's job to assign objectives and delegate supplies on a priority basis. Creation of another ground forces headquarters below SHAEF would have placed the designated commander in "an anomalous position." A ground forces commander would have been fighting battles and coming back to the supreme commander for assignment of supplies and airpower. Acknowledging that his decision contradicted established British practice, Eisenhower noted that the British accepted it for the most part. Eisenhower obviously recalled Fox Conner's advice based on the World War I example of Marshal Ferdinand Foch. Eisenhower accepted his mentor's warning that coalition warfare required one man to be in charge in order to overcome nationalistic considerations.[35]

Montgomery's final call for a ground forces commander occurred during the Battle of the Bulge, and *Crusade in Europe* continued the false impression that Montgomery's press conference brought the command question to a climax. Retaining the confused chronology established by Moorehead and de Guingand, Eisenhower's narrative placed Montgomery's press conference before the secret ultimatum of late December. According to the supreme commander, American commanders believed that the field marshal had "deliberately belittled them," and they reacted with "scorn and contempt." "I do not believe that Montgomery meant his words as they sounded," Eisenhower wrote, "but the mischief was not lessened thereby." Eisenhower concluded: "This incident caused me more distress and worry than did any similar one of the war."[36]

American military attaches in London kept the War Department informed of Fleet Street's criticism of SHAEF's command organization and call for a ground forces commander.[37] Preoccupied by the German counteroffensive, Eisenhower was unaware of the comments in the British press until 30 December, when Marshall called them to his attention. Eisenhower reproduced Marshall's telegram:

They may or may not have brought to your attention articles in certain London papers proposing a British deputy commander for all your ground forces and implying that you have undertaken too much of a task yourself. I am not assuming that you had in mind such a concession. My feeling is this: under no circumstances make any concessions of any kind whatsoever. I just wish you to be certain of our attitude. You are doing a grand job, and go on and give them hell.[38]

The chief of staff had little reason to worry, for Eisenhower had no intention of appointing a deputy ground commander. "Our present difficulties," he responded, "are being used by a certain group of papers and their correspondents to advocate something that they have always wanted but which is not in fact a sound organization."[39] Eisenhower, for example, did not believe that a ground forces commander would have made a whit of difference in the case of the German counteroffensive, which came not at an army group boundary but at the "center of a single group command." The depth of the German attack, combined with Bradley's refusal to evacuate his tactical headquarters in Luxembourg, necessitated Eisenhower putting separate generals in charge of the northern and southern halves of the salient because Bradley could not reach Hodges' and Simpson's armies as readily as Montgomery could.

The British Chiefs of Staff were worried, however. They returned to the twin issues of ground forces command and concentration of forces in January 1945 when they requested both a progress report on the campaign thus far and Eisenhower's plan for the final operations of the campaign. At this point *Crusade in Europe* combined two separate events that took place in December 1944 and January 1945. The first was Eisenhower's 12 December appearance (along with Tedder, his deputy) before the British Chiefs of Staff Committee to discuss his plans for closing to and crossing the Rhine. Present at the meeting with Eisenhower and Tedder were Prime Minister Churchill, who doubled as minister of defense;

Field Marshal Brooke, CIGS; First Sea Lord Admiral of the Fleet Sir Andrew B. Cunningham; Chief of the Air Staff Marshal of the Royal Air Force Sir Charles Portal; and General Ismay, Churchill's chief of staff.[40] The second event was Eisenhower's appreciation of future operations of 20 January 1945, drawn up partially as a result of the British Chiefs' dissatisfaction with what they heard on 12 December.[41]

Eisenhower's reader learned that Brooke took him to task for "the planned dispersion of our forces" without knowing when or where their conversation took place.[42] Brooke contended that if Eisenhower insisted on closing to the line of the Rhine on a broad front, then the Allies would be too weak to break through and to cross the river on a timely basis. *Crusade in Europe* quoted an exasperated Brooke: "I wish that the Twelfth Army Group were deployed north of the Ruhr and the British forces were in the center."[43] To Brooke's way of thinking, transposition of Montgomery's and Bradley's troops would have ensured the prevalence of sound strategy, that is, concentration along a single axis of advance, rather than what Brooke regarded as "nationalistic considerations," which was a broad front with its multiple lines of advance. Eisenhower remained adamant about closing to the Rhine on a broad front, and maintained that the so-called glory of taking the Rhine or the Ruhr, what he took to be Brooke's "nationalistic considerations," had nothing whatever to do with his plan. Brooke again brought up the issue of a ground forces commander, and again Eisenhower rejected it.

During his discussion with the British Chiefs, the supreme commander mentioned that the planning date for crossing the Rhine was 1 May 1945, which he attributed to dire warnings from SHAEF engineers based on the anticipated flow of the Rhine. Brooke was not as blasé about the May date as we shall see subsequently. Montgomery's planned crossing of the Rhine in the 21st Army Group sector actually occurred on 23-24 March. According to Eisenhower, when they stood next to one another on the west bank of the Rhine observing Montgomery's crossing, Brooke paid him a compliment: "'Thank God, Ike, you stuck by your plan. You were completely right and I am sorry if my fear of dispersed effort added to your burdens. The German is now licked. It is merely a question of when he chooses to quit. Thank God you stuck by your guns.'"[44]

The final crisis concerning strategy and command occurred when SHAEF decided to cut Germany in two, north from south, to advance on Dresden and Leipzig rather than Berlin, and to put Bradley in command of the final main attack. Furthermore, once the encirclement of the Ruhr was completed, Eisenhower returned Simpson's Ninth Army to Bradley, decreasing the size of Montgomery's command. Given that the Russians were on the Oder, some thirty miles from Berlin, while the Allies were 300 miles away on the Rhine, Eisenhower decided against forcing Anglo-American units into the German capital. In all probability, the supreme commander argued, the Russians would have surrounded Berlin before the British or Americans arrived. Moreover, owing to the distance involved, to supply a Berlin spearhead would have required immobilizing units on the rest of the front, a repeat of September's single-thrust dilemma. Eisenhower called such a thrust "stupid." Furthermore, SHAEF had reports concerning a possible Nazi last stand in the Bavarian Alps, the so-called National Redoubt, and Eisenhower feared that Hitler would attempt to drag out the war, hoping to win better peace terms than unconditional surrender. To prevent a Nazi last stand in southern Germany with potential risks to the coalition, Eisenhower decided to take the entire area.[45]

Prime Minister Churchill and the British Chiefs of Staff totally disagreed with the assumptions behind the conduct of Eisenhower's final battle. Churchill was upset by Eisenhower's strategy and by the supreme commander's communicating with Stalin directly, informing the Soviet leader of SHAEF's plan and Allied halt-lines. Montgomery's loss of the American Ninth Army infuriated the British Chiefs of Staff, while it merely irritated the prime minister, who believed that Montgomery should have been strengthened and sent on to Berlin ahead of the Russians. Eisenhower's 1948 memoir, written during the Berlin Airlift, developed a defensive tone on these matters, and he reprinted large portions of his 1945 telegrams to General Marshall, justifying his actions. The messages pointed out that SHAEF plans had always called for a push east from the area of Kassel, and that the approaches to Berlin from the west were swampy and unsuitable to rapid exploitation. Furthermore, Eisenhower argued that Berlin had been largely destroyed and had lost its value as an objective.[46] Eisenhower wanted a river obstacle as a halt-line because the Western Allies could not depend on radios to communicate with the Russians because of language differences. There had already been instances where the air forces of the Allies had fired on one another. Therefore, Eisenhower chose the Elbe and Mulde rivers as the halt-line and demarcation point between the Anglo-Americans and the Russians.[47]

Eisenhower's final chapter, entitled "Russia," noted that he believed that at Yalta the Anglo-Americans ought to have received a larger area of Germany to occupy; the line to have asked for would have been the Elbe. The problem was that during the Yalta Conference in February 1945, the Western Allies were still held up by rivers and dams in western Germany. "Except for a fear that we could advance no farther eastward," Eisenhower wrote, "there would seem to have been little reason for agreeing to an occupational line no deeper into Germany than Eisenach."[48] The general noted that it was pure speculation on his part and he never discussed the matter with any of the decision makers. Given the Anglo-American positions in northwest Europe in February 1945 relative to the Russians' propinquity to Berlin, Eisenhower failed to realize that a line of occupation at Eisenach, about fifty miles northeast of Fulda, was probably as far east as the Anglo-Americans could get the Russians to accept.

THE SUNDAY TIMES

There were those in 1948 who believed that it was Eisenhower's fault that the line between the former allies had been drawn as far west as it had been. In its review of *Crusade in Europe* of 21 November 1948, *The Sunday Times* took Eisenhower to task for a multitude of alleged sins, one of which involved the postwar geographical division of Europe. Entitled "Eisenhower's Book: The Facts," the review, by the paper's unnamed military correspondent, pronounced Operation ANVIL, the American-sponsored invasion of southern France, a disaster of the first magnitude. Indeed, it was partly responsible for preventing Montgomery from winning the war before Christmas, and it also was significant in the Anglo-Americans' forfeiting their chance to reach Vienna ahead of the Russians.[49]

Evidently, Montgomery fed the review to Sir Denis Hamilton, who would become the paper's editor in 1961. De Guingand identified Hamilton as the military correspondent in a letter to Eisenhower. On 20 January 1949, de Guingand wrote, "I was very angry about this article as it was obvious that Hamilton (the Military Correspondent) had been to see Monty and the latter had put over a lot of the old 'war cries.' I recognized some of the very expressions."[50] Sir Denis went on to become the director of the Thomson Organization, which owned the *Times* and in December 1962 purchased Montgomery's papers.[51] He was also the father of Nigel Hamilton, the official biographer of Field Marshal Montgomery. Nigel Hamilton quoted his father in relation to his paper's syndication of Montgomery's 1958 memoir: "'I could see he was going to get into trouble with the Eisenhower stuff--but it suited me as a [newspaper] publisher to sell copies. Besides, I'd been through it all in reverse in 1948/9 when I reviewed Eisenhower's book.'"[52]

Concerning Eisenhower's ability as a ground forces commander, *The Sunday Times* picked up where Ingersoll left off: "He insisted on commanding the land armies himself; he is not in any way a battle commander, and he had no previous experience; in fact, he did not understand how to command *in the field*."[53] Borrowing Montgomery's August 1944 phrase, the review said that a supreme commander "sits on a lofty perch," meaning he should not have meddled in the conduct of ground operations.[54] Montgomery believed that Eisenhower made a mistake in trying to exercise strategic and operational command at the same time, and *The Sunday Times* reviewer added that the results were "disastrous in their post-war setting." Moreover, the reviewer stated that Ingersoll was correct to maintain that the lack of a real supreme commander had prolonged the war past Christmas 1944.

The Sunday Times maintained that Eisenhower further erred when he said that Montgomery imagined he could retain command of the 21st Army Group while simultaneously commanding the ground forces. Calling Eisenhower's charge "untrue," the review noted that Montgomery had offered to serve under Bradley, if Eisenhower would not have an English ground commander. While it is true that the field marshal offered to serve under Bradley most of his comments regarding ground forces command were nowhere near as magnanimous. There is no suggestion in the field marshal's papers that he ever imagined he would have to give up the 21st Army Group in order to command the ground forces.

Eisenhower's reference to Montgomery's single thrust as "pencillike" came under attack by *The Sunday Times*. Referring to Montgomery's single thrust, its reviewer noted, "The right flank was to be on the Ardennes and the left flank on the North Sea; over a million men would have been involved in the movement."[55] From a nationalistic perspective, the Montgomery single thrust was patently impossible for Eisenhower; even if he had wanted to do it the War Department would have insisted otherwise. The number of divisions demanded by Montgomery varied between half and *all* of the expeditionary force, depending on what day in August 1944 was under discussion. That was far from "pencillike" to Montgomery, but it was "fantastic" to Eisenhower. Patton had believed that SHAEF prolonged the war by not giving his three to six divisions free reign in September, and Eisenhower's "pencillike" reference was a deservedly oblique comment on the claim of his dead friend. In June 1948 Eisenhower wrote Winston Churchill, and his choice of words leads to the conclusion that Patton's memoir weighed on Eisenhower's mind: "I was finally persuaded that I should try to set down my personal account of the *war as I knew it*. Chiefly because so many biased and prejudiced accounts were written by irresponsible people."[56]

Taking Eisenhower's directive of 4 September 1944 out of context, *The Sunday Times* military correspondent wrote that Montgomery received a letter from Eisenhower in mid-September 1944 calling on the Englishman to launch a rapid thrust to Berlin. This letter named Berlin as the final objective of the campaign, not his immediate objective, and definitely not, as the review implied, "the next move." Furthermore, Eisenhower mentioned alternative lines of attack on the axes Ruhr-Hanover-Berlin or Frankfurt-Leipzig-Berlin, or both. To clear up any confusion that might exist, Eisenhower's letter, which he sent to all three army group commanders, stated, "Should the Russians beat us to Berlin, the Northern Group of Armies [Montgomery's 21st Army Group] would seize the Hanover area and the Hamburg group of ports. The Central Group of Armies [Bradley's 12th Army Group] would seize part, or the whole, of Leipzig-Dresden, depending upon the progress of the Russian advance."[57] This was exactly what happened seven months later.

The Sunday Times review also noted that Kay Summersby's *Eisenhower Was My Boss* had appeared in America. In December 1948 Montgomery wrote de Guingand what he thought about both Eisenhower's and Summersby's books: "My own view is that he has been very foolish to open up on controversial issues many of which are bound to be hotly contested. The war leaders had far better remain silent for some years to come. Winston told me privately that he considers that Ike's book, *plus* the Summersby book, have finished Ike as far as the Presidency is concerned."[58]

Hamilton's *Sunday Times* review expressed publicly much the same doubt about Eisenhower's judgment as Montgomery would express in his diary:

It can do no good to General Eisenhower. If American generals were in the habit of confiding in women car drivers and secretaries as Eisenhower and others appear to have done if this book is true, then their characters must slump in the eyes of the world. Mrs. Summersby, Eisenhower's woman driver, alleges that Eisenhower discussed with her his views on generals under him and also disclosed to her the most secret matters. Her views on the leading war figures are enlightening, since they are presumably Eisenhower's; the British come out badly, the Americans always win.[59]

GRIGG'S *PREJUDICE AND JUDGMENT*

The Sunday Times review also alluded to the memoir of Churchill's secretary of state for war, Sir James Grigg. The significance of P. J. Grigg's memoir, *Prejudice and Judgment*, lay in the political questions it raised concerning Eisenhower's command of the land battle. At the time the Russian blockade of Berlin and the Anglo-American airlift to the city were in full swing, *The Sunday Times* told its readers that "Had Montgomery's plan been adopted it would have shortened the war. It also held great possibilities of bringing about the end of the war in Europe with a political balance much more favourable to an early and stable peace than the actual outcome. With a proper plan we could have been in Berlin, Prague, and Vienna before the Russians."[60] Grigg's memoir, which went to the publisher in October 1947, was the first postwar memoir to put SHAEF's alleged failure to end the war in the context of the cold war and the so-called Iron Curtain. "For what it is worth then I believe that the war might have been over by Christmas 1944 if Montgomery had been given his head and that we should have got to Berlin before the Russians, with the probable corollary that the effective iron curtain could have been drawn further to the east."[61]

Arguments against single thrust, Grigg said, came partly from British officers at SHAEF who viewed Montgomery from Alamein onward as slow and timid, which Grigg called "absurd." Montgomery's single thrust also received criticism from Eisenhower and others concerned about the danger of German flank attacks. Grigg answered that "a force of a million men or more hasn't got such a narrow frontage as all that."[62]

Even though he sympathized with Montgomery's case for single thrust, Grigg realized it would have been difficult for Eisenhower to have adopted it. Grigg pointed out that Montgomery failed to consider the trouble Eisenhower would have encountered from "that modern Jeb Stuart," General Patton. Even if Eisenhower had begun a single thrust under Montgomery, Grigg argued, Washington would have overruled the supreme commander. "It is all very well for the latter [Montgomery] to point out that victories and not public opinion win wars but in democracies public opinion cannot be lightly ignored even when it is wrong."[63]

As far as Montgomery's campaign to be named ground forces commander was concerned, Grigg admitted that there was a good deal of "cross purposes" to the argument. In other words, a single thrust on the northern axis of advance was virtually the same thing to Montgomery as his being named ground forces commander. When the Eisenhower strategy of October proved a stalemate, Montgomery renewed the issue of ground forces command. Grigg said that Montgomery contended it was impossible for Eisenhower to command armies from his headquarters at Versailles; the command structure was faulty no matter what the strategy was. Grigg, however, had more understanding of Eisenhower's political and operational dilemma: "The national distribution of command meant that armies from two groups and under two commanders were concerned with the single objective of encompassing the Ruhr."[64]

When the German Ardennes counteroffensive intervened, Montgomery gained temporary command of two American armies, the American First and Ninth. Grigg incorrectly informed his readers that when the emergency was over Bradley took back both armies and thereby reestablished the system of command that Montgomery found so deplorable. In actuality, Montgomery's retention of the Ninth Army continued to infuriate Bradley's 12th Army Group. On the basis of this misunderstanding over command of one or both of the American armies, Grigg proffered the following explanation of the controversies before and after Montgomery's press conference, which so angered Bradley:

It must have been about this period that the incident occurred which is hinted at by both de Guingand (Montgomery's Chief of Staff) in *Operation Victory* and Moorehead in *Montgomery*. It is suggested that the Field-Marshal made some remarks reflecting on Bradley and possibly on Eisenhower too at an off-the-record talk to journalists. I know the former believes to this day that Montgomery used a phrase about the folly of entrusting the control of military operations to amateurs, which he regarded and still regards as unforgivable. Whatever the truth about this, it is established that Eisenhower--though very tactfully through de Guingand--felt it necessary to read the Riot Act to Montgomery and that the latter for the good of the cause abandoned the argument.[65]

CONCLUSION

The battle lines had now been joined. Eisenhower had attacked the "crackpot" theories only to be attacked in turn. British opinion following the field marshal's lead in *The Sunday Times* and P. J. Grigg's memoir now added losing central Europe to Eisenhower's sins; the reader should note that this was four years prior to Chester Wilmot's 1952 *The Struggle for Europe*. When the Russians stopped Allied traffic in and out of occupied Berlin in June 1948, the former German capital acquired a grail-like quality in subsequent books on the campaign. Arguments that Eisenhower had prolonged the war now also maintained that Eisenhower had allowed the Russians to beat the Anglo-Americans to Berlin. The ethnocentrism of the western front, which virtually ignored the eastern front and led its adherents to argue that only Eisenhower and SHAEF saved the German army from annihilation in September 1944, was now joined by its 1948 corollary that argued only one man prevented the Anglo-American liberation of central Europe.

Crusade in Europe was not as strong as it might have been had General Smith been in Washington rather than Moscow, but it was frank enough to convince Field Marshal Montgomery that he had been played for a fool because his own *Normandy to the Baltic* had deliberately avoided controversy. The level of Montgomery's disappointment with *Crusade in Europe* shows in his 10 January 1949 letter to Eisenhower:

I am sorry that you felt it necessary to analyze the characters of some of your colleagues and subordinates, and to indulge in criticism of them. The British Army will take some time to get over your description of Alanbrooke as a person who "lacked the ability to weigh calmly the conflicting factors in a problem and so reach a rocklike decision." It is definitely not true.

For myself, of course, I am by now quite used to having my ideas, and methods of working, misrepresented and twisted to convey an untrue picture: and even described as "fantastic."

But I agree with de Guingand; I think it is a pity that you should have thought it necessary to criticize me and my ways, just at this time in the history of the Western Union, when things are not too easy for any of us.

I am also sorry that you should have opened up a number of very controversial issues, which were lying dormant.[66]

NOTES

1. Dwight D. Eisenhower, *Crusade in Europe* (Garden City, N. Y.: Doubleday, 1948), 306.

2. Stephen E. Ambrose, *Eisenhower,* vol. 1, *Soldier, General of the Army, President-Elect, 1890-1952* (New York: Simon and Schuster, 1983), 67-119; J. R. Henderson, "Morning, Noon and Night," in T.E.B. Howarth, ed., *Monty at Close Quarters: Recollections of the Man* (London: Leo Cooper in association with Martin Secker and Warburg; New York: Hippocrene Books, 1985), 40, recounts Montgomery's trip to Washington in December 1946 when he stayed with Eisenhower. According to Henderson, who served as the field marshal's aide on the trip: "Monty greatly appreciated Ike's remarkably extensive knowledge of British military history."

3. Alfred D. Chandler and Louis Galambos, eds., et al., *The Papers of Dwight David Eisenhower: The Occupation,* 9 vols. (Baltimore and London: Johns Hopkins University Press, 1978), 6:242-43; Stephen E. Ambrose, *Eisenhower,* 1: 458-75; for Eisenhower's two-signed articles, see Ambrose, *Eisenhower,* 1:610, "A Tank Discussion," *Infantry Journal,* November 1920, and "War Policies," *Cavalry Journal,* November-December 1931; the Eisenhower Library believes that Eisenhower was the author of another article in the *Infantry Journal,* "The Leavenworth Course," By a Young Graduate (June 1927).

4. Louis Galambos, ed., et al., *The Papers of Dwight David Eisenhower: The Chief of Staff,* 9 vols. (Baltimore and London: Johns Hopkins University Press, 1978), 7:1070.

5. Ibid., 7:1121.

6. Ibid., 7:1216, n.8; Professor Rodney C. Loehr of the University of Minnesota sent Eisenhower an advance copy of his critical review of *Top Secret,* which appeared in *The American Historical Review* 52 (October 1946):105-107; for Eisenhower's response to Loehr see Galambos, ed., et al., *The Papers of Dwight David Eisenhower: The Chief of Staff,* 7:1131.

7. Galambos, ed., et al., *The Papers of Dwight David Eisenhower: The Chief of Staff,* 9:2084. Smith was determined to write his own book because as he wrote to Eisenhower, Ingersoll was about as qualified "to express an opinion on high levels of policy and operations" as Smith was qualified to criticize brain surgery. See Galambos, ed., et al., *The Papers of Dwight David Eisenhower: The Chief of Staff,* 7:1216, n.8.

8. Galambos, ed., et al., *The Papers of Dwight David Eisenhower: Columbia University,* 10:40-41, 42 n.5 and n.6.

9. Dwight D. Eisenhower, *At Ease: Stories I Tell to Friends* (Garden City, N.Y.: Doubleday, 1967; reprint, New York: Avon Books, 1968), 309-10.

10. Ambrose, *Eisenhower,* 1: 456.

11. Ibid., 469-75; Eisenhower, *At Ease,* 310; *New York Times,* 2 January 1948, p. 29.

12. Douglas M. Black to Eisenhower, 30 March 1948, Dwight D. Eisenhower, Pre-Presidential Papers, 1916-1952, Principal File, Box 137, *Crusade in Europe,* Correspondence, EL.

13. Dwight D. Eisenhower, Pre-Presidential Papers, 1916-1952, Principal File, Box 137, *Crusade in Europe,* Correspondence, EL; Eisenhower, *At Ease,* 311-12; Ambrose, *Eisenhower,* 1: 475. Nevins was the brother of the Columbia University historian, Allan Nevins; for Eisenhower's dictation, see Louis Galambos, Daun van Ee, and Elizabeth Hughes, "Eisenhower's First Presidency," *Columbia: The Magazine of Columbia University* 10 (February 1985):17.

14. Galambos, ed., et al., *The Papers of Dwight David Eisenhower: Columbia University,* 10:20.

15. *Report by the Supreme Commander to the Combined Chiefs of Staff on the Operations in Europe of the Allied Expeditionary Force, 6 June 1944 to 8 May 1945* (Washington, D.C.: Government Printing Office, 1945; reprint, New York: Arco Publishing, 1946), 8.

16. Galambos, ed., et al., *The Papers of Dwight David Eisenhower: Columbia University,* 10:19-21.

17. Eisenhower, *Crusade in Europe,* 4.

18. Ibid., 18.

19. Ibid., 29.

20. Ibid., 30, for the absence of this legal power; see 75, for the power of persuasion.

21. Ibid., 75.

22. Eisenhower to Emmet John Hughes, 10 December 1953, Dwight D. Eisenhower, Presidential Papers, Ann Whitman File, Box 20, EL.

23. Eisenhower, *Crusade in Europe,* 225.

24. Ibid., 228-29.

25. Ibid., 228, italics in the original.

26. Ibid., 280.

27. Butcher, *My Three Years with Eisenhower: The Personal Diary of Captain Harry C. Butcher, USNR, Naval Aide to General Eisenhower, 1942 to 1945* (New York: Simon and Schuster, 1946), 645.

28. Eisenhower, *Crusade in Europe,* 292.

29. Ibid., 305.

30. Ibid., 306; for an account of Eisenhower's injury see Ambrose, *Eisenhower,* 1:347-48.

31. Eisenhower, *Crusade in Europe,* 286.

32. Ibid., 387.

33. Eisenhower to Marshall, 5 April 1943, Dwight D. Eisenhower, Pre-Presidential Papers, 1916-1952, Principal File, Box 80, George C. Marshall (10), EL; for the expurgated version of this message see Alfred D. Chandler, Jr., ed., and Stephen E. Ambrose, assoc. ed., et al., *The Papers of Dwight David Eisenhower: The War Years,* 5 vols. (Baltimore and London: Johns Hopkins University Press, 1970), 2:1070-72.

34. Eisenhower, *Crusade in Europe,* 284-85.

35. Ibid., 18.

36. Ibid., 356.

37. "Criticism Command Organization SHAEF," 26 January 1945, Military Intelligence Division WDGS (War Department General Staff), Military Attache Report, NA, RG 165,

War Department General and Special Staff, Operations Division 1942-1945, 384 ETO, Box 1312, Case 46.

38. Eisenhower, *Crusade in Europe,* 356.

39. Ibid., 357.

40 PRO· CAB 79/84, War Cabinet Chiefs of Staff Committee, 12 December 1944.

41. For the request of the British Chiefs of Staff to the Combined Chiefs of Staff for a progress report from SHAEF and a review of strategy for the upcoming campaign, see Marshall to Eisenhower, 10 January 1945, in Chandler and Ambrose, eds., *The Papers of Dwight David Eisenhower: The War Years,* 4:2412-14, n.1; for Eisenhower's progress report, see 2444-49, and 2450-54 for Eisenhower's plans of the upcoming campaign; for the British reaction, see PRO: CAB 80/91 War Cabinet Chiefs of Staff Committee, 22 January 1945, 108.

42. Eisenhower, *Crusade in Europe,* 370.

43. Ibid., 371. Eisenhower's memoir did not specify his meeting with the British Chiefs of Staff because the minutes of the meeting were still classified when he was writing. Field Marshal Brooke commented on the meeting in his diary: "Ike also *quite* incapable of understanding real strategy. To make it worse Tedder talks nothing but nonsense in support of Ike." Contained in "Notes on My Life," by Field Marshal Viscount Alanbrooke, vol. 14, 12 December 1944, 1085, LHCMA. For Alanbrooke's printed comments, see Arthur Bryant, ed., *Triumph in the West: A History of the War Years Based on the Diaries of Field-Marshal Lord Alanbrooke, Chief of the Imperial General Staff* (Garden City, N. Y.: Doubleday, 1959), 266.

44. Eisenhower, *Crusade in Europe,* 372; in 1959 the field marshal vehemently denied saying this to Eisenhower; see Bryant, *The Turn of the Tide,* 332-33.

45. Eisenhower, *Crusade in Europe,* 396-97.

46. Ibid., 399-401.

47. Ibid., 410-11.

48. Ibid., 475.

49. "Eisenhower's Book: The Facts," *The Sunday Times* (London), 21 November 1948, p. 4.

50. De Guingand to Eisenhower, 20 January 1949, Dwight D. Eisenhower, Pre-Presidential Papers, 1916-1952, Principal File, Box 34, Francis de Guingand, EL.

51. Mr. Stephen Brooks, Introduction to The Papers of Field Marshal Viscount Montgomery of Alamein KG, GCE, DSO, DL, 1887-1976, IWM.

52. Nigel Hamilton, *Monty: Final Years of the Field-Marshal, 1944-1976* (New York: McGraw-Hill, 1986), 887.

53. "Eisenhower's Book: The Facts," *The Sunday Times* (London), 21 November 1948, p. 4, italics in the original.

54. Montgomery's M-521, 26 August 1944, letter to Lieutenant General Sir Archibald Nye, VCIGS, Vice Chief Imperial General Staff, read: "I also said that he, as Supreme Comd., could not descend into the land battle and become a ground C-in-C; the Supreme Comd. has to sit on a very lofty perch." Quoted from Nigel Hamilton, *Master of the Battlefield: Monty's War Years, 1942-1944* (New York: McGraw-Hill, 1983), 814; *The Memoirs of Field-Marshal the Viscount Montgomery of Alamein* (London: Collins, 1958), 268, describes Montgomery's meeting with Eisenhower on 23 August 1944: "The Supreme Commander must sit on a very lofty perch."

55. "Eisenhower's Book: The Facts," *The Sunday Times* (London), 21 November 1948, p. 4.

56. Galambos, ed., et al., *The Papers of Dwight David Eisenhower: Columbia University,* 10:98, italics mine.

57. Chandler and Ambrose, eds., et al., *The Papers of Dwight David Eisenhower: The War Years,* 4:2115-16 for the 4 September directive, 2148-49 for the letter of 15 September.

58. Montgomery to de Guingand, 14 December 1948, Papers of Major General Sir Francis de Guingand, IWM, italics in the original.

59. "Eisenhower's Book: The Facts," *The Sunday Times* (London), 21 November 1948, p. 4. Montgomery's diary quoted in the second volume of his authorized biography reads as follows: "This book should never have been written. It can do no good to General Eisenhower. If American generals were in the habit of dealing with women car drivers and secretaries as Eisenhower and others appear to have done if this book is true, then their characters must slump in the eyes of the world. This book makes it clear that Eisenhower discussed with Kay Summersby, his *woman car driver,* his views on Generals under him and also disclosed to her the most secret matters. Her views on the leading war figures are enlightening, since they are presumably Eisenhower's; the British come out badly, the Americans always win." Quoted from Nigel Hamilton, *Master of the Battlefield,* 769, n.1, italics in the original.

60. "Eisenhower's Book: The Facts," *The Sunday Times* (London), 21 November 1948, p. 4.

61. P. J. Grigg, *Prejudice and Judgment* (London: Jonathan Cape, 1948), 377.

62. Ibid.

63. Ibid., 378.

64. Ibid., 374, for the cross purposes of the argument; 375, for two armies against the Ruhr.

65. Ibid., 375-76. Grigg stated incorrectly that Eisenhower returned the Ninth Army to Montgomery for his northern thrust on the Ruhr; it had never left Montgomery's command.

66. Montgomery to Eisenhower, 10 January 1948, Dwight D. Eisenhower, Pre-Presidential Papers, 1916-1952, Principal File, Box 82, Montgomery (5), 10 January 1948, EL.

4

Bradley Takes Command and Wilmot States Strategy

> Although some American subordinates thought him too ready a compromiser, especially in Anglo-American disputes, Eisenhower had demonstrated in the Mediterranean war that compromise is essential to amity in an Allied struggle. I confess that at times I thought Eisenhower too eager to appease the British command, but I admit to having been a prejudiced judge. For as the American field commander I more often than not participated as the Yankee partisan in those disputes.
>
> --General Omar N. Bradley[1]

The Berlin crisis of 1948-1949 focused scrutiny on Eisenhower's decision to halt at the Elbe. The two principal works under discussion in this chapter, Omar Bradley's 1951 *A Soldier's Story* and Chester Wilmot's 1952 *The Struggle for Europe*, expressed opposite conclusions concerning Berlin. Moreover, Bradley's memoir left the impression that Montgomery was more interested in commanding additional American troops than in altering Allied strategy. Wilmot, on the other hand, emphasized strategy almost to the exclusion of command issues.

BRADLEY'S *A SOLDIER'S STORY*

In 1951 General Omar Nelson Bradley became the third American general of the European theater of operations (ETO) to publish his memoir, but unlike Eisenhower, who had retired, and Patton, whose memoir appeared posthumously, Bradley published *A Soldier's Story* while serving as chairman of the Joint Chiefs of Staff. Bradley's 1948 contract with Henry Holt bound him to publication by the summer of 1951, and in late May 1951, he wrote Eisenhower, then SACE (Supreme Allied Commander Europe), warning him that Montgomery would probably not like what *A Soldier's Story* said about him.[2]

During the war, Bradley never betrayed his growing animosity toward

Montgomery. The Missourian continued to call Montgomery "sir" long after they were both army group commanders and he was no longer under the Englishman's command. As a result of his respectful wartime demeanor, Bradley thought that his memoir would surprise the field marshal. Montgomery read all the memoirs of his contemporaries and often let their authors know what he thought about their efforts. In the early 1950s, Bradley visited SHAPE outside of Paris and encountered Montgomery, who, after a brief chat, said, "Now Omar, take care of yourself. Don't stay up too late at night--writing."[3]

Actually, *A Soldier's Story* was written by Bradley's longtime aide, Lieutenant Colonel Chester B. Hansen.[4] During the war, Hansen kept the massive 12th Army Group headquarters diary, which he used as a basis for tape-recorded conversations with Bradley. After transcribing Bradley's remarks onto five-by-eight inch index cards, labeled "Bradley Commentaries," Hansen wrote what was an early example of oral history.[5] General James Moore, secretary of the general staff while Bradley was chief of staff of the army, remembered that when Bradley questioned using some of the manuscript's Montgomery stories, Hansen replied that the book would not appeal to the public without anecdotes of his contemporaries.[6]

A Soldier's Story revealed Bradley's sense of insecurity regarding higher authority and neighboring army groups. SHAEF came in a close second to Montgomery as Bradley's *bête noire*, constantly foraging among 12th Army Group's divisions to reinforce either the 21st Army Group to his north, or Devers' 6th United States Army Group to the south. As the American 12th Army Group commander, Bradley was in an invidious position. Bradley's performance in Sicily led Eisenhower to promote him over Patton, who would advance no further than command of an army. An army group commander with three stars, Bradley was Patton's junior in combat command, having spent World War I in the United States while Patton was wounded in France and highly decorated. Bradley was also Montgomery's counterpart in terms of command, but junior in experience and rank. As a field marshal, Montgomery was the ranking British officer in the theater, the equivalent of an American five-star general.

To the modest Bradley, Montgomery appeared the "most arrogant and egotistical" person he had ever met, and his memoir called the Englishman "a good, if sometimes perverse, soldier." After the war, Bradley compared Patton to Montgomery: "I was always suspicious of Monty's plans because they were so often tied in with what will this do for Monty. Somewhat like Patton in that extent; he wanted to make headlines, and you always had to consider that in considering his recommendations."[7] Bradley preferred General (later Field Marshal) Alexander to Montgomery and speculated that had Alexander commanded the 21st British Army Group he would have avoided the animosity associated with Montgomery's command.[8]

As Dwight Eisenhower's 1915 classmate at West Point, known as "the class the stars fell on" owing to those 57 of its 164 graduates who became general officers, and a protégé of George Marshall, Bradley was well connected. As a result of technology, much of the high-level planning between Bradley and his classmate went undocumented, taking place either over the scrambler telephone or during face-to-face conversations. After October, Eisenhower and Bradley were in almost daily telephone contact. Air Marshal Robb, SHAEF's deputy chief of staff for air, noted that Eisenhower and his chief of staff remained in close phone contact with the 12th and 6th Army Groups, but not the 21st Army Group.[9]

In mid-September 1944, the supreme commander solicited his army group commanders for their strategic opinions prior to a conference at SHAEF's Versailles headquarters on 22 September. Realizing that the strategic approach to the Ruhr was literally up for bids, on 15 September 1944, Bradley sent his most important letter of the campaign to Eisenhower. *A Soldier's Story* listed Bradley's major concerns:

1. Not until we had cleared the Scheldt and secured the port of Antwerp could we hope to sustain any large-scale offensive beyond the Rhine.
2. Any advance into Germany would have to be made with great strength in depth to guard the rear areas against counterattack and sabotage.
3. Wherever the *main* effort might go, it would have to be supported by secondary attacks on the shoulders. For only by pressing the enemy on a broad front could we prevent him from massing his resistance against the *main* attack.[10]

The Ruhr headed Bradley's list of territorial objectives, and he recommended taking it by a double envelopment. In preparation for the assault on the Ruhr, Bradley advocated closing to the line of the Rhine from Cologne to Frankfurt. Bradley's proposed main thrust against the Ruhr would originate from Frankfurt, while his secondary thrust would jump off from the Cologne area.[11] Bradley informed his readers of the competitive nature of Allied strategy making:

Six months later when the Ruhr pocket was closed around more than 300,000 troops of [Field Marshal Walther] Model's Army Group, we knotted it at Lippstadt, only 20 miles from the point we had chosen that previous September. The campaign had developed precisely according to plan. Yet seldom has a plan been subjected to so tiring a succession of crises as those which afflicted this one before Eisenhower gave it a green light.[12]

In fact, the main attack that eventually enveloped the Ruhr was from the vicinity of Wesel in the north under Montgomery. The 12th Army Group's envelopment from the south at Cologne was secondary; it had not been according to Bradley's plan.

According to Bradley's September assessment, the next territorial objective after the Ruhr was Berlin, but Berlin was secondary to the destruction of the German army. Bradley warned Eisenhower that if Allied intelligence was correct, "it will be necessary to occupy all of Germany allotted to the British and American forces."[13] By attacking both the Ruhr and Berlin, Bradley expected that the Allies would destroy enough of the German army to allow them to overrun their occupation zones with only scattered resistance. Both Bradley and Eisenhower envisioned a head-on battle of attrition on the western front.

On 22 September 1944, twenty-three admirals and generals attended SHAEF's conference. Bradley's memoir described SHAEF staff officers betting on the likelihood of Montgomery's attendance. Montgomery said that he could not leave his headquarters during Operation MARKET-GARDEN, and sent de Guingand in his place. Subsequently, Eisenhower ordered Bradley to personally inform Montgomery of what occurred during the meeting. From the start, Bradley viewed the trip as unnecessary, brought on by Montgomery's disinclination to attend conferences and Eisenhower's reluctance to deal personally with the field marshal. Flying to Montgomery's tactical headquarters, Bradley's plane lost its navigation system and flew over German lines, which did not endear Bradley to his mission. Met at the airfield by one of Montgomery's American staff officers, Major Ray BonDurant, the unpublished Hansen diary contained the answer to what must have been preying on Bradley, that is, the field marshal's itinerary of 22 September: "Monty hadn't done a damn thing that day except sit around his C.P. [Command Post]." Years later the incident still rankled: "There was no reason in the world why he couldn't have come down to attend that conference except his own vanity and feeling of importance. He was too good to go to Ike's HQ."[14]

Fueling Bradley's ire in late September was his perception that Montgomery had taken the strategic bid. Lieutenant General Sir Miles C. Dempsey's Second British Army was to make the *main* effort against the Ruhr, supported by Hodges' First United States Army on his right. Bradley was angry because Eisenhower's decision meant that Patton's Third Army had to drastically curtail its operations on the Moselle. To support Dempsey's northern drive, Bradley had to move his army group boundary forty miles to the north and clear out bypassed Germans west of the Meuse. At this point, Bradley put General Simpson's newly arrived Ninth United States Army on Hodges' right flank to take over the Ardennes plateau in Luxembourg.[15]

Even more tragic in Bradley's view was Montgomery's failure to open the port of Antwerp to ship traffic by clearing the Germans from the Scheldt Estuary. On 4 September 1944, the British Second Army, in one of the singular coups of the war, seized the port city of Antwerp before the Germans could carry out its destruction. Antwerp had little value to the Allies, however, because the Germans still controlled over fifty miles of the Scheldt, linking the port to the North Sea. "Indeed of all the might-have-beens in the European campaign," Bradley stated, "none was more agonizing than this failure of Monty to open Antwerp."[16] Bradley told Hansen that if Montgomery had thought about it, he could have opened Antwerp by the 18th of September, by 20 September, at the latest. Montgomery ought to have taken Walcheren Island from the rear, by taking the roadnet leading to the South Beveland peninsula, which Bradley believed the British could have done by 6 September, bagging the Germans in its western end.[17]

Eisenhower's decision to resume the offensive against the Siegfried Line in November under Bradley soon demonstrated Montgomery's criticism of Eisenhower's splitting command of the avenue of advance north of the Ardennes while allowing Bradley to command separate avenues of approach, north and south of the Ardennes. Bradley's memoir called it "the perennial dispute between Montgomery and me over the old issue of a *single* versus the *double* thrust."[18] The inherently political nature of SHAEF's decision-making concerned Bradley as well;

he worried that if Eisenhower designated Montgomery to make the main attack toward the Rhine in November, then Montgomery would probably also conduct the primary assault on the Ruhr. Bradley could not see the point of sitting down Patton behind the Moselle when the Third Army could be clearing the Saar while approaching the Rhine. Eisenhower backed Bradley, who ordered the Third Army to continue its Saar offensive and the First Army to advance on Cologne. To free sufficient troops for separate attacks north and south of the Ardennes plateau, Bradley thinned Major General Troy A. Middleton's VIII Corps, which ran through the Ardennes. Bradley's memoir announced, "This calculated risk was mine and I have never regretted having made it. Indeed were I to live through that decision again, I would make no other."[19]

The Germans called this bluff on 16 December 1944, and four days later Eisenhower placed Montgomery in command of two of Bradley's armies. The command transfer was the paradigm for the campaign in northwest Europe. Bradley's memoir said he learned of the impending transfer from General Smith on the evening of 19 December 1944: "Ike thinks it maybe a good idea to turn over to Monty your two Armies on the north and let him run that side of the Bulge from 21st Group. It may save us a good deal of trouble, especially if your communications with Hodges and Simpson go out."[20] Hansen's unpublished diary for 19 December described a meeting at 12th Army Group's main headquarters at Verdun, including Generals Eisenhower, Tedder, Smith, Bull, and Strong, from SHAEF, as well as Bradley, Patton, Devers, and their key staff. Hansen's diary posited an imaginary *quid pro quo*: "In order to secure the necessary deployment of strength to stop the German attack with British help, I am told the terms prescribed that we turn over control of the First and Ninth Armies to 21 Group."[21] Hansen confirmed SHAEF's estimation of 12th Army Group's communications with its two northern armies, and added a further consideration: "Moreover, it was felt that our headquarters is in danger of being overrun and should such a situation develop, control might suddenly become more difficult."[22]

If 12th Army Group's communications to its First and the Ninth Armies were threatened by the developing German salient, it had no one to blame but itself. Since 14 October 1944, EAGLE TAC, 12th Army Group's tactical headquarters was located in the Alfa Hotel in Luxembourg City, where it had moved from EAGLE MAIN, still in Verdun. EAGLE TAC suddenly found itself twelve miles southeast of the German salient, which required Bradley to drive one way three sides of a square west of the Meuse, then north and east for 160 miles to Maastricht (Ninth Army) and 150 miles to Tongres (First Army). For most of the Bulge, weather precluded flying altogether.[23]

Unwilling to credit the Germans with any offensive power in October 1944 and wanting to be nearby Third Army's upcoming Saar offensive, Bradley placed his tactical headquarters in Luxembourg City. Earlier in October, the Ninth United States Army had been sectored in the Ardennes prior to its placement between the British Second Army and the First United States Army. Major General James Moore, Ninth Army's chief of staff, ruled out Luxembourg City as an army headquarters because it was far too close to the front, and this was months before any German salient existed. Owing to the north-south direction of the paved highways and the scarcity of east-west roads in the Ardennes, the drive from Luxembourg City to Bastogne was virtually as long as the drive from Luxembourg City to St. Vith. Both became the focus of major battles, and both proved inaccessible from the southeast. There were never enough roads out of Luxembourg City to allow for contact with all the divisional headquarters within an army group, and landing at Luxembourg's airport often meant flying over German lines. General Simpson, Ninth Army commander, told Moore that if a student at the Command and General Staff School had placed an army group headquarters there, he would have received a "U," or unsatisfactory.[24] More than any other single factor, the location of EAGLE TAC in Luxembourg City makes a mockery of Bradley's later contention that in stripping the Ardennes to maintain his offensive north and south, he had taken a "calculated risk."[25]

In December 1944, Bradley admitted that the transfer of his two armies to Montgomery was the logical thing to do, but by 1951 the emotional scar of the dilution of his command and Montgomery's subsequent behavior still hurt: "Had the senior British field commander been anyone else but Monty, the switch in command could probably have been made without incident, strain, or tension. Certainly it would never have touched off the Allied ruckus it subsequently did. But Montgomery unfortunately could not resist this chance to tweak our Yankee noses."[26] P. J. Grigg's *Prejudice and Judgment* alluded to Montgomery's reference to American generals as amateurs at war. Bradley's remarks to Hansen showed the depth of his feelings: "Montgomery and the British made the most out of [it] to try to discredit American leadership. And it was taken as a slam at me."[27]

Montgomery inflicted both public and private humiliation on Bradley. At the field marshal's request, Bradley flew to St. Trond, Belgium, on Christmas Day for a meeting at 21st Army Group's tactical headquarters. The 21st Army Group failed to task a staff officer to pick up Bradley at the airfield, and only the timely arrival of Major William Sylvan, aide to General Hodges, facilitated Bradley's arrival via a First Army staff car. Bradley's memoir mentioned that he ate an apple for lunch and had dinner when he returned to Luxembourg. Twenty-first Army Group had also neglected to offer an American three-star general anything to eat. Clay Blair, the author of Bradley's second memoir, pointed out that this Christmas Day performance destroyed any lingering respect Bradley had for Montgomery.[28]

More distressing to Bradley than being chastised like a second lieutenant for failing to concentrate was Montgomery's announced intention to allow the German attack to exhaust itself prior to counterattacking the northern salient of the Bulge. Convinced that Montgomery had already yielded too much ground, Bradley wrote to his old friend Courtney Hodges at First Army, expressing strong misgivings about giving up any more ground in the north.[29] The letter was remarkable because Hodges was no longer under Bradley's command. If the situation had been reversed, and Bradley were in command of Dempsey's Second British Army and Montgomery wrote Dempsey suggesting qualified obedience, Americans would have been outraged.

The next day, 26 December, Bradley called SHAEF to complain about

Montgomery's plan. Since Eisenhower was out, Bradley vented his frustrations on General Smith: "Dammit, Bedell, can't you people get Monty going on the north?" Bradley believed that the Germans would withdraw from the potential trap over the next two days. Smith was all for caution, however, telling Bradley that the Germans would be over the Meuse River within forty-eight hours.[30] The next day when one of Montgomery's liaison officers, Major Tom Bigland, asked Hansen if Bradley had any message for Montgomery, Bradley snapped: "I wish to hell he'd attack up there, but I can't tell him that."[31]

On 6 January 1944, the day after the command shift became public, Hansen summed up the mood at EAGLE TAC in a six-page entry titled, "Monty Takes Command." SHAEF's announcement of the command shift, made only after *Time* broke the story, failed to call the shift temporary: "When the German penetration through the Ardennes created two fronts, one substantially facing south and the other north, by instant agreement of all concerned that portion of the front facing south was placed under command of Montgomery and that facing north under command of Bradley." Again SHAEF's PRD blundered, and, according to Hansen, "precipitated a crisis in our allied relationships."[32] By failing to mention that the command shift was temporary, SHAEF allowed the impression that it might be permanent.

SHAEF thought nothing of moving units from American command to British command; in fact, it was normal military practice. Thirty-three American divisions fought under Montgomery's operational command during the campaign in northwest Europe. Montgomery commanded American troops in Normandy and in Operation MARKET-GARDEN; SHAEF gave him American troops for clearing the Scheldt, the Bulge, and the Rhineland. Finally, Montgomery commanded Americans while crossing the Rhine and closing to the Elbe. For example, the 82nd Airborne, the "All-American" Division, served under Montgomery's command more than it did under Bradley's. It is highly likely, moreover, that Montgomery commanded more Americans in the campaign than did Jacob Devers, the 6th United States Army Group commander. Bradley anticipated Montgomery's call on an American army for the Ruhr offensive and purposely placed Simpson's green Ninth United States Army on the right flank of 21st Army Group's Second British Army to protect the more veteran First Army under Hodges.[33]

The shock and surprise of the German counteroffensive led to press speculation about command. Elements of the British press were recommending Montgomery as deputy supreme commander, or ground forces commander, as cited in Chapter 1. On 7 January 1945, the American papers ran a story by James McGlincy, the United Press (UP) staff correspondent at SHAEF, that Montgomery "may yet be named Deputy Supreme Commander of the whole Western Front with jurisdiction over ground forces." McGlincy said it was impossible to predict the shape of command once the Bulge was straightened, but changes were rumored, stemming from either the recent criticism of the ground command or an attempt to relieve Eisenhower of some of his excessive responsibilities. The only certainty, according to UP's correspondent, was that the changes in command had nothing to do with assigning blame for the success of the German attack.[34]

The mere suggestion of blame, however, brought out the Anglophobia of 12th Army Group headquarters. According to the Hansen diary, Major Henry Munson, aide to Major General Leven C. Allen, the 12th Army Group's chief of staff, spoke for many: "Hank Munson summed up the command here when he said Monty goes running to the PM when he wants something; the PM goes running to FDR and FDR to the Joint Chiefs of Staff which carry it on to Ike." Hansen thought that Montgomery was behind the campaign in the British press: "It is apparent now, however, that the Prime Minister . . . is exerting strong pressure on Ike to have Monty named the field commander. The public clamor for this appointment is obviously officially inspired."[35]

Montgomery's press conference on 7 January 1945 proved to be the straw that broke 12th Army Group's back. *A Soldier's Story* understated the case when it said "the acutely sensitive EAGLE TAC staff exploded with indignation." Bradley later told Hansen, "It was a very, very poor press conference. From then on I was somewhat bitter toward him, and still am. I don't think I can ever forgive his apparent attempt to discredit me so he could get command of the whole operation on the continent."[36] Bradley had to personally reassure his staff that there was no likelihood of Eisenhower or Marshall permitting Montgomery being named ground forces commander: "Ike has assured me of this," Bradley said, "General Marshall has assured me of this. I am absolutely certain that General Marshall will not stand for it."[37]

To counteract the British buildup of Montgomery, Hansen felt someone in the American command had "to crow Yankee Doodle Dandy."[38] Hansen, Ingersoll, and Munson handed Bradley the *Washington Post* editorial of 28 December that said, "The American people need an authoritative interpretation of what the Rundstedt offensive is all about. . . . But no authoritative interpretation has been advanced by the War Department. The result has been a babel of voices each with a sovereign explanation of what is going on and with the end result of increasing confusion."[39] Ingersoll and Hansen told Bradley that only he could speak for the integrity of the American command, owing to his position as the senior American field commander; 12th Army Group had about six weeks seniority on General Devers' 6th Army Group. "We urged the General to remember that the US has no spokesman on the Western Front," Hansen wrote. "Montgomery can speak as a Briton while Eisenhower must speak as an Allied Commander."[40] Furthermore, as Ingersoll pointed out, Montgomery had established the precedent by holding his on-the-record press conference. Ingersoll asked Bradley if he thought Montgomery had cleared his press release with Eisenhower. Bradley responded with a question of his own: "Do you think he cleared it? You know damned well he didn't."[41]

A Soldier's Story described Bradley's press conference in detail. First, Bradley informed his readers that Eisenhower could have avoided the entire episode simply by stating the command shift was temporary; second, he mentioned that he threatened to resign if Montgomery were SHAEF deputy for ground forces. Bradley told Eisenhower that after all that had transpired he could not serve under Montgomery, and neither would Patton; Eisenhower would have to send him home because he would have lost the confidence of his command. *A Soldier's Story* gave the impression that Bradley's resignation threat followed his press conference, but Hansen's unpublished diary shows that it actually preceded it by a day. The former West Point center fielder still knew how to play hard ball; it was impossible for Eisenhower to discipline him for violating press regulations, no matter how remote that might have been.[42]

Twelfth Army Group staff officers determined to seek more publicity for their commander to prevent their general's role in the campaign from "sinking into oblivion." Hansen blamed SHAEF, the press, and especially Eisenhower's press aide, Harry Butcher, for allowing Bradley's role in the campaign to escape public notice. *A Soldier's Story* stated that Butcher feared that a 12th Army Group press camp would snipe at Montgomery, or undercut SHAEF, to which 12th Army Group responded that Montgomery had consolidated his correspondents at the army group level since Normandy. After heavy lobbying, SHAEF relented, and in late February 1945, 12th Army Group finally set up its own press camp at EAGLE TAC to provide Bradley the same press access as his counterpart to the north. Bradley's memoir passed off the press camp as ensuring a more timely flow of information to the correspondents than they gained at SHAEF.[43]

When Bradley failed to reach press parity with Montgomery or Patton, Hansen judged 12th Army Group's Public Relations officer ineffectual. Bradley and Hansen concluded that correspondents preferred covering the war either down at the army level or up at SHAEF. An army group, Hansen had to admit, was "sort of a bastard headquarters." Objectivity might have caused Hansen to notice that Montgomery's headquarters suffered no lack of top-notch correspondents, because Montgomery was good copy.[44]

The month-long Battle of the Bulge left Bradley's ego badly bruised, and his memoir took Eisenhower to task for failing to refer to the transfer as a temporary measure. Eisenhower's silence over the politically sensitive command issue dated from August 1944 and Bradley's promotion to army group command. "That unfortunate August split never completely healed," Bradley wrote in 1951. "It persisted throughout the winter war in a subtle whispering campaign that favored Monty's restoration to over-all ground command."[45] *A Soldier's Story* maintained that British prestige rested on Montgomery's retaining command of the ground forces for as long as possible. During the winter of 1944-1945, Bradley said Eisenhower found Montgomery's persistence regarding ground forces command astonishing. Pointing out that the field marshal intended to take on the ground forces command in addition to his army group, Bradley quoted Eisenhower as saying, "Monty wants to have his cake and eat it too."[46] Bradley's memoir left no doubt where he stood on the issue of command. By January 1945, following the Bulge, Bradley could not have subordinated himself to Montgomery because the American army was as competent as the British, and it had fifty divisions in the European theater compared to fifteen British or Commonwealth divisions.[47]

In February 1945 rumors suggesting a change in command again made the rounds of EAGLE TAC, and Hansen's diary contained the staff's speculations. The G-3 Operations officer, Brigadier General A. Franklin Kibler, opposed the establishment of a ground forces command because it would require the interposition of another headquarters, while the G-2 Intelligence officer, Brigadier General Edwin Sibert, simply distrusted Montgomery, believing him ambitious and envious. On 4 February, Montgomery came to Bradley's headquarters for a luncheon conference with Eisenhower and Bradley. Hansen noted that since the German counteroffensive, dislike of Montgomery had grown "among command echelons" owing to his refusal to compromise on tactical decisions taken while in command of First and Ninth Armies. Perfidious Albion reared its head when Hansen attributed Montgomery's special "diplomatic position" within the British government with preventing SHAEF from commanding the 21st Army Group as it did the American 12th and 6th Army Groups.[48]

Always alert to British pressure on SHAEF, Bradley blamed SHAEF's guarantee that the northern thrust under Montgomery would be the main attack on the Rhine and the Ruhr on British lobbying at the Malta Conference in January 1945. Bradley worried that the 12th Army Group would be gobbled up and relegated to a secondary role, since in closing to the Rhine and for its crossing, Montgomery commanded the Canadian First, the British Second, and the American Ninth Armies. Bradley's memoir stated that a 21st Army Group staff study showed that "Monty could support no more than 21 divisions in that northern offensive."[49] Bending to British pressure, *A Soldier's Story* alleged that SHAEF arbitrarily boosted this figure to thirty and then thirty-six divisions. Meanwhile, Bradley's southern pincer of the Ruhr attack was limited to twelve divisions. Bradley's Commentaries told a different story. First, the study referred to was a SHAEF study that limited the number of divisions supportable on the northern axis of advance to twenty-five, not twenty-one. Bradley told Hansen, "I think arbitrarily somebody back at SHAEF, I don't know whether [General Walter Bedell] Smith or [Lieutenant General John F. M.] Whiteley, arbitrarily made it thirty divisions."[50]

On 7 March 1945, the First United States Army threw a monkey wrench into SHAEF's plan for crossing the Rhine and enveloping the Ruhr. First Army's capture of the Ludendorff Railway Bridge at Remagen set in motion a chain of events that from Bradley's point of view finally ended the six-month-long argument over strategy and command. Montgomery's set-piece crossing was not scheduled to jump off for another two weeks, until 23-24 March. The Remagen crossing, however, represented a chance to shorten the war and consequently set off a new round of debate over where to begin the envelopment of the Ruhr, in the north or the south.

In the midst of this debate, Montgomery demanded that SHAEF constitute a ten-division reserve from the First United States Army and allow him to draw from it in support of his northern offensive. From Bradley's perspective this amounted to a repetition of the Battle of the Bulge, when Montgomery commanded four armies, two of them American, one British, and one Canadian albeit with British divisions. Had Eisenhower acceded to Montgomery's demand, the 12th Army Group would have been left commanding only Patton's Third Army. It seemed as if Montgomery were insinuating that the American army was not entitled to its own commanders. Without mentioning ground forces command, the field marshal would have been the *de facto* ground forces commander.[51]

"Fortunately Eisenhower called Montgomery's bluff," Bradley concluded. The supreme commander informed Montgomery that if any more American divisions went north of the Ardennes, then Bradley's 12th Army Group would be in command of them *and* the Ninth Army, which would have put Bradley in control of the main effort. *A Soldier's Story* said that Montgomery instantly dropped his request. Bradley's Commentaries claimed that Eisenhower's threat turned Montgomery into "a two-thrust proponent." From Bradley's point of view, Montgomery went along with the broad-front strategy when faced with the loss of command of the Ninth United States Army. Therefore, Bradley concluded that the field marshal was interested primarily in command and only secondarily in strategy. Owing to Eisenhower's calling Montgomery's bluff, Bradley said that the six-month struggle over broad front versus single thrust went to Eisenhower by forfeit.[52]

The great strength of Bradley's memoir is his portrayal of the struggle for command among a handful of proud and ambitious men. Under the watchful gaze of Marshall, Eisenhower was not about to allow an Englishman to command for him the greatest ground force that the United States had ever assembled. Neither was Bradley about to let his army group become a replacement depot for Montgomery or Devers, while he was convinced that Patton and he were better matched to end the war quickly. More than anyone else, Omar Bradley was in a position to observe the effects of Montgomery's plans. Whenever a new Montgomery plan went into action, Bradley invariably had fewer troops, a wider frontage, a secondary role, time on his hands, or all of the above. More than any other contemporary, Bradley believed that the argument was not about strategy as much as it was about command.

WILMOT'S *THE STRUGGLE FOR EUROPE*

The Struggle for Europe more than any other book in the postwar years fashioned the public perception of the strategic debate between Eisenhower and Montgomery. Prior to the appearance of Chester Wilmot's *The Struggle for Europe* in 1952, the major works dealing with the campaign in northwest Europe were primarily personal memoirs produced rapidly by famous soldiers often with the help of a team of researchers and editors. Spending nearly six years in research and writing, Wilmot interviewed participants and utilized official British documents to a greater extent than any previous author. Begun by the Australian BBC correspondent in 1945 as a history of the 21st Army Group, it developed into an explanation of why the Anglo-Americans won the war but lost the struggle for Europe to Stalin and the Russians.[53]

The British counterattack on the American postwar memoirs begun by Grigg and Denis Hamilton gained strength from Wilmot. Wilmot urged a generation of readers to believe that a series of American political and military decisions prolonged the campaign in northwest Europe and thereby led to the decline of Britain's position relative to the rest of the world as well as the enslavement of eastern Europe. Because of the manner in which Montgomery shaped Wilmot's argument and because of its contribution to the study of the campaign, Wilmot deserves a special place in this study. John Keegan, the military historian, pointed out recently that Wilmot effectively invented the contemporary writing of military history by mixing social, economic, and political factors with both strategy and tactics.[54]

In the process of writing, Wilmot was fortunate to interview Montgomery three times. The field marshal had a reputation for keeping historians at arm's length and for keeping his cards close to his vest. Colonel (later Brigadier General) S.L.A. Marshall, the U.S. military historian, took Montgomery to task for placing restrictions on combat historians at 21st Army Group headquarters during the war. Dr. Forrest Pogue, the American official historian, has pointed out that Montgomery was the only officer who refused to see him when he was in London in 1947 conducting interviews and researching his official history, *The Supreme Command.* Montgomery also refused to see British historian Correlli Barnett in relation to Barnett's *The Desert Generals.* Sir Arthur Bryant's researcher, Mrs. M. C. "Buster" Long, wrote Lady Alanbrooke in November 1954, "Apropos Monty his the *only* refusal I have had. Even Winston has said he will help when he has a moment! Also the President of the USA!!!"[55]

Two flattering postwar broadcasts helped Wilmot establish a relationship with the field marshal. Two weeks after Wilmot broadcast "Montgomery's Great Day" for Radio Newsreel, marking the anniversary of the German surrender at his tactical headquarters, Montgomery granted the first of several interviews. On 8 October 1948, Wilmot's BBC broadcast, "The First Soldier of Europe," hailed the field marshal's appointment as permanent military chairman of the Commanders-in-Chief Committee. Wilmot would interview Montgomery twice more in March 1949.[56]

By allowing Wilmot to see his correspondence with Eisenhower for the period 4 September to 28 October 1944, Montgomery made *The Struggle for Europe* a singularly important book. The Chester Wilmot Papers at the Liddell Hart Center for Military Archives at King's College in London contain twelve typed pages entitled "The Conduct of the Campaign after the Change in Command." The title referred to Eisenhower's assumption of command on 1 September 1944, and all of the Montgomery documents cited by Wilmot dealt exclusively with strategy rather than command. Reaching 14 October 1944, Wilmot recorded the following comment: "There was an exchange of letters about this time on the subject of command (letters not on the file)."[57] Wilmot did not see Eisenhower's rebuke of 13 October 1944, but he was aware that Montgomery stated on 16 October, "I have received your letter of Oct. 13th. You will hear no more on the subject of command from me."[58]

Basing his discussion of broad front versus single thrust largely on Montgomery's papers for September and October 1944 and three interviews with the field marshal, the BBC correspondent naturally focused on the strategic debate. In the process, Wilmot paid scant attention to Montgomery's campaign to be named ground forces commander.[59] To Wilmot's readers, Montgomery appeared to have been carrying on an operational debate with Eisenhower over the course to follow to conclude the war. Indeed, Wilmot's contention that Montgomery's strategy would have ended the war sooner and saved eastern Europe from the Russians gave the book much of its political appeal and vouchsafed the British claim to higher moral authority. *The Struggle for Europe* spared Eisenhower much contemporary criticism leveled at him by Montgomery, but in the process it also elevated the debate to a level that it did not really enjoy in the fall and winter of 1944-1945, when it was often mean-spirited and dominated by personality.

As a consequence of the American direction of the war, Wilmot argued, the strategy of the campaign was simply to steamroll the Germans in an unsophisticated and costly frontal assault. America's material advantage allowed the United States Army to attack with massive firepower in the strategic tradition of General Ulysses S. Grant, whom Wilmot called the "apostle of the direct approach."[60] General George C. Marshall had designated sixty divisions for Europe and his protégé, General Eisenhower, had to create the opportunity for their employment. This led to Eisenhower's insistence on a broad front, including the ANVIL landings of August 1944, which cost the British the opportunity to exploit recent victories in Italy. Wilmot believed that if the Allies had invaded the Balkans with troops from Italy, they could have beaten the Russians to Vienna and liberated eastern Europe.[61] How the Anglo-Americans might have launched a single-thrust attack on Berlin, or even the Ruhr, deprived of these divisions in the primary theater is anyone's guess.

Even more damning than frittering away the postwar advantage relative to the Russians, Wilmot believed that Eisenhower's broad-front strategy prevented Montgomery from ending the war in 1944. Broad front was a defensive strategy, and it was Hitler, not Eisenhower, who was required to use it. Wilmot's chapter, "The Great Argument," summarized both Eisenhower's and Montgomery's positions, and concluded that between 17 August and 4 September a deep advance on a narrow front would have succeeded with almost no risk. Wilmot accepted at face value Montgomery's single-thrust plan, which he put forward to Bradley and Eisenhower between 17 and 23 August 1944. Montgomery said to Bradley that their two army groups combined should attack north after crossing the Seine. Together they would form "a solid mass of forty divisions, which would be so strong that it need fear nothing."[62] Taking Montgomery's proposal at face value, Wilmot overlooked the fact that on 17 August 1944 Eisenhower simply did not have forty divisions under his command and would not until some time in September.

When Eisenhower and Kay Summersby referred to this particular Montgomery proposal as "fantastic" and "crazy," they meant it literally.[63] On 4 September Montgomery advocated "one powerful and full-blooded thrust towards Berlin."[64] Even Wilmot admitted that in advocating an advance on Berlin, Montgomery was overplaying his hand.[65] Montgomery was a better golfer than Eisenhower, but not a better poker player, and Eisenhower knew a bluff when he saw one. On 10 September the two men held their famous meeting at the Brussels airfield. According to Wilmot's account, Montgomery insisted that Major General Sir Miles Graham, his chief Administrative officer, be allowed to stay, but not Eisenhower's

counterpart, Lieutenant General Sir Humphrey Myddleton Gale. In 1949 Wilmot
interviewed Graham, who said that the meeting got off to a bad start when Monty
produced a handful of telegrams and asked Eisenhower if he had sent them. Re-
plying that he had, Montgomery exploded, "Well they're nothing but balls, sheer
balls, rubbish." Eisenhower let Montgomery get it off his chest and then reached
out and touched his knee and said, "Steady, Monty, you can't speak to me like that,
I'm your boss."[66] Wilmot cleaned up the published version in 1952.

Montgomery's heated reaction was to Eisenhower's directive of 4 September
that listed the Ruhr and the Saar as simultaneous objectives. Convinced that there
could be only one advance on the Ruhr, and it ought to be in the north,
Montgomery persuaded Wilmot that a single thrust had been feasible. Wilmot
wrote that the German army had been so thoroughly defeated south of the Seine
that an attack against the Ruhr would have had nothing to fear. Rather than choose
between the Saar or the Ruhr, Eisenhower continued both attacks until they failed
as Montgomery had predicted they would. Echoing Ingersoll, Wilmot concluded,
"The occasion called for a man with a bold plan, a Commander-in-Chief who knew
what was essential and had the will to impose his strategic ideas without regard for
personalities or public opinion."[67]

Eisenhower compromised on strategy during the 10 September meeting by
approving Montgomery's planned airborne assault on Arnhem, Operation
MARKET-GARDEN. In March 1949 Montgomery told Wilmot, "I hoped that
[Eisenhower] would reinforce my success but I knew now that we could not hope
to get much more than a bridgehead beyond the Rhine before the winter, and be
nicely poised to break out in the New Year. By the time MARKET-GARDEN was
undertaken its significance was more tactical than strategic."[68]

It is highly likely that Wilmot exaggerated Montgomery's belief that the war
might have ended as a result of a single thrust in September 1944. As time passed
and positions hardened, it seemed that Montgomery always maintained that the war
could have been won in September. Yet in his first interview with Wilmot, the
field marshal seemed somewhat ambivalent about the likelihood of ending the war
in 1944:

The war was prolonged for five or six months because of the broad-front decision. If we had
gone on with my policy we might not have forced the Germans to surrender in 1944, but
at least we should have isolated the Ruhr; there would have been no German
counteroffensive in the Ardennes, no battle of the Rhineland, no battle of the Rhine. It
would have been a comparatively easy matter to finish Germany early in 1945.[69]

Convinced that the Germans were totally defeated by late summer 1944 and that
Eisenhower's lack of a plan permitted them to recover, the Wilmot-Montgomery
argument contained several assumptions: (1) that August 1944 was October 1918,
and the Germans only had to be pushed another month and they would collapse
and surrender; (2) that the Anglo-Americans had the necessary supplies to win the
war against Germany by themselves in early September; (3) that the Western Allies
could have delivered those supplies to the frontline troops in time to complete

number one; and (4) that the western front not, the eastern front, held the war's time clock. In early September, the Allies had simply outrun their administrative tails; their supply equipment had worn out, and the terrain had changed. Instead of the French plain they now encountered the Low Countries, Belgian ports, and Germany's West Wall. The irony of the totally defeated argument is that, while the German Seventh Army was destroyed by September 1944, the British had already begun breaking up divisions in order to obtain infantry replacements.[70] Furthermore, Montgomery's fixation with the Ruhr allowed the German Fifteenth Army to escape and to hold the Scheldt Estuary and to counterattack from the west during his ground assault on Arnhem.

By September 1944, the British army had been at war for five years. Wilmot recognized that Eisenhower and other Americans doubted that the British and Canadians were up to conducting the rapid movements called for by Montgomery's strategy, and his depiction of a tired British army called into question his own argument. For instance, the commander of the 11th Armored Division, Major General G.P.B. Roberts, failed to secure the bridges over the Albert Canal when his division took Antwerp on 4 September. Wilmot attributed the lack of orders for Roberts to cross the Albert Canal to the "confusion and conflict within the Allied High Command." Furthermore, outside of Oosterhout, Holland, during MARKET-GARDEN on 22 September, lead elements of the British 43rd Division were held up for over eight hours by a company of Germans, one Mark III tank, an 88 millimeter gun, and five smaller antiaircraft guns. With the fate of the 1st Airborne Division in Arnhem and the entire operation at stake, Wilmot pointed out that regimental casualties totaled nineteen wounded. During MARKET-GARDEN, Wilmot acquired a reputation by driving on the side of the road from the Valkenswaard Bridge to the Meuse-Escaut Canal to file a story. Road signs announcing that the verges had not been cleared of mines kept hundreds of British trucks road bound, even though the verges were wide enough and safe enough for vehicular use as Wilmot had proven by driving on them.[71] Wilmot's advocacy of single thrust suffered by comparison not only from his own depiction of the British army, but also from his own personal example.

Montgomery would later blame Eisenhower's failure to halt Patton's movement against the Moselle for the tenuous condition of the right flank of the Second British Army during MARKET-GARDEN. According to the field marshal, Bradley was evasive, and Eisenhower was too weak to make up his mind to halt Patton. Therefore, First United States Army's XIX Corps lacked the necessary gasoline to protect the Second British Army's right flank in the Arnhem operation. The American XIX Corps commander, Major General Charles H. Corlett, had no prior knowledge of MARKET-GARDEN and was taken off guard when the British moved to the north rather than the northeast. Subsequently relieved of his command, Corlett was understandably upset with both First Army and the British.[72]

Further complicating his own argument against a broad front, Wilmot also informed his reader that Patton's Moselle offensive had attracted to it two German divisions from Italy and two *Schutzstaffel* (SS) brigades from Germany. "In the last weeks of August . . . ," Wilmot wrote, "every division that could then be mustered, some seven in all, had been sent to the Upper Moselle to stop Patton."[73] Furthermore, the ground assault on Arnhem was jeopardized by German attacks on both its right and left flanks. Attacks on its right flank came out of Germany, while attacks from the left flank originated entirely from troops ignored by Montgomery when he opted not to seize the South Beveland peninsula and seal off the German Fifteenth Army.

If these seven German divisions had not gone in against a moving and dangerous Patton, it stands to reason that an equivalent number of divisions, not necessarily the same ones, could have gone against either Montgomery or Devers. There was some synergistic effect to the broad-front approach. The point is that even in the dark days of September the Germans retained the ability to reinforce their endangered western front with reserves from either Germany or Italy, or both. Had Patton been stopped as Montgomery urged, it is highly likely that the Germans would have inflicted even greater damage on the First Allied Airborne Army around Arnhem or on the Third United States Army itself. However much Eisenhower and Bradley assumed that a broad front enabled the Anglo-Americans to maintain their advantage in maneuverability, the Germans constantly redeployed forces along the front and even managed to create a strategic reserve, something Eisenhower was unable to do.

CUNNINGHAM'S *A SAILOR'S ODYSSEY*

Several highly placed contemporaries of Montgomery believed that it had been a mistake to go for Arnhem. The Royal Navy's first sea lord, Admiral Sir Andrew Browne Cunningham, agreed with Admiral Sir Bertram Ramsay, the Allied naval forces commander, that Montgomery should have taken more seriously the job of cleaning out the German garrisons on Walcheren Island and South Beveland. Cunningham was sarcastic: "For the time being one of the finest ports in Europe was of no more use to us than an oasis in the Sahara desert."[74] Cunningham's 1951 memoir, *A Sailor's Odyssey: The Autobiography of Admiral of the Fleet Viscount Cunningham of Hyndhope,* did not go into great detail on the debate between Montgomery and Eisenhower. The first sea lord, a member of the British Chiefs of Staff Committee, disagreed with a supreme commander also having direct operational command of armies in the field but felt that it was a political decision. As far as the single-thrust strategy was concerned, Cunningham was suspicious of subsequent claims to the effect that it would have ended the war in 1944. "This was not claimed at the time," Cunningham wrote, "and is an afterthought on the part of someone who agreed with Montgomery's views."[75]

Two contemporaries of Montgomery's who disagreed with him over Arnhem and Antwerp never had the opportunity to write their memoirs. Admiral Ramsay believed that Montgomery was being facetious when he stated at SHAEF's 5 October conference that the Allies did not have to clear the Scheldt Estuary and open Antwerp before they took the Ruhr. Both SHAEF and Montgomery had ignored Ramsay's warning of a month before that more attention had to be paid to opening the Scheldt Estuary. Ramsay, usually a supporter of the field marshal's, laid into Montgomery in front of Brooke, Eisenhower, Tedder, Smith, Leigh-Mallory, Bradley, and Devers. In his diary for 5 October, Ramsay wrote:

This afforded me the cue I needed to lambast him for not having made the capture of Antwerp the immediate objective at [the] highest priority and let fly with all my guns at the faulty strategy we had allowed. Our large forces are now practically grounded for lack of supply and had we now got Antwerp and the rest of the Corridor we should be in a far better position for launching the knockout blow. . . . I got approving looks from Tedder and Bedell Smith and both of them together with the CIGS told me after the meeting that I had spoken their thoughts and it was high time that some one expressed them.[76]

Ramsay died in a plane crash outside of Paris on 2 January 1945. Had he lived his acerbic diary and incisive views, just as often critical of Eisenhower as of Montgomery, would have provided the basis of an incomparable memoir. His death and that of Leigh-Mallory meant that only one of the Allied ground, air, and naval commanders of Operation OVERLORD produced a postwar memoir, that is, Montgomery. In their last meeting together, on 30 September 1944, Leigh-Mallory told Ramsay that Montgomery had made a great mistake in pushing for the Arnhem assault. First, Arnhem took gasoline away from Patton, who would have pierced the Siegfried Line and crossed the Rhine; and second, the airborne operation was a futile use of the aircraft that were more profitably employed in airlift to aid the ground troops. Ramsay concurred with Leigh-Mallory and told him that Montgomery's plan had been badly orchestrated and far too weak; Arnhem had been a waste of time.[77] On 14 November 1944, accompanied by his wife, Leigh-Mallory flew off to Burma for a new command, but all on board were killed when the plane struck a French mountain near Grenoble.

CONCLUSION

By late June 1950, the cold war had become a hot war in Korea, and both the Soviet atomic bomb and Communist China were nearly one year old. The Anglo-American Berlin Airlift had succored that city until the Russians called off their blockade. The West felt besieged, and criticism of Eisenhower's refusal to take Berlin ahead of the Russians became more vitriolic. As the man who had played the key role in Eisenhower's decision not to go into Berlin, and the chairman of the Joint Chiefs of Staff during the Korean War, General Bradley stressed that his advice to Eisenhower was motivated by saving American lives. Bradley told his readers: "When Eisenhower asked me what I thought it might cost us to break through from the Elbe to Berlin, I estimated 100,000 casualties. 'A pretty stiff price to pay for a prestige objective,' I said, 'especially when we've got to fall back and let the other fellow take over.'"[78] After the war, Bradley told Hansen that besides the political considerations, there were sound military reasons behind Eisenhower's announcing a demarcation line at the Elbe. It was essential that the

Russians not advance into the American area of occupation, Bradley said, because no one was certain of our ability to get them to leave.[79]

The next chapter investigates Churchill's opinions concerning Berlin. By the time the sixth and final volume in his history of the Second World War appeared, the Berlin issue dominated the final chapters of books on the campaign. Suffice it to say that militarily Bradley was proved correct. The Russians took Berlin in a house-to-house battle, and their casualties were nearly three times what Bradley had predicted.[80] Between the Red Army's broad front and the Anglo-Americans' broad front, the German army was essentially destroyed. As far as Eisenhower and Bradley were concerned, the military destruction of the German army paralleled the political destruction of Nazi Germany, which was an additional consideration of the American strategic option. Eisenhower had hoped to destroy the Germans west of the Rhine, and Bradley wanted the German army destroyed to ease the occupation to follow.

NOTES

1. Omar N. Bradley, *A Soldier's Story* (New York: Holt, 1951), 206.

2. Bradley to Eisenhower, 22 May 1951, Dwight David Eisenhower, Pre-Presidential Papers, 1916-1952, Principal File, Box 13, Omar Bradley, EL. Concerning Bradley's publishing while still in uniform, Eisenhower said to Montgomery that Bradley "'was a little bit touched in the head.'" Nigel Hamilton, *Monty: Final Years of the Field-Marshal, 1944-1976* (New York: McGraw-Hill, 1986), 797.

3. For the surprise factor, Bradley Commentaries (S-16, 39-A), Papers of General of the Army Omar N. Bradley, USAMHI; for calling Montgomery "sir," Hansen Diary [hereafter HD], 23 September 1944, CBHP, USAMHI; for Montgomery's comment to Bradley see Barney Oldfield, *Never a Shot in Anger* (New York: Longmans, 1956; reprint, Santa Barbara, Calif.: Capa Press, 1989, Battle of Normandy Museum Edition), 173, n.4.

4. Omar N. Bradley and Clay Blair, *A General's Life: An Autobiography by General of the Army Omar N. Bradley and Clay Blair* (New York: Simon and Schuster, 1983), 9; James E. Moore, General, United States Army (Ret.), Oral History Interview, 106, Senior Officers Oral History Program [hereafter SOOHP] Project 84-19, Interview by Lieutenant Colonel Larry F. Paul, USAMHI.

5. Bradley Papers, USAMHI; Bradley and Blair, *A General's Life,* 11.

6. For the Hansen remark, see James E. Moore, General, United States Army (Ret.), Oral History Interview, 106, SOOHP (84-19), USAMHI; for Bradley on Montgomery, see Bradley, *A Soldier's Story,* 138.

7. For Bradley's "arrogant and egotistical" comment, see Bradley Commentaries (S-12, 39-A), USAMHI; for a "perverse soldier," see Bradley, *A Soldier's Story,* 138; for the comparison between Montgomery and Patton, see Bradley Commentaries (S-18, 40-B), USAMHI.

8. Bradley, *A Soldier's Story,* 207.

9. For the Class of 1915, see *Register of Graduates and Former Cadets, 1912-1991* (West Point: Association of Graduates, 1991), 190-93; for contact with Eisenhower, see Diary of Air Marshal Robb, Meeting in Supreme Commander's Office, 12 January 1945, Papers of Air Chief Marshal Sir James Robb, AC 71/9/26, RAFM; Bradley, *A Soldier's*

Story, 354-55.

10. Bradley, *A Soldier's Story,* 420; Bradley's letter called for an advance "on a very wide front," but his memoir described a "broad front," which was now the vogue; see Bradley to Eisenhower, 15 September 1944, Butcher Diary [hereafter BD], Dwight D. Eisenhower, Pre-Presidential Papers, 1916-1952, Principal File, Harry C. Butcher, Box 169 (31 August-15 October) (3), EL.

11. Bradley to Eisenhower, 15 September 1944, BD, Dwight D. Eisenhower, Pre-Presidential Papers, 1916-1952, Principal File, Harry C. Butcher, Box 169 (31 August-15 October) (3), EL.

12. Bradley, *A Soldier's Story,* 420-22.

13. Bradley to Eisenhower, 15 September 1944, BD, Dwight D. Eisenhower, Pre-Presidential Papers, 1916-1952, Principal File, Harry C. Butcher, Box 169 (31 August-15 October) (3), EL.

14. For Major BonDurant, see HD, 24 September 1944, CBHP, USAMHI; Eisenhower's sending him to see Montgomery is in Bradley, *A Soldier's Story,* 422-23; for Montgomery's schedule and unwillingness to visit Eisenhower's headquarters, see Bradley Commentaries (S-19, 40-A), USAMHI.

15. Bradley, *A Soldier's Story,* 423.

16. For Eisenhower's failure to order Montgomery, see Bradley, *A Soldier's Story,* 423; for Montgomery's failure to open Antwerp, see 425.

17. Bradley Commentaries (S-0, 39-B), USAMHI.

18. Bradley, *A Soldier's Story,* 434-35, italics in the original.

19. Ibid., 438.

20. Ibid., 476.

21. HD, 19 December 1944, CBHP, USAMHI.

22. Russell F. Weigley, *Eisenhower's Lieutenants: The Campaign of France and Germany, 1944-1945* (Bloomington: Indiana University Press, 1981), 505.

23. Hugh M. Cole, *The Ardennes: Battle of the Bulge (United States Army in World War II: The European Theater of Operations.* Washington, D.C.: Center of Military History, United States Army, 1993), 424.

24. Moore believed that a regiment was the largest force that should have gone into Luxembourg City. See James E. Moore, General, United States Army (Ret.), Oral History Interview, 110, SOOHP (84-19), USAMHI.

25. Bradley, *A Soldier's Story,* 464; the first mention in the Hansen Diary of the "calculated risk" is 23 December 1944, one week after the opening of the German counteroffensive.

26. Bradley, *A Soldier's Story,* 477-78.

27. Bradley Commentaries (S-25, 42-B), USAMHI.

28. For Bradley's memoir treatment see Bradley, *A Soldier's Story,* 480-81; for Major Sylvan's car, see HD, 25 December 1944, CBHP, USAMHI; for Clay Blair, see Bradley and Blair, *A General's Life,* 369.

29. Bradley, *A Soldier's Story,* 480.

30. Ibid., 482.

31. Bradley and Blair, *A General's Life,* 376; HD, 27 December 1944, CBHP, USAMHI.

32. The SHAEF statement is in Bradley, *A Soldier's Story,* 484; Hansen calling it a crisis is in "Monty Takes Command," HD, 6 January 1945, 1, CBHP, USAMHI.

33. Dispositions of troops are in *Order of Battle of the United Sates Army: World War II (European Theater of Operations: Divisions)* (Paris: December 1945), 285-86, Center for Military History, Washington, D.C.; for steps to maintain the First Army, see Bradley, *A*

Soldier's Story, 436-37.

34. "No Allied Generals to Be 'Sacked'," *San Francisco Chronicle,* 7 January 1945, p. 2.

35. "Monty Takes Command," 6 January 1945, HD, 3-4, CBHP, USAMHI.

36. Bradley Commentaries (S-16, 39-A), USAMHI; for indignation, see Bradley, *A Soldier's Story,* 485.

37. For General Marshall's assurances, see HD, 8 January 1945, 7, CBHP, USAMIII.

38. For someone to crow Yankee Doodle, see "Monty Takes Command," 6 January 1945, HD, 4, CBHP, USAMHI.

39. Bradley, *A Soldier's Story,* 485.

40. HD, 8 January 1945, 7, CBHP, USAMHI.

41. HD, 8 January 1945, 8-9, CBHP, USAMHI; for the published version, see Bradley, *A Soldier's Story,* 485-86. I could find no evidence in either the Eisenhower Library or among Montgomery's papers at the Imperial War Museum that Montgomery cleared his press conference with Eisenhower; see Nigel Hamilton, *Monty: Final Years of the Field-Marshal, 1944-1976* (New York: McGraw-Hill, 1986), 298. Montgomery did clear it with Churchill, however; see, PRO: CAB 65/49, War Cabinet Conclusions, 8 January 1945.

42. For Bradley's threat to resign, see HD, 8 January 1945, CBHP, USAMHI; for the memoir's chronology, see Bradley, *A Soldier's Story,* 487-88.

43. The printed account of the press camp is found in Bradley, *A Soldier's Story,* 475-76, 498-99. For "sinking into oblivion," see HD, 17-21 January 1945; for the press camp, see HD, 22 February 1945 and 28-29 March 1945, CBHP, USAMHI.

44. Bradley Commentaries (S-24, 41-B), USAMHI.

45. Bradley, *A Soldier's Story,* 353.

46. Ibid., 355.

47. Ibid., 488.

48. HD, 4 February 1945, CBHP, USAMHI. Hansen had in mind Montgomery's ordering the 82nd Airborne out of the area around St. Vith against the wishes of the XVIII Airborne Corps commander, Major General Matthew B. Ridgway, and Montgomery's steadfast refusal to attack earlier than 3 January 1945, despite urging by General Hodges, First Army commander, Major General J. Lawton Collins, VII Corps commander, and Bradley himself.

49. Bradley, *A Soldier's Story,* 513-14.

50. Bradley Commentaries (S-10, 45-A), USAMHI.

51. Bradley, *A Soldier's Story,* 517-18.

52. For Bradley's printed recollections, see Bradley, *A Soldier's Story,* 517-18; for Montgomery becoming a "two-thrust" man, see Bradley Commentaries (S-10, 39-A), USAMHI. Montgomery approved because the forces were concentrated; see "Notes on Conversation with Monty," 18 May 1946, 5, Chester Wilmot Papers, 15/15/127, Montgomery, Liddell Hart Collection, LHCMA.

53. Wilmot to Eisenhower, 15 October 1945, Dwight D. Eisenhower, Pre-Presidential Principal File, Box 120 (Williamson-Wilson, F.), EL; Chester Wilmot, *The Struggle for Europe* (London: Collins; New York: Harper and Brothers, 1952).

54. John Keegan, *The Second World War* (New York: Viking Press, 1989), 598.

55. S.L.A. Marshall, "Military Memoirs," *The Yale Review* 37 (June 1948): 757-60; for Pogue and Barnett, see Carlo D'Este, *Decision in Normandy* (New York: E. P. Dutton, 1983), 491; Mrs. M. C. Long to Lady Alanbrooke, 19 November 1954, Alanbrooke Papers, 10/2/69, Letters of Congratulation, 1945-1963, LHCMA.

56. For Wilmot's broadcasts, see Chester Wilmot Papers, 15/15/127, Montgomery,

Liddell Hart Collection, LHCMA; for Wilmot's Montgomery interviews, see Chester Wilmot Papers, 15/15/53, Ardennes Offensive, 15/15/127, Montgomery, Liddell Hart Collection, LHCMA.

57. "The Conduct of the Campaign after the Change in Command," 11, 15/15/127, Montgomery, Chester Wilmot Papers, Liddell Hart Collection, LHCMA.

58. Ibid.

59. Wilmot acknowledged Montgomery's assistance in conducting research in the British zone of occupied Germany in the fall of 1945; see *Appendix A,* "A Note on Sources," 724, in Chester Wilmot, *The Struggle for Europe* (London: Collins; New York: Harper and Brothers, 1952). Footnotes alert the reader to the Wilmot-Montgomery interviews.

60. Wilmot, *The Struggle for Europe,* 339, n.1.

61. For ANVIL and the broad front, see Wilmot, *The Struggle for Europe,* 454; Wilmot quoted the postwar opinion of General Mark W. Clark, Fifth United States Army commander in Italy, 455.

62. Ibid., 460. Churchill said that Eisenhower had "more than 37 divisions" at the fall of Paris, 25-27 August 1944, see Winston S. Churchill, *The Second World War,* vol. 6, *Triumph and Tragedy* (Boston: Houghton Mifflin; Cambridge, Mass.: Riverside Press, 1953), 190.

63. Summersby Diary, 12 September 1944, noted: "Monty's suggestion is simple, give him everything, which is crazy." Dwight D. Eisenhower, Pre-Presidential Papers, 1916-1952, Principal File, Box 140, Summersby Diary, EL; Eisenhower had called "fantastic" both Patton's and Montgomery's notions for a single thrust; see Dwight D. Eisenhower, *Crusade in Europe* (Garden City, N. Y.: Doubleday, 1948), 292.

64. Wilmot, *The Struggle for Europe,* 483.

65. Ibid., 489.

66. Interview with Major-General Sir Miles Graham, 19 January 1949, 15/15/48, Chester Wilmot Papers, Liddell Hart Collection, LHCMA; for the published version, see Wilmot, *The Struggle for Europe,* 488-89.

67. For the condition of the German army, see Wilmot, *The Struggle for Europe,* 460-61; for a man with a bold plan, see 468.

68. Wilmot-Montgomery Interview, "Allied Strategy after Fall of Paris," 23 March 1949, 5, 15/15/127, Montgomery, Chester Wilmot Papers, Liddell Hart Collection, LHCMA.

69. Notes on Conversation with Monty, 18 May 1946, 4, 15/15/127, Montgomery, Chester Wilmot Papers, Liddell Hart Collection, LHCMA.

70. See Carlo D'Este, *Decision in Normandy* (New York: E. P. Dutton, 1983), 262-63. Montgomery's drive to gain control of American divisions began in earnest after 14 August 1944, the date that he asked for permission to break up the British 59th Infantry Division.

71. For the Albert Canal, see Wilmot, *The Struggle for Europe,* 486; the Somersets are 518; for Wilmot's driving habits, see 516, n.1.

72. "To make matters worse, the English started on their ill-advised jaunt to end the war over a single good road to Arnheim [sic]. Without a word of notice to me they pulled out and opened my flank for fifty miles," was how Corlett put it in his *Cowboy Pete: The Autobiography of Major General Charles H. Corlett,* edited by Wm. Farrington (Santa Fe, N. M.: Sleeping Fox Enterprises, 1974), 101.

73. First Army's gas is in Wilmot, *The Struggle for Europe,* 495; Patton and the Germans is 478.

74. Andrew Browne Cunningham, *A Sailor's Odyssey: The Autobiography of Admiral of the Fleet Viscount Cunningham of Hyndhope* (New York: E. P. Dutton, 1951), 609.

75. For Cunningham's views on a supreme commander see Cunningham, *A Sailor's*

Odyssey, 620.

76. Diary of Admiral Sir Bertram Ramsay, 5 October 1944, 5, PRO: CAB 106/1124.

77. Diary of Admiral Sir Bertram Ramsay, 30 September 1944, 5, PRO: CAB 106/1124.

78. Bradley, *A Soldier's Story,* 535.

79. Bradley Commentaries, Berlin--Decision to Halt on Elbe, USAMHI

80. Cornelius Ryan, *The Last Battle* (New York: Simon and Schuster, 1966; reprint, New York: Pocket Books, 1967), 490, gives a figure near to Bradley's; however, John Erickson, *The Road to Berlin: Continuing the History of Stalin's War with Germany* (Boulder, Colo.: Westview Press, 1983), 622, puts Russian losses during the Berlin campaign at 304,887 killed, wounded, and missing.

5

Antwerp and Berlin, A Tale of Two Cities: Churchill's *Triumph and Tragedy* and Pogue's *The Supreme Command*

> The Russian armies will no doubt overrun all Austria and enter Vienna. If they also take Berlin will not their impression that they have been the overwhelming contributor to our common victory be unduly imprinted in their minds, and may this not lead them into a mood which will raise grave and formidable difficulties in the future? I therefore consider that from a political standpoint we should march as far east into Germany as possible, and that should Berlin be in our grasp we should certainly take it.
>
> --Prime Minister Churchill to
> President Roosevelt, 1 April 1945[1]

Decorum ruled in the works of the British head of state in 1953 and an American official historian in 1954. Prime Minister Churchill limited his criticism of President Eisenhower to what had already appeared in Butcher's *My Three Years with Eisenhower*. Dr. Forrest C. Pogue bent over backwards in writing *The Supreme Command* to fairly represent both nations involved in running SHAEF, and it is still the only history of that wartime institution. Taken in tandem, these two works made a strong case that it would have been impossible to get to Berlin without first opening Antwerp to ship traffic.

CHURCHILL'S *TRIUMPH AND TRAGEDY*

Sir Winston Leonard Spencer Churchill, Knight of the Garter, had reason to look back fondly on 1953. Queen Elizabeth II knighted him in April; in September, *Triumph and Tragedy*, the sixth and final volume of *The Second World War*, appeared in print; and in October his memoirs won the Nobel Prize for literature. A Conservative, then a Liberal, then again a Conservative, twice wartime first lord of the admiralty, and twice simultaneously prime minister and minister of defense, the most controversial British politician of his time had become the great literary statesman of his age. Following each of the century's world wars, Churchill produced a multivolume personal history. After the First World War, he authored *The World Crisis*.[2] From 1948 to 1951, Churchill turned out five volumes in spite of suffering a stroke, and on 31 October 1951, at the age of seventy-six, he became prime minister for the second time. His writing pace slowed over the next two years, however, due to his added responsibilities and the effects of further strokes.[3]

Churchill was the only member of the Big Three--Roosevelt, Stalin, and himself--to produce a memoir. Roosevelt died of a cerebral hemorrhage in April 1945, and the closest thing to a memoir was Robert E. Sherwood's *Roosevelt and Hopkins: An Intimate History* (1948). Emery Reves, Churchill's European literary agent, understood the singular importance of Churchill's work: "In view of the fact that Roosevelt is dead and Stalin will never publish his documents, you are the only man who can reveal the decisive issues of the last war."[4]

When his Conservative Coalition government was voted out of power in July 1945, Churchill was unemployed. Not yet a rich man, he faced the sale of his beloved estate, Chartwell. Thanks to a trust raised by Lord Camrose, William Ewert Berry, the editor-in-chief and publisher of the *Daily Telegraph* of London, Churchill was able to sell Chartwell as well as live in it. Under terms of the trust, Chartwell passed to Britain's National Trust upon his death and became his monument. As part of the arrangement of his memoirs, Churchill also established a trust to receive royalties. On 31 July 1951, the trust was five years old and matured; thereafter, in the event of his death, his wife Clementine would pay a 50 percent tax on the trust rather than the 80 percent inheritance rate. Churchill lived fourteen more years until 1965 as an independently wealthy man, partly from the sale of Chartwell but largely from the syndication rights to *The Second World War*, which alone brought him at least $1 million.[5]

Anticipating the style and format of his memoirs, in late May 1946 Churchill sent Prime Minister Clement Attlee the following request:

In my own case an unusually large proportion of my work was done in writing, i.e. by shorthand dictation, and there is therefore in existence an unbroken series of minutes, memoranda, telegrams, etc., covering the whole period of my Administration, all of which were my own composition, subject to Staff or Department checking. . . . These pieces, written at the moment and under the impact of events, with all their imperfections and fallacies of judgment, show far better than anything composed in subsequent years could do, the hopes and fears and difficulties through which we made our way.[6]

Permission to use his official papers seemed all the more urgent owing to the works of Ingersoll and Butcher. On 23 September 1946, Churchill wrote the Cabinet secretary, Sir Edward Bridges, asking the government to permit him to publish official papers that he had written. "I feel I have a right, if I so decide to tell my tale and I am convinced that it would be to the advantage of our country to have it told, as perhaps I alone can tell it."[7] The Cabinet quickly approved Churchill's request, with the condition that His Majesty's Government would review each volume prior to publication, and the United States would approve publication of the Churchill-Roosevelt correspondence.

Even before he had permission to publish his documents, Churchill formed his team of research assistants. In March 1946, Churchill hired F. W. Deakin, who had helped with previous books and was on leave from Wadham College, Oxford. General Ismay, his former chief of staff, served as principal military advisor while Lieutenant General Sir Henry Pownall and Commodore George R. G. Allen worked on army and naval matters, respectively. Sir Edward Marsh read each chapter for style, and to catalogue his personal papers, Churchill hired a young barrister, Denis Kelly.[8]

Kelly's first act was to move Churchill's papers away from Chartwell's oil burner, which Churchill kept roaring winter and summer. Kelly finished the catalogue in four months but spent another month stopping what was known as "rummaging." Documents were ordered up from the basement storeroom by Churchill and his staff, who treated them as raw material, writing on some, cutting up others, and discarding unwanted parts. Certain that "rummaging" was destroying the documents as well as his catalogue, Kelly developed a system to request, deliver, pick up, and return documents on a daily basis.[9]

Churchill's retired proofreader, Charles Carlyle Wood, was sorely missed when Churchill's publisher turned his reference to the French army in 1940 as "the *prop* of the French nation" into "the *poop* of the French nation." To prevent further use of errata slips, Churchill talked Wood out of retirement.[10]

Dictation was Churchill's method for all his speeches and books. After drawing up the contents of each chapter as a guide, Churchill ordered key documents from Kelly. Churchill's dictated narrative linked together the documents, and his experts set to work with blue pencil for deletions and red pencil for additions. At that point, the chapter went to his printer, Cassell of London, which turned the typed chapters into galley proofs. Churchill treated galley proofs as drafts and thought nothing of going through five galleys per chapter.[11] Churchill told Walter Graebner, "I write a book the way they built the Canadian Pacific Railway. First I lay the track from coast to coast, and after that I put in all the stations." One eyewitness to this procedure remarked, "A publisher had to be confident that he had a best-seller on his hands before he was willing to meet Churchill's far-reaching demands."[12]

Churchill titled volume six *Triumph and Tragedy* because victory failed to produce a lasting peace. Focusing on Berlin, Churchill implied that Eisenhower's decision not to take the city worsened the cold war. Acutely aware of the potential damage to then President Eisenhower during the McCarthy period, Churchill wrote him in late March 1953 when *Triumph and Tragedy* was in its final galleys. The prime minister assured the president that he had withheld the book on account of the presidential election. Furthermore, as Eisenhower was now president, he had "taken great pains to ensure that it contains nothing which might imply that there was in those days any controversy or lack of confidence between us." Churchill said he described their differences in a way "that even ill-disposed people will be unable to turn them to mischievous account." Churchill had confided to his secretary, John Colville, some months before that "owing to Eisenhower winning the presidency he must cut much out of Volume 6 of his War History and could not tell the story of how the United States gave away, to please Russia, vast tracts of Europe they had occupied and how suspicious they were of his pleas for caution."[13]

As far as strategy and command were concerned, *Triumph and Tragedy* picked up where *My Three Years with Eisenhower* left off with the long-delayed invasion of southern France, Operation ANVIL, later renamed DRAGOON. Churchill pleaded with Eisenhower to call off the invasion along with its redeployment of several divisions from Italy to France; he wanted the troops in Italy to seek a decision in Italy. In 1947 Lord Alanbrooke told the American official historian, Forrest Pogue, that Churchill believed that Britain stood to gain more prestige in the Mediterranean theater where it "predominated." Another wartime member of the British Chiefs of Staff Committee, Marshal of the Royal Air Force Lord Charles Portal, told Pogue that Churchill was "upset because he had envisaged two rather equal theaters when he let Ike have the European show for Alex [Field Marshal Alexander] in the Med."[14]

When DRAGOON went off six weeks after the Normandy landing (6 June-15 August), as if that qualified for the diversion and pincers approved at the Teheran Conference in November 1943, Churchill felt betrayed. The prime minister believed that the mere threat of an invasion tied down German troops in southern France. The American fixation with northwest Europe caused the Allies to miss the opportunity to advance up the Po Valley in Italy and then launch an amphibious invasion against the Istrian peninsula. Such an invasion, Churchill said, offered "attractive prospects of advancing through the Ljubljana Gap into Austria and Hungary and striking at the heart of Germany from another direction." The Americans thus prevented not only the opportunity to strike a heavy blow against the Germans, but also "to reach Vienna before the Russians, with all that might have followed therefrom."[15]

Triumph and Tragedy summarized the differences between Eisenhower and Montgomery without taking sides, concluding that, "Strategists may long debate these issues." Relative to Montgomery's forty-division gamble of 23 August, only Churchill noted that at the time of the liberation of Paris, 25 August 1944, Eisenhower commanded "more than thirty-seven divisions." Allotting the main thrust to the British, Eisenhower wanted their northeastward movement to overrun the Channel coast, the Germans' flying bomb sites and the port of Antwerp. "Without the vast harbour of this city," Churchill said, "no advance across the lower Rhine and into the plains of northern Germany was possible."[16]

Triumph and Tragedy showed that on 8 September Churchill focused on the port issue in rejecting the optimistic conclusions of the British Joint Intelligence Committee's report, "German Capacity to Resist." "Apart from Cherbourg and Arromanches," Churchill wrote, "we have not yet obtained any large harbours. The Germans intend to defend the mouth of the Scheldt, and are still resisting in the northern suburbs of Antwerp." The former first lord of the Admiralty simplified the issue and implied criticism of Montgomery's subsequent handling of the campaign: "It is difficult to see how the Twenty-first Army Group can advance in force to the German frontier until it has cleaned up the stubborn resistance at the Channel ports and dealt with the Germans at Walcheren and to the north of Antwerp." In conclusion, Churchill predicted that September: "*It is at least as likely that Hitler will be fighting on January 1 as that he will collapse before then.*"[17]

Churchill edited documents in *Triumph and Tragedy* that contained criticism of Eisenhower's failure to concentrate. Montgomery's reservations concerning Eisenhower's plan to advance on both the Ruhr and the Saar reached the *Queen Mary* on 7 September, as the British delegation neared the Second Quebec Conference: "I am not (repeat not) happy about the general strategic plan for further conduct of operations but I do not (repeat not) see how I can do anything more in the matter and must now do the best I can to carry out the orders of the Supreme Commander." Churchill shared these misgivings in 1944, but he hid them in 1953.[18]

The prime minister deleted from *Triumph and Tragedy* the first paragraph of his 3 December 1944 message to his old friend, Field Marshal Sir Jan Christian Smuts, prime minister of the Union of South Africa, because it questioned Eisenhower's conduct of the campaign and mentioned the possibility of altering command:

Before this offensive was launched we placed on record our view that it was a mistake to attack against the whole front and that a far greater mass should have been gathered at the point of desired penetration. Montgomery's comments and predictions beforehand have in every way been borne out. I imagine some readjustments will be made giving back to Montgomery some of the scope taken from him after the victory he gained in Normandy.[19]

Triumph and Tragedy reprinted Churchill's second paragraph, describing the situation on the western front as a "strategic reverse," which was Montgomery's term for the situation on the western front in his cable to Eisenhower of 30 November that Butcher had already mentioned in 1946.[20] Clearly, Churchill was more concerned with the conduct of the campaign by early December 1944 than he could divulge with Eisenhower in the White House. On the day before he cabled Smuts in December 1944, he had dictated two messages that were never sent. One was for Eisenhower, reproduced here for the first time, dealing with command and strategy; the second was addressed to the CIGS and dealt with the politics of command which Churchill wanted forwarded to Montgomery. By the first week of December 1944, Churchill contemplated dividing the front into two commands and returning to the Normandy command setup minus Montgomery's title of ground forces commander:

Prime Minister to General Eisenhower
2 Dec. 44

The following is at present entirely personal to you and off the record in every way.

1. I thought I would let you know at this juncture how my mind is moving about the Western Front. Considering its vast extent, it would be better to divide it into two fronts, a northern and a southern. I consider it indispensable that you should command both these fronts directly and that no other staff should be interposed between you and the two front

commanders. The addition of such a staff would simply be a complication, probably many more staff officers and office delays, whereas you enjoy the complete confidence of the British armies, of me and of the Chiefs of Staff. Furthermore it would be a misfortune to remove Omar Bradley from the headship of a group of armies which he discharges so admirably, which armies will have very severe fighting.

2. I should hope that the northern front would be given to Montgomery, and the southern front to Devers or whoever is chosen by the American authorities. I repeat I am entirely opposed to the interposition of any command between you and the two commanders of fronts which will be under you. Of course I will at appropriate times make any representations that may be necessary to the President, but I wish to let you know the line I shall take in any controversy that may develop.

3. I think there will be a great advantage in giving Montgomery the northern front. He and Omar Bradley work together so well and have mutual liking and confidence. Both Bradley and Montgomery have offered to serve under each other, in the true spirit which governs all Anglo-American relations, for the inculcation of which you bear the chief honour. However I shall suggest as opportunity requires that Montgomery should command the northern front and should have the same direct contact with you as he has hitherto enjoyed, whether in command of Anglo-American troops or simply of the 21st Group of Armies.

4. I never expected that the final battle would be won, before Christmas, and I was impressed with the arguments that we were spreading our forces too widely. Nevertheless I am glad that it was fought and the results have carried us another good step towards our goal. Everything in my opinion should now turn to reinforcement, regrouping and preparation for the spring, which I hope will mean not later than the end of February.

5. There seem to me however to be two important strokes which might be delivered in the interval. First, I presume you intend to exploit the brilliant successes from Strasbourg and the Belfort gap and perhaps press harder with the victory already gained east of Metz. Secondly, although I have not examined this in detail, there seems to be high strategic and political arguments for clearing up the Dutch situation by a kind of backhanded stroke of the 21st Army Group with any support they may need. If there is a frost this winter, as some predict, the crossing of the canals and swampy fields ought to be much easier.[21]

When the CIGS read it, he was so furious that Churchill had divulged Montgomery's confidences that he threatened to withhold Montgomery's wires from the prime minister. Brooke convinced Churchill not to send the message that day, and subsequently the message was never sent.[22]

On 4 December, Churchill dictated a second message, which Brooke also persuaded him to not dispatch. Churchill knew from reading Montgomery's strategic-reverse message, as well as the British newspapers, that the field marshal and Eisenhower had held far-ranging talks at 21st Army Group.[23] The prime minister's personal minute of 2 December addressed the political nature of the command issue:

1. With regard to our conversation tonight about the changes in high commands, the changes now under discussion cannot be effected by the military authorities themselves but only by the Governments concerned. The visit by General Eisenhower to General Montgomery was publicized in a remarkable manner and cannot be treated as mere conversation between high officers. In order to regularise the situation you should inform General Mont-

gomery that he should inform me officially of the conversations he has had with, and the letter he has written to, General Eisenhower. Alternatively you can do so. What cannot possibly be allowed is that the Governments concerned should not be consulted about changes so far-reaching in the high commands.

2. You were perfectly justified in acquainting me when you did of the proceedings, but I do not think matters should have gone so far without my being informed.[24]

Churchill's reservations concerning the stalemate on the western front in December 1944 were muted in *Triumph and Tragedy*. He included his message to Roosevelt of 6 December 1944, which called the situation serious. Borrowing Montgomery's theme, the prime minister pointed out that the Allies had not yet reached the Rhine in the north, their objective of late October. Churchill published Roosevelt's upbeat response of 10 December 1944, which admitted to being less upset over the progress of the campaign because he had been less optimistic about crossing the Rhine in the first place. Roosevelt recalled that as a young man he had "bicycled over most of the Rhine terrain," and his recollection of its geography convinced him that closing to the west bank of the Rhine would be very difficult. Given his paralysis, it must have been a bittersweet memory; it was certainly accurate.[25]

On 16 December 1944, the German Ardennes counteroffensive intervened. Subsequently, Eisenhower appointed Montgomery to command two American armies, and Montgomery held his press conference. *Triumph and Tragedy* included Churchill's speech to the House of Commons on 18 January 1945, pointing out that the battle and the casualties had been primarily American. Yet by omitting any reference to Montgomery's press conference, his comments on the Battle of the Bulge appeared devoid of context. In his secret minute to the British Chiefs on 10 January, Churchill called the press conference unfortunate and patronizing and added that it "completely overlooked the fact that the US have lost perhaps 80,000 men and we but 2000 or 3000." Far more worrisome, he warned that "Eisenhower told me that the anger of his Generals was such he would hardly dare to order any of them to serve under Montgomery. This of course may cool down, but also it may seriously complicate his being given the leadership of the northern thrust."[26] Churchill's unpublished minute advised the British Chiefs to hold all discussion of command and strategy for the meeting of the Combined Chiefs of Staff on Malta at the end of January.

Triumph and Tragedy's next major complaint about General Eisenhower concerned the supreme commander's telegram to Marshal Stalin of 28 March 1945: "We all thought this went beyond the limits of negotiations with the Soviets by the Supreme Commander in Europe as they had previously been understood." The British Chiefs of Staff were also appalled at Eisenhower's change of strategy. In order to shift the major thrust from Montgomery's to Bradley's army group, Eisenhower returned Simpson's Ninth Army to Bradley after over three months under Montgomery's command. Aware that Montgomery would miss the chance to march on Berlin, the British Chiefs protested to the Combined Chiefs of Staff. This, more than any other incident in the campaign, demonstrated the extent to which the

British military assumed the use of American armies. Both the British Chiefs and Churchill worried about being condemned to a static role at the war's end. Churchill realized that there was no prospect of entering Berlin with the Americans.[27]

Because of the declining size of the British army, Churchill and the British Chiefs of Staff wanted to keep control of the Ninth United States Army. In the War Cabinet on 4 December 1944, Churchill regretted turning the British 50th Infantry Division into a holding division owing to a lack of manpower; a holding division was a euphemism for a noncombat force that provided replacements for combat units. Churchill warned that over the next six months it was vital to maintain the size of the British army. "Reductions in our effective fighting strength might well be reflected in our influence at the Peace settlement," Churchill worried out loud.[28] On 6 April in a letter to his wife, who was in Moscow, Churchill returned to the size of His Majesty's forces in the last days of the war:

I have also had a wrangle between our Staffs and the Americans . . . about a change of plan Eisenhower introduced on the Western Front . . . taking away the 9th US Army from Montgomery's command and leaving him with a rough but considerably restricted and unspectacular task. . . . Undoubtedly I feel much pain when I see our armies so much smaller than theirs. It has always been my wish to keep equal, but how can you do that against so mighty a nation and a population nearly three times your own?[29]

Churchill's single greatest complaint about Eisenhower, according to *Triumph and Tragedy*, grew out of the decision to leave Berlin for the Russians. Notwithstanding their strategic differences with Eisenhower, Churchill reminded his Chiefs on 31 March that Eisenhower's standing with the Joint Chiefs was very high. "He may claim to have correctly estimated so far the resisting strength of the enemy and to have established by deeds, (a) the 'closing' . . . of the Rhine along its whole length, (b) the power to make the double advance instead of staking all on the northern advance." Combined with the continuing arrival of fresh American divisions, Eisenhower's strategic success made it virtually impossible to question his conduct of the campaign. On 1 April, when Churchill wrote the admonition heading this chapter, he did not know that the president was so weakened that General Marshall drafted Roosevelt's reply.[30]

At some point during his postwar writing and speaking, Churchill must have wondered whether life was imitating art. Berlin evolved into a symbol of Churchill's disappointment over both the conclusion of the war in Europe and the origin of the cold war. Since he had failed to convince Eisenhower to take Berlin in 1945, the Russians had acted every bit as churlish as he had expected they would, most recently closing off Anglo-American access to the city, provoking the Berlin Airlift. Berlin was on Churchill's mind on 9 October 1948 when he traveled to North Wales to speak at a Conservative party rally. History and politics merged as Churchill told his audience:

In fact, as we can all now see, the growing aggressiveness and malignity of the Soviet Government and its complete breaches of good faith at that time should have made both the

British and American Governments refrain from dispersing their armies so completely. Nor should they have carried out their great withdrawals in Germany until after there had been a general confrontation along the line upon which the Western and Eastern Allied armies had met.

It would also have been wiser and more prudent to have allowed the British Army to enter Berlin, as it could have done, and as many good judges thought would be done, and for the United States armoured division to have entered Prague, which was a matter almost of hours.[31]

Referring to the Berlin blockade, then in its fourth month, Churchill commented that a Conservative government would never have allowed the crisis to develop as it had. Instead of flying goods into Berlin, Churchill said it would be preferable to use British seapower to cut off Soviet imports! By taking a hard line with the Russians, the Anglo-Americans would have been better able to bargain with the Russians from a position of strength. If the Soviets wanted peace and security in a postwar world unthreatened by the atomic bomb, Churchill argued they could have it by simply going back to their border.[32]

Alone of all the generals and statesmen of the war, Churchill was in the unique position where his memoir's hard-line pronouncements on Berlin were so similar to his postwar political speeches that they were interchangeable; they clearly increased interest in the final volume of his memoir. By 1953 the strategic debate over Berlin had taken on an additional literary significance as exemplified by *Triumph and Tragedy*, which superseded the military significance of the German capital in the closing days of 1945 when Eisenhower never seriously contemplated going there. Moreover, as Tuvia Ben-Moshe pointed out in *Churchill: Strategy and History*, Churchill advanced his postwar arguments to make himself appear more prescient regarding Soviet intentions than he had been in 1945. Ben-Moshe also noticed that by 19 April 1945 Eisenhower had convinced the prime minister that the Anglo-Americans were not operationally situated to take Berlin, whereas the Russians were. In 1953 Churchill was engaged in a literary exercise rather than a genuine debate.[33]

POGUE'S *THE SUPREME COMMAND*

The present study was conceived as an analysis of the debate over strategy and command through the memoirs, diaries, biographies, and autobiographies of participants, largely primary sources. Though not a memoir, Forrest C. Pogue's official history, *The Supreme Command,* qualifies as the seminal work for the twin issues of strategy and command.[34] Pogue earned his Ph.D. in international relations and history from Clark University in 1939 and throughout most of the campaign was a combat historian in the First United States Army, attached to V Corps. Pogue made extensive use of both War Department records and Eisenhower's personal files. Through the facilities of the Office of the Chief of Military History

(OCMH), *The Supreme Command* also benefited from translation of captured German records.

More than any other volume in the official histories of the *United States Army in World War II*, Pogue's volume depended on oral history. Eisenhower wrote to Pogue on 26 July 1946, "Much of the story of SHAEF Headquarters rests in the memories of the officers involved. You are urged to interview as widely as possible."[35] From December 1946 through March 1948 Pogue interviewed field marshals, generals, and admirals in Europe: Only one man refused to see him, Field Marshal the Viscount Montgomery of Alamein, then CIGS. Pogue conducted over 100 interviews, a dozen of which he judged sensational or malicious. When he turned over his interviews to OCMH a decade later, Pogue warned the chief historian of their potential to damage Anglo-American relations.[36]

Brigadier General (later Major General) Harry J. Malony, chief of the Historical Section, briefed General Eisenhower on the concept of *The Supreme Command*. The volume would tell the story of an Allied headquarters and also "refute the false accusations in many recent publications." Although the book was originally to have a British collaborator, owing to SHAEF's Anglo-American composition, Field Marshal Sir Henry Maitland Wilson, who was in charge of the British part of the project, judged Pogue competent to represent the British as well. In the spirit of cooperation, British official historians answered requests for documents by supplying originals or paraphrases, and when the Americans had documents that the British needed they returned the favor. For example, in the 1950s the British official historians requested from OCMH several documents originating in Montgomery's headquarters addressed to Eisenhower that were not in their files. Pogue checked with the White House, and President Eisenhower approved sending copies to the British. As a result of both the wartime cooperation between the two nations and the expressed intent of the volume, Pogue felt he had an obligation to stress the collaborative nature of the alliance.[37]

Strong disagreements occasionally marked the meetings of the Combined Chiefs of Staff, but Pogue contended that these differences were based on doctrine, principle, and world view, not ambition or pride. The Allies had very different strategic concepts, and Pogue cautioned his readers that "A failure to understand this fact could reduce the story of this great allied coalition, perhaps the most successful in history, to a study in personal and national recriminations." Personalities did not become a strategic issue until Montgomery's press conference of 7 January 1945.[38] Influenced by his two years of interviewing, Pogue cautioned his reader that studies based entirely on documents gave an impression of personal animus at the highest levels of Allied command. Documents lacked the personal touch; for example, they could not record a smile during a tedious debate, signaling that the points under discussion may have been intended largely for the record. Pogue noted that the vast cooperative effort was often overlooked by both historians and the general public "who turn rapidly through pages of dull agreement and seek out the more interesting pages of controversy."[39]

The American official historians soon realized that the Anglo-American intelligence was very good, but contrary to speculation they were not party to the

ULTRA secret. Brigadier Edgar T. Williams, Montgomery's Intelligence officer, described to Pogue the optimism prevalent at the end of August 1944: "We tended to be hysterical about the fold up of Germans. First Army had a lot of enemy stuff they got from Germans in the Mons pocket. Little ULTRA. Lost our disillusionment we usually had when operations got excited."[40] ULTRA referred to the level of intelligence classification (confidential-secret-top secret-ultra) given to the British ability to read German signal ciphers throughout the Second World War. Eisenhower's memorandum to Pogue advised that *The Supreme Command* would have an appended chapter concerning the OVERLORD cover and deception plan, which would not be published with the rest of the book. No such chapter was written, however, and the Allied ability to read top-secret German radio signals was not known until 1974.[41] Pogue and his fellow official historians simply guessed that ULTRA referred to a very accurate level of intelligence, most likely signals intelligence.

Brigadier Williams also told Pogue that Eisenhower was too patient with Montgomery, that he "let him get away with too much for the sake of the alliance." Had the supreme commander simply said "Shut up, Monty," he would have done so. Pogue believed that Eisenhower undoubtedly added to his problems "by failing to make clear" to Montgomery when the time for discussion had ended and the time for execution had begun. Owing to Montgomery's unique position as the senior British officer in the theater as well as his direct link to the CIGS, Pogue believes, Eisenhower was reluctant to say, "Here is an order: execute it."[42]

The reader will recall from Chapter 2 that Montgomery was not the only Allied general with a single-thrust scheme in September 1944; Patton also believed he could have crossed the Rhine at that time. In 1946 Eisenhower told Colonel S.L.A. Marshall, the chief historian of the European theater, that Patton had talked to him in a vague way about going to Metz. However, Patton never pressed his plans, as did Bradley or Montgomery. Instead, Patton would complain to his staff about Eisenhower and then call to apologize before word of the outburst reached SHAEF. Eisenhower told Marshall that Patton's behavior and his reluctance to push his views made him difficult to deal with, but his abilities as a commander made up for his deficiencies.[43] Eschewing Eisenhower's confidential criticism of Patton's style, Pogue addressed Patton's claim that the Third Army could have crossed the Rhine in September. The official historian quoted a letter written in July 1946 to Ralph Ingersoll by Colonel Herbert W. Ehrgott, chief of staff of IX Engineer Command:

Had Patton continued through the Saar Valley and the Vosges it must have been without close air support and with a very small contribution in the way of air supply beyond the Reims-Epernay line. . . . I would not have liked to tackle the job of supplying Patton over the Vosges and through the Pfalz during that October. I don't doubt that we could have carried about 2 armored divisions and one [motorized] division up to Köln [Cologne], but then where. Certainly not across the Rhine. A good task force of Panzerfaust, manned by Hitler youth could have finished them off before they reached Kassel.[44]

Concerning Montgomery's single thrust, Pogue believed it was impossible to determine whether a diversion of all available supplies to Montgomery would have allowed him to cross the Rhine before the Germans reorganized their defenses. At a minimum, it meant halting the Third Army near Paris, delaying the linkup with Franco-American forces near Dijon, and possibly exposing the right wing of the OVERLORD forces to a German attack. If Montgomery's single thrust had led to a Rhine crossing that caused Germany to surrender, then, in Pogue's view, its attendant risks would have been well worth taking. But if Germany did not surrender once the Allies put troops on the east bank of the Rhine, it was doubtful that the exposed forces could have been maintained at operational levels.[45]

The calmness of Pogue's treatment of Montgomery's single-thrust proposal varied widely from what General Smith told Pogue: "Monty's August proposal for the single thrust was the most fantastic bit of balderdash ever proposed by a competent general. . . . We had made the most careful logistical studies which showed that it was impossible. The best we could hope for was that we could establish a bridgehead . . . at the expense of our failure to take Antwerp."[46] Bedell Smith's intemperate dismissal of Montgomery's single thrust was probably nearer SHAEF's 1944 opinion than Pogue's politically correct version published during the Korean War, when good relations with Great Britain were essential. Pogue conceded a point to the proponents of single thrust: The German defense of the Rhine by reserve troops of dubious quality was aided by SHAEF's decision to advance on a broad front. The official historian argued that by the time of the Arnhem attack, 17 September, the Germans had already recovered and were clearly capable of confronting with considerable force either a single or double thrust by the Allies.[47]

In September 1944, SHAEF planners concluded that the Allies might push three corps to Berlin by the end of September, at the expense of grounding five corps in Normandy and Brittany, but only if Antwerp and the Pas de Calais ports produced 7,000 tons of supplies a day and if the airlift accounted for another 2,000 tons per day. Pogue pointed out that the administrative system had been designed for a "slower, more ponderous drive," and it could not keep up with the pursuit of late August and early September. The official historian cited the continuation of Third Army's attack on the French port of Brest as an example of this conservatism. Patton and Bradley questioned the value of besieging the German garrison occupying the port city of Brest at the tip of the Brittany peninsula in terms of both time and divisions, but to call it off would be seen as a defeat. *The Supreme Command* concluded that "In hardly any respect were the Allies prepared to take advantage of the great opportunity offered them to destroy the German forces before winter."[48]

The Belgian port of Antwerp was the key to any successful offensive that September 1944, either single thrust or broad front. Unfortunately, Montgomery's Administrative officer, General Graham, told the field marshal that the 21st Army Group did not require Antwerp for its operations beyond the Rhine. General Gale, SHAEF's deputy chief of staff and chief Administrative officer, said, "I told General Eisenhower that there was no way we could comply with Monty's view to stop everything on the right while he went to Berlin. You couldn't move the

stuff to him in the first place. . . . We needed as soon as possible to open up Antwerp. We were operating on lines of communication which were too long. Besides
Monty didn't see that the stuff wasn't his . . . it was American stuff."[49] Bedell
Smith criticized Montgomery's notion that the Allies need not take Antwerp prior
to forcing the Rhine and advancing on the Ruhr: "Only Sir Miles Graham
supported it. He was not a sufficiently able man to say that what Monty wanted
was impossible logistically."[50]

Commenting on Eisenhower's language in *Crusade in Europe* regarding
Montgomery's single thrust, *The Supreme Command* stated, "The Supreme
Commander refused to consider what he called a 'pencil like thrust' into the heart
of Germany." Eisenhower believed that German reserves would destroy any solitary
advance over the Rhine. Pogue discussed the difference between Montgomery's
proposed "full-blooded" thrust and Eisenhower's "pencil like" description. Owing
to Montgomery's call for both the Second British Army and two corps of the First
United States Army, Pogue thought that "full blooded" was more accurate, but the
official historian noted that "pencil like" aptly described Patton's proposed two-
corps thrust.[51]

Pogue maintained that the 10 September 1944 Eisenhower-Montgomery meeting
at Brussels airfield marked "a new phase in Allied operational planning." At the
beginning of September, stress had been on pushing two thrusts to the Rhine, but
the focus shifted on 4 September, following the capture of Antwerp. According to
Pogue, on 13 September the supreme commander now gave priority to the clearing
of the Scheldt Estuary, when he ordered Montgomery to capture the approaches to
Antwerp and Rotterdam, as well as several Channel ports. Clearing the Scheldt had
to await the outcome of Montgomery's Arnhem operation, after which the Allied
offensive against Germany's borders came to a complete stop.[52]

While the Scheldt awaited in October, Montgomery debated command with
Eisenhower, and Pogue paraphrased Montgomery's suggested reworking of command to give himself greater latitude in clearing Antwerp's approaches.
Eisenhower's response of 13 October, Pogue called, "one of his most explicit
letters of the war." *The Supreme Command* quoted Eisenhower's admonition: "I am
quite well aware of the powers and limitations of Allied Command, and if you, as
the senior commander in this theater of one of the great Allies, feel that my conceptions and directives are such as to endanger the success of operations, it is our
duty to refer the matter to higher authority for any action they may choose to take,
however drastic."[53] Eisenhower's implication was clear. If Montgomery wished to
reestablish a ground forces command, then he would have to take it up with the
Combined Chiefs of Staff. Pogue noted that Eisenhower's letter brought a prompt
response from Montgomery promising that Eisenhower would "hear no more on
the subject of command from me."[54] Daniel Crosswell pointed out in his study of
Walter Bedell Smith that a visit by General Marshall to the western front happened to coincide with Smith's facilitating Eisenhower's get tough approach with
Montgomery.

Later in October, Marshall cabled Eisenhower inquiring as to the soundness of
an all-out offensive in October to win the war before the end of the year. Marshall

wondered whether use of ammunition reserves and the secret proximity-fuse artillery shells along with concentration of the strategic air forces might bring about victory in 1944. To study Marshall's proposal, the British Chiefs turned to their Joint Planning Staff (IPS). In a critical paper indicating high-level British opinion regarding the war's termination, the JPS concluded that the earliest date for ending the war was 31 January 1945 and the latest date was 15 May 1945. The JPS specified opening Antwerp to shipping as the one factor governing all of Eisenhower's plans. Pogue quoted the warning of the British planners that to launch an all-out offensive without first opening Antwerp to ship traffic "would be to court failure, and would probably have the effect of prolonging the war well into 1945."[55]

On 30 November 1944, Montgomery sent his strategic-reverse message to Eisenhower, and *The Supreme Command* published much of their subsequent correspondence. Montgomery's shibboleth was concentration: "In the new plan we must get away from the doctrine of attacking in so many places that nowhere are we strong enough to get decisive results. We must concentrate such strength on the main selected thrust that success will be certain. It is in this respect that we failed badly in the present operations."[56]

Misconstruing Montgomery's strategic-reverse remark as applicable to the campaign since Normandy, Eisenhower on 1 December made his strongest defense of the broad-front strategy during the war:

I do not agree that more strength could have been thrown to the North than was actually maintained there during early September. Lines of communication in the north were so stretched that even delivery of five-hundred tons to you at Brussels cost Bradley three divisions, the possession of which might have easily placed him on the Rhine in the Worms area. . . . Had we not advanced on a relatively broad front, we would now have the spectacle of a long narrow line of communication, constantly threatened on the right flank and weakened by detachments of large fighting formations.[57]

Eisenhower added that he had no intention of stopping either Patton or Devers while they were cleaning up the right flank and thereby giving to the Allies the *"capability of concentration."*[58]

Montgomery's message also questioned command arrangements. While acknowledging Eisenhower's refusal to employ a ground forces commander, Montgomery pointed out that he and Bradley had worked well together in Normandy. "Things have not been so good since you separated us," Montgomery wrote. The field marshal suggested that Eisenhower should bring them together again and that either he or Bradley "should have full operational control" north of the Ardennes. Implicit in Eisenhower's response was the difference between an army group command and a theater command, Eisenhower wrote: "We must look at this whole great affair stretching from Marseilles to the lower Rhine as one great theater. We must plan so when our next attack starts we will be able to obtain maximum results from all our forces, under the conditions now existing."[59]

The next time the field marshal raised the ground forces command issue with the supreme commander was aboard the latter's heavily guarded train at Hasselt, Belgium, on 28 December, and Montgomery's persistence finally found the limit of Eisenhower's patience. Enlarging on de Guingand's account in *Operation Victory*, Pogue named General Smith as leading a group of officers who wanted a showdown with Montgomery. As outlined in Chapter 2, de Guingand warned his superior that someone would have to go, and it would not be Eisenhower. Subsequently, Montgomery promised Eisenhower his 100 percent cooperation, and Eisenhower thought he had heard the end of the command issue. Pogue informed his reader that Montgomery and the British Chiefs brought it up "on at least two other occasions," and each time Eisenhower refused to consider it.[60]

Pogue pointed out that the British Chiefs of Staff were about to call for a ground forces commander, and General Marshall discussed it with Eisenhower. Some in Whitehall wanted to trade Tedder, the present deputy supreme commander, for Alexander, currently Eisenhower's Mediterranean counterpart. On 10 January 1945, Eisenhower cabled Marshall that a ground commander would merely complicate matters, but he conceded that it would be more convenient at the moment if his deputy supreme commander were a ground officer rather than an air force officer. In fact, as we will see in Chapter 7, Eisenhower would inform Tedder of his coming replacement. Marshall wired that he had considered showing Eisenhower's message to President Roosevelt because he was worried about the supreme commander's resolve on the ground command issue. If there were any questions as to the possibility of a British field marshal taking the place of a British air marshal as deputy supreme commander, Marshall removed them in his most direct statement on the command issue of the war. Pogue omitted the following politically sensitive remarks by Marshall:

Frankly, Alexander's appointment as a deputy would mean two things I think. First, that the British had won a major point in getting control of the ground operations in which their divisions of necessity will play such a minor part and, for the same reason, we are bound to suffer very heavy casualties; and second, the man being who he is and our experience being what it has been, you would have great difficulty in offsetting the direct influence of the P.M.[61]

The British Chiefs of Staff on 10 January 1945 formally requested that the Combined Chiefs of Staff call upon Eisenhower for a progress report on his strategy and a summary of his future plans. The request marked the entrance of the British Chiefs of Staff into the debate between Eisenhower and Montgomery. "In presenting their questions," Pogue noted, "they appeared to be in the position of championing Montgomery against his superior." The strategic significance of their action would be lost, however, if the Joint Chiefs of Staff viewed it as disloyalty to the supreme commander. If that happened, Pogue believed the question of strategy would have taken a back seat to supporting Eisenhower. Since Montgomery's plans involved overturning Eisenhower's conception of the campaign and employing two American armies, Pogue said it was doubtful that the

Joint Chiefs would agree with their British counterparts calling for both concentrating in the north and appointing a ground forces commander.[62]

Pogue cited Eisenhower's argument to the Combined Chiefs that the first
requirement for the assault north of the Ruhr was a firm defensive line on the
Rhine capable of being held with a minimum number of troops. Eisenhower
estimated that he would have eighty-five divisions in the theater by the spring,
enough to win the war in the West provided that the Russian offensive was
successful. Established on the entirety of the Rhine, the Allies could hold it with
just twenty-five divisions, allowing fifty-five divisions in the attack. To remain
static in Alsace, where not all the American units had reached the Rhine, would
require twenty more divisions, a total of forty-five. In other words, there would be
an economy of scale in holding the entire line of the Rhine. Eisenhower slated
thirty-five divisions for the northern offensive under Montgomery and twenty divisions for the secondary offensive against Frankfurt under Bradley. To adopt a static
position south of Bonn, Eisenhower contended, would leave him insufficient divisions for the secondary attack.[63]

Strategy and command loomed large at the Malta Conference at the end of
January 1945. Eisenhower did not attend the conference; instead, he sent his chief
of staff, General Smith. On the strategic question, Smith wired that the British
Chiefs wanted a written guarantee that the main effort would come in the north and
that Eisenhower would not delay the crossing of the Rhine merely to clear the west
bank of Germans along the entire length of the river. Concerning command,
General Ismay told Pogue in December 1946 that he had warned the British Chiefs
at Malta: "If I were George Marshall I would regard anything of this sort as a vote
of no-confidence in Ike. We can't do this sort of thing." Smith had a lengthy
discussion at Malta with Brooke and told him that a directive requiring Eisenhower
to maintain a prescribed number of troops under Montgomery was a "vote of no
confidence" and if he felt that way then he should recommend Eisenhower's relief
to the Combined Chiefs.[64]

The final controversy over strategy and command involved Eisenhower's
decision not to advance on Berlin but to have Bradley clear central Germany.
Putting the issue into an editorial context, Pogue devoted two chapters of thirty-
four two-column pages to "The Drive to the Elbe." The Berlin question remained
moot, according to Pogue. There was never any American consideration of going
back on the 1943 agreement on occupation zone boundaries in Germany or on the
1944 Yalta accords in order to forestall the Russians. The official historian believed
that having made concessions to the Russians at Yalta to enlist them in the effort
against Japan, President Roosevelt would not have reversed course regarding
Berlin, even if the Joint Chiefs of Staff agreed with the British Chiefs on the issue,
which they did not.[65]

The official historian provided the clearest explanation of halt-lines and
occupation zones yet in print. For military reasons, Eisenhower wanted a river between the onrushing Anglo-American and Russian armies. Fighter bombers had
already strafed Russian units in Yugoslavia, and as early as November 1944 the
Anglo-Americans took strong precautions to prevent such incidents from reoc-

curring.[66] In 1947 General Smith told Pogue, "I told the British we can't go on. What if the Russians say please move off the road. So we decided a month and a half before we met that we would have to have a river line." The occupation zones did not correspond to military operations or stop-lines, and Eisenhower did not believe it was militarily sound to halt operations simply because the halt-line had been reached. "Rather," as Pogue wrote, "both sides should be free to advance until contact was made." Once contact was made with the Russians, one side or the other would then fall back behind the prearranged halt-line that had been temporarily bypassed. The British Chiefs argued that the Western armies drive as far east as possible and stand in place until ordered to withdraw by their respective governments. The United States Departments of State and War pointed out to Whitehall that the Anglo-Americans had more to lose than to gain by that proposal. What was to keep the Russians from bypassing Berlin altogether and simply racing westward to pick up as much land as possible, and dealing with Berlin later?[67]

On 21 and 22 April 1945, General Eisenhower communicated through the Combined Chiefs of Staff to Moscow the procedures that the Western forces would follow as they approached junction with the Soviets. The central army group would halt at the Elbe, his northern group would turn northward into the Jutland peninsula, and his southern force would drive into Austria via the Danube Valley. The British Chiefs were upset and pointed to the alacrity with which the Soviets responded to Eisenhower's message.[68]

General Marshall, in passing on the views of the British Chiefs to Eisenhower, added, "Personally and aside from all logistic, tactical or strategic implications I would be loath to hazard American lives for purely political purposes." The chief of staff was fighting a two-front war and wanted to redeploy American armies to the Far East. Quoting Eisenhower's directive from the Combined Chiefs of Staff, which stated he was to "undertake operations aimed at the heart of Germany and the destruction of her armed forces," Pogue concluded that the war aims of the Western Allies in 1945 were beyond Eisenhower's province as supreme commander.[69]

The Office of the Chief of Military History sent the draft of *The Supreme Command* to the historians of the United Kingdom Official Histories, whereupon General Dempsey read it and called Montgomery's attention to it. On 28 October 1951, Montgomery wrote Eisenhower expressing his "grave concern." Montgomery said that the book was not written from an Allied point of view because Pogue had not had access to British documents, which was not entirely true. Should the book be published in its present form, full of criticism for himself, Dempsey, and the British army, Montgomery contended that it would be a tragedy. Unlike Bradley's book, which was a private work, Pogue's official history carried the stamp of the United States Army. "I would ask you, most earnestly," Montgomery wrote, "to use your influence to see that 'The Supreme Command', as written in its present form by Forrest C. POGUE, is not issued."[70]

Two days later Lieutenant Colonel Roy Lamson, Jr., an army historian serving at SHAPE, informed Pogue of Montgomery's objections. Lamson mentioned that he had told Eisenhower that the version was a draft and would be undergoing revision. Eisenhower asked to see the manuscript before it was published, and he requested that the passages dealing with Montgomery and Dempsey be marked. Pogue wrote Eisenhower that the manuscript had been sent to the British to correct errors of fact, not for censorship. Furthermore, Pogue said that Montgomery's Intelligence officer, Brigadier Edgar T. Williams, had read the manuscript and suggested changes, many of which Pogue incorporated.[71] According to Pogue, Eisenhower never pressured him to change anything in his manuscript.

CONCLUSION

Triumph and Tragedy and *The Supreme Command* made it clear that two cities stood out in the conduct of the campaign, Antwerp and Berlin. Both Churchill and Pogue caused readers to conclude that Montgomery believed he could get to Berlin without opening the approaches to Antwerp. What is so striking half a century later is Montgomery's inability to realize that in order to get Eisenhower to consider allowing him to take Berlin he would first have had to open Antwerp to the sea, whether or not the 21st Army Group required it. Without Antwerp, Montgomery's messages about going to Berlin were just so much brave talk. Based on the field marshal's comments to Chester Wilmot cited in Chapter 4, it is highly likely that Montgomery never had any real intention of going to Berlin in September 1944. If Montgomery had intended to get to Berlin, he would probably have cleared Antwerp. Instead, the Ruhr loomed large at 21st Army Group, just as large as it did at SHAEF, and Montgomery felt he might stand a chance to take the Ruhr without Antwerp.

Writing in 1953 with the advantage of being able to say "I told you so" about the Russians and Berlin did not make Churchill more prescient in 1945, but it certainly seemed that way to the public. The Soviet closing of Berlin and the subsequent Berlin Airlift permanently changed the writing of the Berlin chapter in all succeeding books. Pogue pointed out that both the United States Departments of War and State realized the risks inherent in taking a hard line with the Soviets over Berlin. At no point between 1945 and 1953 did Churchill ever seem to consider that the policy he advocated in the spring of 1945 risked more than diplomatic unpleasantness with Stalin, given the extent of Soviet suspicion of the West. Similarly, Churchill never seems to have worried very much what Marshal Joseph Broz Tito, the communist partisan and later dictator of Yugoslavia, would have thought about a British line of communications running through his country and into Austria. Discounting any meaningful reaction by Stalin or Tito seems a rather ethnocentric notion, as if the opinion of the Western Allies was the only one that counted in 1945, as if the only sins were sins of omission. The notion carried over into the postwar writings, advanced by Churchill's memoir, which argued that it was mainly American domination of strategy from 1944 onward that created the tragedy in the triumph. Churchill's memoir set the stage for the ultimate in this school of thought, Montgomery's memoir and the second volume of Alanbrooke's diaries.

NOTES

1. Winston S. Churchill, *The Second World War,* vol. 6, *Triumph and Tragedy,* 6 vols. (Boston: Houghton Mifflin; Cambridge, Mass.: Riverside Press, 1948-1953), 465.

2. Winston S. Churchill, *The World Crisis,* 4 vols. (New York: Charles Scribner's Sons, 1923-1927).

3. Lord Moran [Sir Charles Wilson], *Churchill Taken from the Diaries of Lord Moran: The Struggle for Survival, 1940-1965* (Boston: Houghton Mifflin; Cambridge, Mass.: Riverside Press, 1966); see 431, n.10 for knighthood; 544 n.5 for the Nobel Prize; 838 for the sequence of publication and medical problems.

4. The Reves quotation is in Martin Gilbert, *Winston S. Churchill,* vol. 8, *Never Despair, 1945-1965* (Boston: Houghton Mifflin; Cambridge, Mass.: Riverside Press, 1988), 484; Robert E. Sherwood, *Roosevelt and Hopkins: An Intimate History* (New York: Harper and Brothers, 1948).

5. Gilbert, *Never Despair;* for Chartwell and Lord Camrose, see 256-57, for the trust and taxes, see 603; for profits from serialization, see Robert Payne, *The Great Man: A Portrait of Winston Churchill* (New York: Coward, McCann and Geoghegan, 1974), 353.

6. Gilbert, *Never Despair,* 235.

7. Ibid., 268, for Churchill's dictated memoranda; for correspondence to or from Roosevelt, 269-70. Ismay encouraged Churchill to use his secret material to refute inaccuracies by Elliot Roosevelt, the president's son, who had written *As He Saw It* (New York: Duell, Sloan and Pearce, 1946), see Interview with General Sir Hastings Ismay, 17 December 1946, OCMH Collection, *Supreme Command,* Pogue Interviews, USAMHI.

8. Gilbert, *Never Despair,* 221, for Ismay's role; for other advisors, see 339.

9. Ibid.; for storage of documents at Chartwell, see 331; for "rummaging," see 332.

10. Ibid., 344.

11. Ibid., 343.

12. Putting in the stations after the track is in Walter Graebner, *My Dear Mr. Churchill* (Boston: Houghton Mifflin; Cambridge, Mass.: Riverside Press, 1965), 60; for needing to have a best-seller, see Maurice Ashley, *Churchill as Historian* (New York: Charles Scribner's Sons, 1968), 29.

13. Churchill, *Triumph and Tragedy,* v; for Churchill's letter to Eisenhower, see Gilbert, *Never Despair,* 810-11; for remarks to Colville, see John Colville, *The Fringes of Power: 10 Downing Street Diaries, 1939-1955* (New York and London: W. W. Norton, 1985), 658.

14. For Alanbrooke, see Interview with Field Marshal Viscount Alanbrooke, 28 January 1947; for Portal, see Interview with Viscount Portal of Purfleet, 7 February 1947, OCMH Collection, *Supreme Command,* Pogue Interviews, USAMHI.

15. For the Ljubljana gap, see Churchill, *Triumph and Tragedy,* 61; for reaching Vienna ahead of the Russians, see 100. Tuvia Ben-Moshe's *Churchill: Strategy and History* (Boulder, Colo.: Lynne Rienner Publishers; Hertfordshire, Harvester Wheatsheaf, 1991), 297-99, 323 dismisses this Balkan myth and points out that the British Chiefs rejected any movement on Vienna on operational grounds.

16. For strategists long debating the issue, see *Triumph and Tragedy,* 192; for the likelihood of an advance without Antwerp and the number of divisions, see 190.

17. The entire minute of 8 September is in Churchill, *Triumph and Tragedy,* 195-96, italics in the original.

18. For Montgomery's message of 7 September, see Martin Gilbert, *Winston S. Churchill,* vol. 7, *Road to Victory, 1941-1945* (Boston: Houghton Mifflin; Cambridge,

Mass.: Riverside Press, 1986), 942; Churchill's concern over Eisenhower's failure to concentrate is on 1081.

19. Martin Gilbert, *Road to Victory,* 1081; Gilbert's narrative dates the telegram as of 1 December 1944, but his footnote dates it 3 December; compare to Churchill's version in *Triumph and Tragedy,* 266-68.

20. For a "strategic reverse," see Churchill's *Triumph and Tragedy,* 267. Harry C. Butcher, *My Three Years with Eisenhower: The Personal Diary of Captain Harry C. Butcher, USNR, Naval Aide to General Eisenhower, 1942 to 1945* (New York: Simon and Schuster, 1946), 718; "Notes on My Life," by Field Marshal Viscount Alanbrooke, vol. 14, 28 November 1944, 1077, LHCMA.

21. PRO: CAB 106/1106, "The Broad Front versus Narrow Front Controversy," Appended Notes, Copies of Extracts of Important Documents Not Available Elsewhere from Churchill Papers, File 341, "OVERLORD Operations Post D-Day."

22. "Notes on My Life," by Field Marshal Viscount Alanbrooke, vol. 14, 2 December 1944, 1080, LHCMA; for Alanbrooke's published reaction, see Arthur Bryant, *Triumph in the West: A History of the War Years Based on the Diaries of Field-Marshal Lord Alanbrooke, Chief of the Imperial General Staff* (Garden City, N. Y.: Doubleday, 1959, 261-62.

23. For example, "Eisenhower Holds 'Zero' Talk, Planning the Last Battle in Germany, Secret Visit to Montgomery," *Daily Mail* (London), 29 November 1944, p. 1.

24. The Papers of Field Marshal Viscount Alanbrooke, 14/1-9, Western Front, Montgomery (17 November 1944-24 January 1945), LHCMA.

25. Churchill's cable to Roosevelt is in Churchill, *Triumph and Tragedy,* 268; for Roosevelt's bicycling,see 271.

26. Churchill, *Triumph and Tragedy,* 282 for Churchill's speech to Commons; for complications concerning Montgomery commanding the northern thrust, see PRO: PREM 3, 341/2, Churchill to Ismay for COS Committee, 10 January 1945, 185-86.

27. Ibid. For Eisenhower's cable to Stalin, see 458; for chances of Allied troops entering Berlin, see 461.

28. For breaking up the 50th Infantry Division see Nigel Hamilton, *Monty: Final Years of the Field-Marshal, 1944-1976* (New York: McGraw-Hill, 1986), 158-59; for the effect of the British army's size on the peace conference, see PRO: CAB 65/44/161, War Cabinet Conclusions, 4 December 1944, 129.

29. Gilbert, *Road to Victory,* 1283.

30. For Eisenhower's standing, see Churchill, *Triumph and Tragedy,* 461; for General Marshall's response, see 466.

31. Gilbert, *Never Despair,* 436-37.

32. Ibid., 437-38.

33. Ben-Moshe, *Churchill: Strategy and History,* 316 for Berlin and 330-33 for *Triumph and Tragedy.* Ben-Moshe points out that Churchill transformed a dialogue of memoranda into a monologue devoid of critical responses from his chiefs or ministers.

34. Forrest C. Pogue, *The Supreme Command (United States Army in World War II: The European Theater of Operations,* Washington, D.C.: Office of the Chief of Military History, Department of the Army, 1954).

35. Louis Galambos, ed., et al., *The Papers of Dwight David Eisenhower: The Chief of Staff,* 9 vols. (Baltimore and London: Johns Hopkins University Press, 1978), 7:1209-10.

36. Interview with Dr. Forrest C. Pogue, 17 March 1991; Eisenhower had written Pogue a "To Whom It May Concern" letter of introduction that was good enough for Charles de Gaulle but not Montgomery, who demanded a letter from Pogue's principal. For Pogue's

interviews, see Pogue's letter to Dr. Kent R. Greenfield, 26 August 1958, OCMH Collection, *Supreme Command,* Pogue Interviews, USAMHI; for a complete list, see Pogue, *The Supreme Command,* 565-68.

37. Malony's briefing is in Galambos, ed., et al., *The Papers of Dwight David Eisenhower: The Chief of Staff,* 7:1210, n.2; for cooperation with British historians, Interview with Dr. Forrest C. Pogue, 17 March 1991.

38. For Pogue's comment on recriminations, see Pogue, *The Supreme Command,* 50; for the effect of Montgomery's press conference on personalities, see 389.

39. Ibid. For Pogue's warning on the impersonality of documents, see xii; for seeking out controversy, see 290.

40. Interview with Brigadier Edgar T. Williams, 30-31 May 1947, OCMH Collection, *Supreme Command,* Pogue Interviews, USAMHI.

41. Galambos, ed., et al., *The Papers of Dwight David Eisenhower: The Chief of Staff,* 7:1210. F. W. Winterbotham, *The Ultra Secret* (New York: Harper and Row, 1974) first broke the ULTRA secret; for the British official history pertinent to this study, see F. H. Hinsley et al., *British Intelligence in the Second World War,* vol. 3, part 2, *Its Influence on Strategy and Operations* (London: Her Majesty's Stationery Office, 1988).

42. For telling Montgomery to "shut up," see Interview with Brigadier Edgar T. Williams, 30-31 May 1947, OCMH Collection, *Supreme Command,* Pogue Interviews, USAMHI; for Eisenhower's reluctance to give orders to Montgomery, see Pogue, *The Supreme Command,* 289.

43. Colonel S.L.A. Marshall, Interview with General Dwight D. Eisenhower, 7 June 1946, OCMH Collection, *Supreme Command,* Pogue Interviews, USAMHI.

44. Pogue, *The Supreme Command,* 258-59.

45. Ibid., 259. Students of the debate over Patton's single-thrust chances should consult Ronald Andidora's "The Autumn of 1944: Boldness Is Not Enough," *Parameters* 17 (December 1987): 71-80, and the exchange of opinion that followed between Andidora and General Andrew P. O'Meara, USA (Ret.) in *Parameters* 18 (June 1988): 101-03.

46. Interview with Lieutenant General Walter Bedell Smith, 13 May 1947, OCMH Collection, *Supreme Command,* Pogue Interviews, USAMHI.

47. Pogue, *The Supreme Command,* 302.

48. Ibid.; for the SHAEF planners and ports, see 254; for "more ponderous drive," see 259; defeating the Germans before winter is on 260.

49. Interview with Lieutenant General Sir Humfrey Gale, 27 January 1947, OCMH Collection, *Supreme Command,* Pogue Interviews, USAMHI.

50. Interview with Lieutenant General Walter Bedell Smith, 13 May 1947, OCMH Collection, *Supreme Command,* Pogue Interviews, USAMHI.

51. Pogue, *The Supreme Command,* 255; for the differences between "full-blooded" and "pencil like," see 255 n.29.

52. Ibid., 256.

53. Pogue, *The Supreme Command,* 297. The fullest treatment of the message, written by Whiteley at Smith's behest, is in D.K.R. Crosswell, *The Chief of Staff: The Military Career of General Walter Bedell Smith* (Westport, Conn.: Greenwood Press, 1991), 262-63.

54. Pogue, *The Supreme Command,* 298; Crosswell, *The Chief of Staff,* 262-63.

55. Pogue, *The Supreme Command,* 308.

56. Ibid., 312.

57. Ibid., 313-14.

58. Ibid., italics in the original.

59. Ibid., Montgomery's one man in control, 312-13; Eisenhower's response is on 314.

60. Ibid., 387.

61. Eisenhower and Whitehall is in Pogue, *The Supreme Command,* 389-90; for Marshall's response, see Marshall to Eisenhower, 11 January 1945, BD, Dwight D. Eisenhower, Pre-Presidential Papers, 1916-1952, Principal File, Harry C. Butcher, Box 169 (1 January-28 January) (2), EL.

62. Pogue, *The Supreme Command,* 409; for the British Chiefs' call for a ground forces commander, see 389.

63. Ibid., 412. Eisenhower's total number of divisions was five more than he had assigned missions to under this proposal.

64. Interview with General Sir Hastings L. Ismay, 20 December 1946; Interview with Lieutenant General Walter Bedell Smith, 8 May 1947, OCMH Collection, *Supreme Command,* Pogue Interviews, USAMHI.

65. Pogue, *The Supreme Command,* 445.

66. Ibid., 462-63.

67. Interview with Lieutenant General Walter Bedell Smith, 13 May 1947, OCMH Collection, *Supreme Command,* Pogue Interviews, USAMHI; movement to contact and State Department concerns, see Pogue, *The Supreme Command,* 465.

68. Pogue, *The Supreme Command,* 467.

69. Ibid., 468.

70. Interview with Dr. Forrest C. Pogue, 17 March 1991; for Montgomery's letter see, Montgomery to Eisenhower, 28 October 1951, Dwight D. Eisenhower, Pre-Presidential Papers, 1916-1952, Principal File, Box 82, Bernard Montgomery (2), EL.

71. Lamson to Pogue, 30 October 1951, Dwight D. Eisenhower, Pre-Presidential Papers, 1916-1952, Box 93, Forrest C. Pogue, EL; interview with Dr. Forrest C. Pogue, 17 March 1991.

Signal Corps, SC 192606–S, released 16 August 1944, taken 15 August 1944. Valley Forge Military Academy and College Collection. At his 15 August 1944 press conference in France, Eisenhower has just announced that General George Patton was in command of the Third U.S. Army. Eisenhower also attempted to cool the notion that the war would soon end. Following this conference, Captain Harry Butcher's leak to Gallagher began the press flap over Montgomery's command of the ground forces.

British official photo from ACME Bur Spec # 1A MGS CAN 3–15–45 ML. UPI/CORBIS–BETTMANN. Picture No. U753648ACME. Photograph of Gen. of the Army Dwight D. Eisenhower, Supreme Allied Commander in Western Europe, Sir Bernard L. Montgomery (at left), and Lt. Gen. Omar Bradley (at right), during ceremonies in Holland.

U.S. Army Signal Corps, National Archives. Front row, left to right: Tedder, Eisenhower, Montgomery; back row, left to right: Bradley, Ramsay, Leigh-Mallory, Smith. Eisenhower meets with his commanders prior to the invasion of Normandy. Of the three Allied Expeditionary Forces commanders (Leigh-Mallory, Ramsay, Montgomery), only Montgomery survived the war. Both Leigh-Mallory and Ramsay had favored Patton's single-thrust in September 1944.

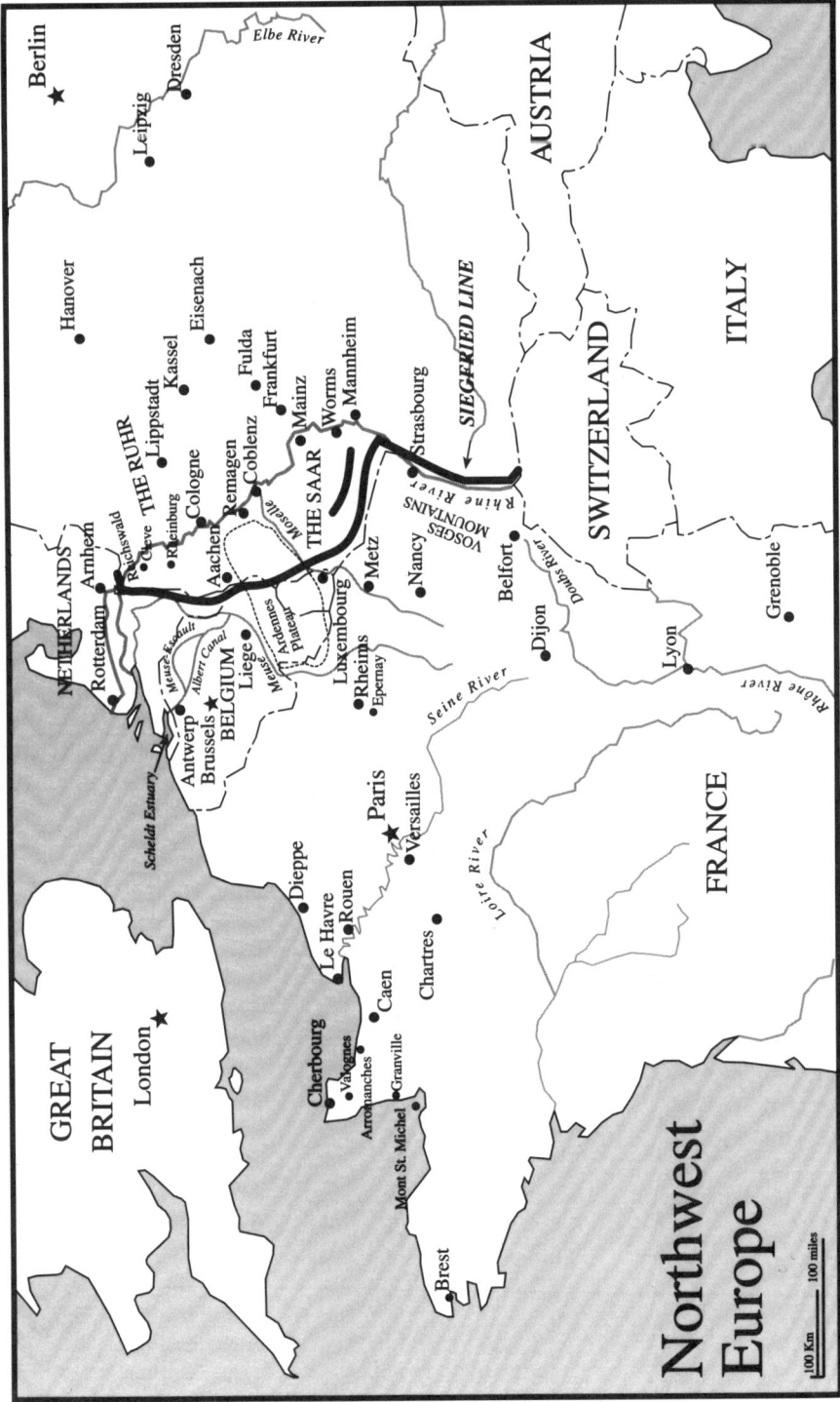

Map 1. Map prepared by Donald S. Frazier, Abilene, Texas.

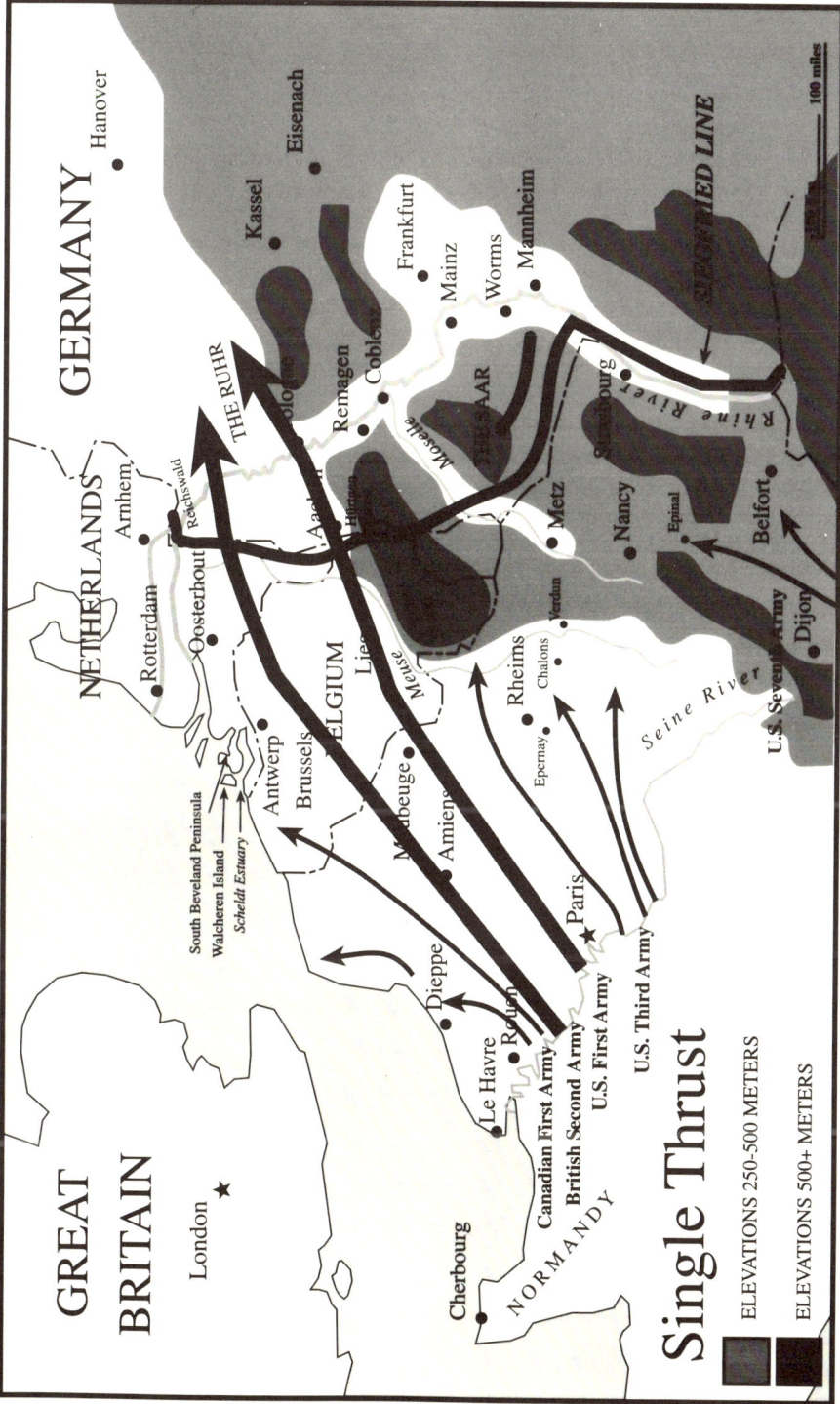

Map 2. Map prepared by Donald S. Frazier.

GREAT BRITAIN

London

NETHERLANDS

GERMANY

Hanover

Eisenach

Kassel

Frankfurt

Mainz

Worms

Mannheim

Coblenz

Remagen

Cologne

THE RUHR

SIEGFRIED LINE

Rhine River

Arnhem

Reichswald

Oosterhout

Rotterdam

Aachen

Huesen

Moselle

THE SAAR

Strasbourg

Metz

Nancy

Epinal

Belfort

Verdun

Dijon

Rheims

Chalons

Epernay

Seine River

U.S. Seventh Army

Cherbourg

NORMANDY

Le Havre

Rouen

Dieppe

Paris

Amiens

Maubeuge

Brussels

Antwerp

BELGIUM

Liege

Meuse

South Beveland Peninsula

Walcheren Island

Scheldt Estuary

Canadian First Army

British Second Army

U.S. First Army

U.S. Third Army

Single Thrust

ELEVATIONS 250-500 METERS

ELEVATIONS 500+ METERS

100 miles

The Ardennes

Front Lines, 15 December 1944

German Advance

Command and Control Split 20 December 1944

Cologne

Remagen

Coblenz

Moselle River

Aachen

Prüm

Elsenborn

Malmedy

St. Vith

Maastricht

Zonhoven

Bastogne

Luxembourg

ARDENNES

Hasselt

Spa

Houffalize

St. Trond

Liege

Bradley's 12th Army Group Tac Headquarters

Patton's Third Army

Namur

Givet

Hodges' First Army

Meuse River

Montgomery's 21st Army Group Headquarters

Simpson's Ninth Army

Meuse-Escault

Albert Canal

BELGIUM

Brussels ★

Horrocks' XXX Corps.

Antwerp

20 Km   20 Miles

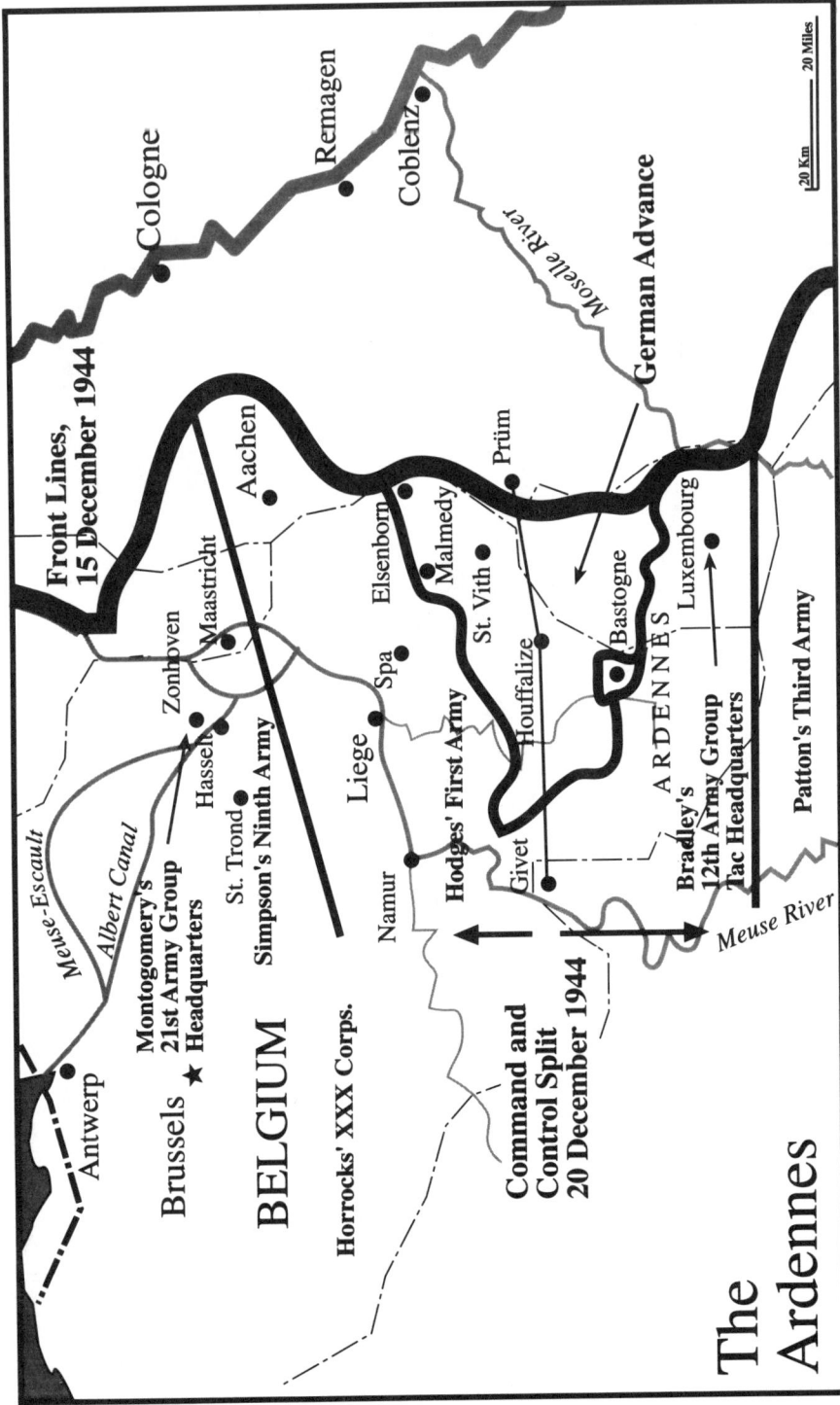

Map 3. Map prepared by Donald S. Frazier.

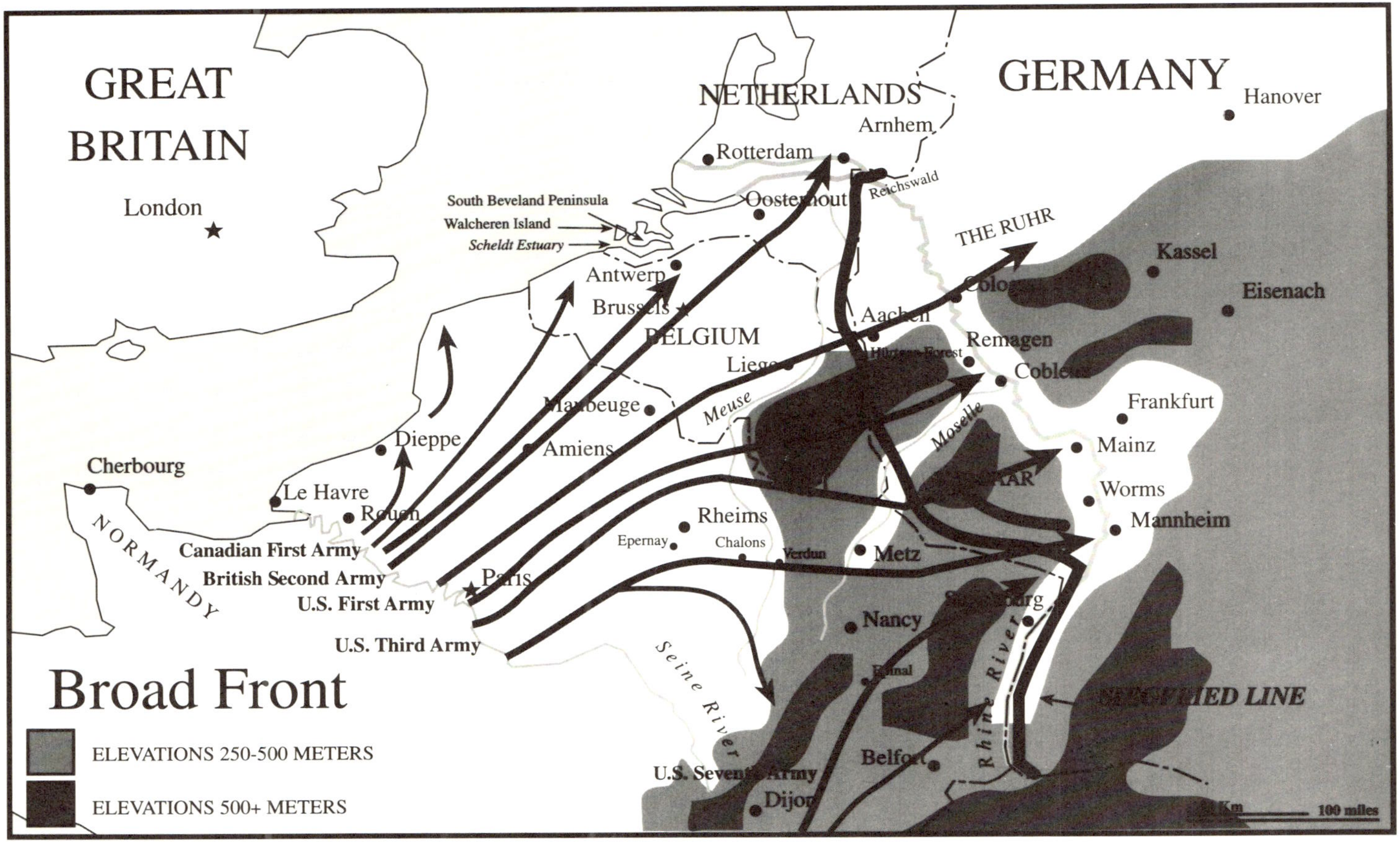

Map 4. Map prepared by Donald S. Frazier.

6

The British Field Marshals Counterattack: Montgomery and Alanbrooke

I would not class Ike as a great soldier in the true sense of the word. He might have become one if he had ever had the experience of exercising direct command of a division, corps, and army--which unfortunately for him did not come his way. But he was a great Supreme Commander--a military statesman. I know of no other person who could have welded the Allied forces into such a fine fighting machine in the way he did, and kept a balance among the many conflicting and disturbing elements which threatened at times to wreck the ship.

--Field Marshal the Viscount Montgomery of Alamein[1]

The British counterattack on Eisenhower as ground forces commander gained momentum with the appearance of *The Memoirs of Field-Marshal the Viscount Montgomery of Alamein* in 1958 and within a year Sir Arthur Bryant's second volume in his edition of Field Marshal Lord Alanbrooke's wartime diary, *Triumph in the West*. Taken together, they pictured the supreme commander as a charming man who was most influenced by the last man with whom he spoke; however, Brooke's oft-cited aphorism was largely the result of Montgomery's legerdemain. One thing is certain, and that is by November 1944 both field marshals wanted Eisenhower replaced as ground forces commander.

The Memoirs of Field-Marshal the Viscount Montgomery of Alamein was an instant best-seller in Britain in 1958 and continued the argument against Eisenhower's strategy and command that Montgomery began in November 1948 in *The Sunday Times* and repeated through Wilmot's *The Struggle for Europe*. Montgomery's *Memoirs* went beyond his wartime charges that Eisenhower had prolonged the war and wasted lives and added that Eisenhower had also worsened the position of the Western Allies relative to the Soviet Union through his failure to take Vienna, Prague, and Berlin. When the second volume of Alanbrooke's diaries appeared a year later, the historical counteroffensive was complete.

MONTGOMERY'S *MEMOIRS*

Originally titled "The Sparks Fly Upward," Montgomery prefaced his memoir with a quotation from the Book of Job, Chapter Five, Verse Seven: "Yet man is born into trouble, as the sparks fly upward."[2] Bernard Law Montgomery was born to trouble on 17 November 1887, the fourth child in a family of nine children, and his *Memoirs* described an unhappy childhood marked by a clash of wills with his mother. Throughout his life Montgomery adored his father, an Anglican bishop, and shunned his mother; when she died in 1949 he did not attend her funeral. Ultimately, tragedy helped make him a field marshal. Marriage at thirty-nine to Mrs. Betty Carver, a widow with two young sons, brought Bernard both a normal home life and love. A widower at forty-nine in October 1937, Montgomery described the effects of his wife's death: "I was utterly defeated. I began to search in my mind for anything I had done wrong, that I should have been dealt such a shattering blow. I could not understand it; my soul cried out in anguish against this apparent injustice. I seemed to be surrounded by utter darkness."[3]

By the time the Second World War began, Montgomery enjoyed a wealth of command experience. Wounded in World War I and awarded the Distinguished Service Order, his country's second highest medal, Montgomery was appalled by the callousness of staff officers who wasted lives by the thousands without ever visiting the front. Colonial service in Ireland, India, and Palestine interspersed with study and teaching at the Staff Colleges at Camberley and Quetta rounded out his interwar career. He returned to France in 1939 as the commander of the British 3rd Division.

Throughout most of the British retreat to Dunkirk in May 1940, Montgomery fought under General Sir Alan Brooke. Brooke turned over II Corps to Montgomery when ordered out of France, and Montgomery fought alongside Major General (later Field Marshal) Alexander, the I Corps commander. In England after Dunkirk, Montgomery acquired a reputation for single-mindedness and professionalism. Fate intervened in August 1942 just as Montgomery was ordered to take over command of the British First Army for the Anglo-American invasion of North Africa. His orders were countermanded the next day, when he received command of the British Eighth Army in Egypt under Alexander's Middle East Command. Churchill's first choice to command the Eighth Army, Lieutenant General William Henry E. (Strafer) Gott, had been killed.[4]

In remaking the Eighth Army, and inflicting on the Germans the defeat at El Alamein, 23 October to 4 November 1942, Montgomery became the greatest British hero of the war--hence his title. Under Montgomery's command, the Eighth Army invaded Sicily and southern Italy in the summer and fall of 1943. In December 1943, Montgomery returned to England to command both the Allied ground forces and the 21st Army Group in the invasion of France. Following the Second World War, Montgomery commanded the British Army of Occupation in Germany and served as CIGS. In September 1948, he became the chairman of the Western Union Commanders-in-Chief Committee. When Supreme Headquarters Allied

Powers Europe (SHAPE) opened in April 1951, Eisenhower was named supreme commander and Montgomery deputy supreme commander.[5]

In the summer of 1954, thinking about his retirement, Montgomery arranged with the Kemsley newspapers to serialize his memoirs and to become their military consultant.[6] He began writing in the summer of 1955, and as his foreword announced, "Every word of the book was written in the first instance in pencil in my own handwriting."[7] Montgomery obtained the advice of three readers: his former Intelligence officer, Brigadier Edgar T. "Bill" Williams, then warden of Rhodes House, Oxford; the former Secretary of State for War Sir P. J. Grigg; and historian Sir Arthur Bryant. Arguments over documentation left Williams concerned: "His idea of fairness, and more particularly of truth, did not always march in step with mine." Unable or unwilling to produce evidence, Montgomery would announce, "Well, it's going in! They're *my* Memoirs!"[8]

Montgomery modeled his *Memoirs* after the style of Churchill's *The Second World War*, especially his chapters dealing with the war. Making extensive use of his wartime directives, speeches, lectures, and correspondence, Montgomery connected the documents with narrative. In the process, Montgomery's chapter titled "Allied Strategy North of the Seine" would become fundamental to the student of the debate over strategy because it published the following: SHAEF's Intelligence summary of 25 August; Eisenhower's Directive of 4 September (FWD-13765); Montgomery's plan of 17 August (M-99); Montgomery's notes for de Guingand's meeting with Eisenhower of 22 August; Montgomery's M-160 of 4 September; Eisenhower's cable of 5 September (FWD-13889); Eisenhower's Directive of 15 September 1944 (FWD-13765); Montgomery's response of 18 September (M-526); Eisenhower's reply of 20 September; and Montgomery's response of 21 September (M-223).[9] Of 529 pages of text in the 1958 edition by Collins, only 104 pages dealt with the campaign in northwest Europe. Montgomery devoted 130 pages to the desert and the Mediterranean campaigns of Sicily and Italy. The largest part of the autobiography, eleven chapters and 174 pages, dealt with the postwar period; the remaining pages covered his boyhood and early career.

Concerning his *Memoirs'* place in the historiography of the campaign in northwest Europe, Montgomery pointed to the national bias prevalent in works by American writers who felt free to criticize British operations in general and his own in particular. Montgomery accurately predicted that the conduct of the war in northwest Europe would remain "a happy hunting ground for historians" for years to come. In a style all his own, the field marshal wrote, "My friend Ike has agreed that it is now my turn to put my own point of view."[10]

By the time Montgomery took over the 21st Army Group and turned out its staff, he had the reputation of an ambitious and self-centered man. In the London clubs that winter, it was said that "'the Gentlemen are out and the Players are just going in to bat.'"[11] Sparks flew in his relations with the Royal Air Force throughout the Normandy campaign, particularly with Air Marshal Sir Arthur Coningham, commander of the RAF's Second Tactical Air Force. Montgomery refused to deal with Coningham and went over his head to the Allied Expeditionary Air Forces commander, Air Chief Marshal Sir Trafford Leigh-Mallory, because, as he correctly pointed out, Coningham was not his equal in France and had not been his equal in North Africa.

"Not only did I have two badges in my beret: I was wearing two berets," Montgomery wrote, "I was at once C.-in-C. 21 Army Group and the Ground Force Commander for Normandy."[12] On 7 July 1944, anticipating the arrival of another American army into the campaign, Montgomery wrote Brooke, "[Eisenhower] has decided to form the United States Army Group and to put it under me. I will then command: First US Army Group; Second British Army; First Canadian Army. And I see no difficulty in this."[13] Montgomery, by virtue of his training and inclination, was prepared to command more than the sixteen divisions that Great Britain and Canada could provide. Eisenhower may have intended to allow Montgomery to command temporarily the First United States Army Group, renamed the 12th Army Group; he soon changed his mind when prodded by General Marshall and Secretary of War Stimson.[14]

Prefacing his specific differences with Eisenhower, Montgomery described their approaches to battle. Eisenhower, Montgomery pointed out, had been likened by Bedell Smith to a football coach, up and down the bench encouraging his players to drive through the opponent's line. Montgomery, however, sought to unbalance his opponent while remaining balanced himself. The 21st Army Group commander planned to make the Germans deploy on a wide front while he concentrated on a narrow front to strike a crushing blow. Montgomery maintained that his method was cautious with men's lives, while Eisenhower's was expensive.[15]

By August 1944, the British army could no longer bear the price of battle and had to find infantry replacements from active units. On 14 August 1944, Montgomery informed the War Office that he had to break up the 59th British Infantry Division. The War Office had predicted that by the end of 1944 the 21st Army Group would be forced to disband two infantry divisions and three independent armored brigades to provide replacements. During August 1944, as Carlo D'Este pointed out in his *Decision in Normandy*, "The independent 56th Infantry Brigade became part of the 49th Division when its 70th Brigade was disbanded; the 33rd Armoured Brigade lost two battalions; the 8th and 34th Tank Brigades each lost a regiment, and the 27th Armoured Brigade was disbanded."[16] Nigel Hamilton, Montgomery's authorized biographer, concluded that at the heart of Montgomery's call for a single thrust was his belief that only an Anglo-American single thrust and concomitant use of American troops would save the British army from cannibalization.

On 17 August 1944, Montgomery outlined to Bradley a plan envisioning a northeastward movement of their army groups. *The Memoirs* quoted the outline plan: "After crossing the Seine, 12 and 21 Army Groups should keep together as a solid mass of some forty divisions which would be so strong that it need fear nothing." According to Montgomery, Bradley agreed with this notion. In 1958 Montgomery called it a German "Schlieffen Plan" in reverse, after the German offensive of August 1914 that failed to capture Paris and led to a four-year stalemate. The only difference was that this Schlieffen Plan would be launched "against a shattered and disorganized enemy."[17]

On 20 August 1944, at a meeting attended by de Guingand, Eisenhower announced his intention to assume personal command of the ground battle as of 1 September, which complicated Montgomery's single-thrust plan because now he had to address the command issue as well. *The Memoirs* published Montgomery's notes for de Guingand's 22 August meeting with Eisenhower for the purpose of maintaining the status quo. These five points summarized the debate over command and strategy for both the upcoming campaign and posterity:

1. The quickest way to win this war is for the great mass of the Allied armies to advance northwards, clear the coast as far as Antwerp, establish a powerful air force in Belgium, and advance into the Ruhr.
2. The force must operate as one whole, with great cohesion, and be so strong that it can do the job quickly.
3. Single control and direction of the land operations is vital for success. This is a WHOLE TIME job for one man.
4. The great victory in N.W. France has been won by personal command. Only in this way will future victories be won. If staff control of operations is allowed to creep in, then quick success becomes endangered.
5. To change the system of command now, after having won a great victory, would be to prolong the war.[18]

When de Guingand reported no progress with Eisenhower, Montgomery asked the supreme commander to come to his tactical headquarters on 23 August 1944. Montgomery saw Bradley on the morning of 23 August and was "amazed" to discover that Bradley no longer agreed with his northern single thrust. According to Montgomery, Bradley now favored Eisenhower's split offensive that called for the 12th Army Group to attack eastward toward Metz and the Saar. For his part in the debate, Bradley denied ever agreeing to Montgomery's forty-division plan: "Monty deceitfully wrote in his memoir: 'I found to my amazement that Bradley had changed his mind. On the 17th of August he had agreed with me, on the 23rd he was a whole-hearted advocate of the main effort of his Army Group being directed eastwards on Metz and the Saar.' I had not changed my mind. I had *never* agreed to the main features of Monty's plan."[19] When the supreme commander came to Montgomery's headquarters that afternoon accompanied by his chief of staff, Montgomery insisted on speaking to Eisenhower alone.

The field marshal's *Memoirs* missed few chances to say "I told you so," and in recapping his meeting with Eisenhower of 23 August 1944, Montgomery told his readers what he had told Eisenhower. Eisenhower should concentrate the logistical supplies behind Montgomery's plan for a decisive action. The field marshal argued that logistical problems doomed Eisenhower's double-thrust strategy to failure. Montgomery predicted that the attack would "peter out," allowing the Germans to recover. Worse still, a broad-front strategy ran the risk of prolonging the war into 1945. Furthermore, as the supreme commander, Eisenhower should "sit on a very lofty perch" and not "descend into the land battle" and become a ground forces commander. Rather, the supreme commander should let Montgomery run the ground battle for him, or if he deemed American public opinion an obstacle, Montgomery offered to serve under Bradley.[20]

When the two generals got to specifics, Montgomery produced his second proposal in a week. No more talk about forty divisions; now, as Montgomery put it, "I said I wanted an American army of at least twelve American divisions to advance on the right flank of 21 Army Group."[21] To give the First United States Army enough gasoline to be useful to the 21st Army Group, Eisenhower would have to stop Patton's Third Army. Montgomery advocated a 21st Army Group attack, with three armies, to clear the Channel coast, West Flanders, Antwerp, and South Holland.

When Eisenhower insisted on continuing two separate thrusts, Montgomery said he knew that the war would go on for another winter "with all that entailed for the British people." Montgomery's *Memoirs* expressed contempt for Eisenhower's concern for American public opinion and stressed the effects of American nationalism on Britain as a result of another winter of war: "Why should we throw everything away for reasons of American public opinion and American electioneering (1944 was the Presidential election year)?" A broad front was unnecessary to protect the right flank of the Anglo-American armies; the DRAGOON forces had at least done that. Repeating what he had told Chester Wilmot ten years earlier, Montgomery maintained that, "There was no real risk in doing what I suggested."[22]

Between 30 August and 4 September 1944, optimism gave way to euphoria as General Dempsey's British Second Army stole a march on Patton's Third Army and advanced 250 miles in six days to capture the port of Antwerp intact. Anything seemed possible, and in that regard on 4 September 1944 Montgomery sent Eisenhower a further variation on the theme of 17 August: "We have now reached a point where one really powerful and full-blooded thrust towards Berlin is likely to get there and thus end the German war."[23] There were only two possible thrust lines, the Ruhr and the Saar, and Montgomery was convinced of the superiority of the line of the Ruhr. Montgomery requested Eisenhower come and talk to him about it.

Their meeting would not take place for six days owing to Eisenhower's knee injury, following an emergency landing on the beach near his Granville headquarters. Montgomery's *Memoirs* reproached the placement of SHAEF's headquarters at Granville on the west side of the Cherbourg peninsula, overlooking Mont St. Michel:

This was possibly a suitable place for a Supreme Commander; but it was useless for a land force commander who had to keep his finger on the pulse of his armies and give quick decisions in rapidly changing situations. He was over four-hundred miles behind the battle front. . . . There were no telephone lines, and not even a radiotelephone, between his H.Q. and Bradley and myself. In the early days of September he was, in fact, completely out of touch with the land battle, as far as I could see.[24]

By the time the two men met on 10 September (detailed in Chapter 4) it was too late. The German army in the West was already recovering. Frustrated over losing the ground forces command, which the *Daily Mirror* had called a demotion, Montgomery must have contemplated the dismantling of further British divisions. Montgomery became convinced that Eisenhower's decision to take over the ground forces was a looming disaster. By 5 September, Lieutenant General Henry G. Crerar, commanding general of the First Canadian Army, noticed that the 21st Army Group commander was showing signs of strain: "Monty . . . is very upset at the loss of operational command over the US Armies and his nomination to Field-Marshal's rank has accentuated rather than eased his mental disturbance."[25] Certainly, Montgomery's outburst against Eisenhower at the Brussels airfield on 10 September suggests a man who was temporarily overwrought.

The Memoirs' treatment of September 1944 stressed strategy rather than operational command. For instance, Montgomery's letter to Eisenhower of 18 September (M-526) stated that administrative shortages negated movement by all the Allied armies. The proper objective was the Ruhr and then on to Berlin via the northern route, because it guaranteed capture of the German ports and allowed the Allies maximum use of their seapower. The field marshal now argued that the 21st Army Group plus the *nine* divisions of the First United States Army would be adequate to the job if Eisenhower provided *"everything it needed in the maintenance line."* On the other hand, Montgomery noted that Eisenhower might settle on the Frankfurt approach into central Germany. In that case, the 12th Army Group would need three armies, and the 21st Army Group would do its best with what was left over. Montgomery was certain that he could "from a maintenance point of view" get to Berlin with three armies.[26]

It was his third variation since 17 August, and although it represented a 25 percent decrease in his demands on American divisions, now Berlin reappeared as the objective beyond the Ruhr. Montgomery had positioned himself chameleon-like across Eisenhower's 15 September Directive (FWD-13765) that stated: "Clearly, Berlin is the main prize, and the prize in defence of which the enemy is likely to concentrate the bulk of his forces. There is no doubt . . . that we should concentrate all our energies and resources on a rapid thrust to Berlin."[27]

By stressing strategy and logistics, *The Memoirs* gave Montgomery's single-thrust plan a rationality that Eisenhower did not see in September 1944 because there had been no literary separation between command and strategy during the war. *The Memoirs* omitted Montgomery's cable of 21 September to General Smith suggesting Eisenhower hand over operational control of the First United States Army to Montgomery:

1. Ref. attached. My Chief of Staff will raise the subject at the conference tomorrow.
2. I consider that the organization for command and control of the operations to capture the RUHR is not satisfactory. It is a task for one man, and he should have the operational control and direction of all forces involved. He should be able to adjust boundaries as necessary to suit the changing tactical problem.

3. To achieve success, the tactical battle will require very tight control and very careful handling.

I recommend that the Supreme Commander hands the job over to me, and gives me powers of operational control over First United States Army.[28]

This represented a fourth variation in the plan first proposed on 17 August to Bradley. Moreover, it should be pointed out that for virtually all of August and September 1944 the order of battle of the First United States Army was nine divisions.[29] Implementation of Montgomery's 21 September 1944 proposal would have meant turning over the *entire* First United States Army. If Montgomery were to have received twelve American divisions, that would have required turning over the First Army and presumably four divisions of the Third United States Army. Eisenhower's concern for American public opinion may have seemed incredible to Montgomery, but implementation of the field marshal's proposition would have negated American control over an entire American army and rendered meaningless Bradley's 12th Army Group.

When the Germans repulsed the British airborne landing at Arnhem causing Montgomery to withdraw the survivors of the 1st British Airborne on 25 September 1944, the offensive in the west was over and the initiative lost. On 24 September 1944, in his nightly message to the CIGS, Montgomery noted: "It may well be that we can attain our object [bridgeheads across the Rhine] equally well if not better by developing thrust lines eastwards and we shall have greater resources for these if we abandon the attempt to cross the NEDER RIJN west of ARNHEM."[30]

The field marshal also admitted that he had mistakenly believed that the First Canadian Army could clear the approaches to Antwerp while the rest of the 21st Army Group went for the Ruhr. *The Memoirs* took exception to *Crusade in Europe*'s account of the 10 September Brussels meeting that described the field marshal's duties as follows: "After completion of the bridgehead operation he [Montgomery] was to turn instantly and with his whole force to the capture of Walcheren Island and the other areas from which the Germans were defending the approaches to Antwerp." In 1958 Montgomery said that this point was not brought up at the conference on 10 September.[31]

After the war, Montgomery told Chester Wilmot that there was no one at the meeting but Eisenhower and himself, but Wilmot noticed that talking about it made Montgomery uncomfortable.[32] Again Montgomery's impression of events cannot be verified. Among others present at the meeting were the deputy supreme commander, Air Chief Marshal Tedder, Montgomery's Administrative officer, Major General Sir Miles Graham, and Lieutenant General Sir Humphrey Myddleton Gale, SHAEF's chief Administrative officer. Gale's diary for 10 September attests:

I could not get the opinion of GRAHAM and the opinion of MONTGOMERY to agree as to how far his present system of maintenance would enable him to go. GRAHAM seemed to think he could support the Army to the RHINE and MONTGOMERY seemed to think that he could not be supported much farther than he was now.

However, they made certain proposals for future maintenance all of which disregarded the importance of clearing the approaches to ANTWERP so that we might make use of that important port as a base for our thrust into GERMANY. MONTGOMERY was obdurate and said ANTWERP would have to take its time. I pointed out that for purposes of oil alone ANTWERP was essential to him and also for the U.S. forces but he insisted on taking the view that he could not hurry over it and it would be some weeks before it would fall.[33]

In September 1944, Gale was certain that Montgomery's motive sprang from reasons of command, and the Gale diary entry of 10 September concerning the likelihood of opening Antwerp concluded, "This is all very distressing because it makes General EISENHOWER'S position almost impossible. His strategy is sound, his plans are well laid, but now that MONTGOMERY is no longer the Ground Forces Commander it is perfectly clear to me that he is going to play his own hand regardless of the wider issues involved."[34]

The Memoirs referred to Montgomery's paper dated 10 October 1944 entitled "Notes on Command in Western Europe." Sent to General Smith at SHAEF, *The Memoirs* paraphrased Montgomery's observation that operational command of land armies in war required almost daily contact with subordinate commanders and was therefore "a whole-time job."[35] Montgomery's unpublished paper warned that SHAEF was too far from the front to influence the battle for the Ruhr, and it stated flatly that battles could not be controlled through telegrams. Eisenhower had three choices as Montgomery saw it in October 1944: (1) move forward and take control of the battle; (2) appoint Montgomery to take control; or (3) appoint Bradley to take control. Control to Montgomery meant operational command over the flanking army group, that is, either he or Bradley would have to become de facto ground forces commander of the two army groups advancing on the same axis north of the Ardennes.[36]

On 13 October 1944, Eisenhower's response to Montgomery's most recent criticism on command came in reference to the need to open Antwerp. Eisenhower pointed out to Montgomery that both the CIGS and the chief of staff of the United States Army had come close to giving him a direct order to open Antwerp; both had recently visited the continent. In fact, Montgomery had made it a point to tell General Marshall on 8 October just what he thought of the command setup, but Marshall did not trust Montgomery's motives and backed Eisenhower. Subsequently, Eisenhower informed Montgomery that opening Antwerp had nothing whatever to do with command. Montgomery pledged to Eisenhower on 16 October that "You will hear no more on the subject of command from me."[37]

Montgomery's criticism was apt; moreover, it was basic operations logic. The SHAEF approach put Bradley in command of two axes of advance, Liege-Aachen and the Saar. Meanwhile, north of the Ardennes, SHAEF had two commanders, Montgomery and Bradley, splitting the same axis of advance. The field marshal was merely pointing out what SHAEF had chosen to ignore. A SHAEF report of 22 August 1944 addressed to the chief of staff concerning the 12th Army Group advancing astride the Ardennes said, "The main disadvantage to this course is that all the forces advancing along a single axis of advance would not be under a single commander."[38] Since this was the course followed by SHAEF, it must be added that the report also noted that splitting the avenue of advance between Montgomery and Bradley negated American "political objections to retaining sizable forces under British command."[39]

By November 1944, Montgomery may have pledged to give up the idea of ground forces command, but he and Brooke were about to begin their most concerted effort of the campaign to remove Eisenhower from the role of ground forces commander. On the same page that *The Memoirs* listed British casualties by division from 6 June to 1 October 1944, including the two divisions that were broken up in 1944, the 50th and the 59th, Montgomery alluded to his talks with Eisenhower on 28-29 November in vague terms, stating that the situation at the front was not good.[40] Breaking up a second British division no doubt intensified Montgomery's frustration over the strategic stalemate and his inability to direct the battle for the Ruhr. His frustration expressed itself in his "strategic reverse" message, describing to Brooke his meeting with Eisenhower of 28 November 1944. Alanbrooke's edited diary reprinted nearly all of Montgomery's two-page message:

Ike visited me to-day and we have had a very long talk. I put the following points to him. 1st. That the plan contained in his last Directive had failed and we had in fact suffered a strategic reverse. He agreed. 2nd. That we must now prepare a new plan and in that plan we must get away from the doctrine of attacking all along the front and must concentrate our resources on the selected vital thrust. He agreed. 3rd. That it seemed a pity he did not have Bradley as Land Force Commander to take off him the work of running the operations on land. He did not, repeat, not agree.[41]

The man who took down Montgomery's nightly messages was his MA (Military Assistant), Lieutenant Colonel Christopher P. "Kit" Dawnay. Writing some forty years later, Dawnay described Eisenhower's overnight visit to Montgomery's headquarters and Montgomery's attempt to get Eisenhower to accept a single thrust against the Ruhr. Eventually, after saying "no" every way he knew how, Montgomery "reduced Ike to a condition of speechlessness," and he asked to go to bed. Dawnay showed the general to his room and returned to Montgomery's office:

"Get this message sent to the CIGS." I wrote it down at his dictation and was astonished to discover that he was claiming that Ike had agreed in general with the single-thrust strategy. I read the message back and asked if it was correct. He assented. I said: "May I say something, sir?" "Yes, certainly." "Ike does *not* agree, sir." His only comment was "Send that message, Kit." And so I did. But Ike had not agreed.[42]

According to Montgomery's *Memoirs*, the German Ardennes offensive forced Eisenhower to do what Montgomery had been calling for since August, that is, place Montgomery in operational control of the Anglo-American forces along the northern axis of advance. *The Memoirs* included a frank discussion of the issues that December in a subheading entitled "The Command Problem." During their meeting at Hasselt, Belgium, on 28 December 1944, Montgomery again urged Eisenhower to concentrate all Allied power in the upcoming battle against the Ruhr and to leave him in operational command. The next day Montgomery followed up with a letter pointing out that the Allies had suffered "one very definite failure," owing to Eisenhower's broad front. Rather than suffer another failure, Montgomery suggested that his current temporary command become permanent operational control. He even wrote the sentence for Eisenhower to describe the change in command: "From now onwards full operational direction, control and co-ordination of these operations is vested in the C.-in-C. 21 Army Group, subject to such instructions as may be issued by the Supreme Commander from time to time."[43] This was the high-water mark of Montgomery's persistence, and it needs to be considered in the context of Brooke's warnings against "rubbing it in" to Eisenhower cited later in this chapter. Montgomery related how Eisenhower had received simultaneously Marshall's prohibition against a British ground forces commander, and decided to force the issue. De Guingand informed Montgomery how "het up" Eisenhower was, so Montgomery concluded it best to "pipe down."

The Memoirs included the outline of Montgomery's 7 January 1945 press conference.[44] In retrospect, the field marshal admitted that the press conference was a mistake in that he appeared to have been triumphant over American generals, not the Germans. Following this public apology, Montgomery nevertheless could not resist pointing out that the Americans had suffered 80,000 casualties and adding that "it would never have happened if we had fought the campaign properly," which was a tacit criticism of American generals. By Montgomery's calculus, the Ardennes campaign added six weeks to the war and granted the Soviets much of central Europe.[45]

Montgomery's discussion of the closing days of the war borrowed liberally from Wilmot and Churchill. Concerning Berlin, Montgomery believed that Berlin was lost to the Russians in August 1944 when Eisenhower "mucked it up" by choosing to advance on separate fronts. Montgomery told his readers that war is a political instrument, and it made little sense to win militarily only to lose politically. According to the field marshal in 1958, the political balance of power in the postwar world had required that the "Western nations" liberate the central European capitals of Vienna, Prague, and Berlin ahead of the Russians.[46]

BRYANT'S *TRIUMPH IN THE WEST*

Sparks also flew from the published diaries of Field Marshal Lord Alanbrooke, wartime CIGS and chairman of the British Chiefs of Staff Committee. He was created a baron in September 1945 and adopted the title of Alanbrooke of Brookeborough in Fermanagh (Northern Ireland). In January 1946 he and the other British Chiefs of Staff were made viscounts; in December Alanbrooke was made a Knight of the Garter.[47] In 1954 Alanbrooke teamed with historian and biographer Sir Arthur Bryant for the purpose of producing a biography. In the process, Alanbrooke rewrote his diaries by adding detailed commentaries, "Notes on My Life," which were to form the basis of Bryant's biography. When Bryant read the diaries, he became convinced that they constituted "one of the great original documents of military history," and he urged Alanbrooke to publish them instead. Subsequently, Bryant's publisher, William Collins, agreed to publish the diaries, and that led to *The Turn of the Tide* in 1957 and *Triumph in the West* in 1959. The project lasted five years and was assisted by Mrs. M. C. "Buster" Long, Bryant's research associate, who conducted interviews and documentation searches.[48] Organizing chapters around the chronological exposition of the diary and Alanbrooke's "Notes on My Life," Bryant provided a clear context for the quoted entries and letters.

As part of the fifty-fifty split on the royalties of *Triumph in the West*, Collins structured a buyout of the copyright in exchange for a tax-free trust on the basis that the field marshal was not a professional writer. Unlike de Guingand and Montgomery who wrote several books--writing became Montgomery's livelihood-- Alanbrooke collaborated with Bryant in his spare time. The new Labor government refused the parliamentary grant promised him by Churchill, so after forty-four years of service, Alanbrooke was awarded £311½ and half pay for life. Forced to sell his house, Alanbrooke was hard pressed until he managed to obtain several directorships from banks and corporations, which kept him busy and comfortable.[49]

Bryant explained Alanbrooke's publication of his controversial diaries as both a personal and political decision. Brooke's nightly epistles to his wife, Benita, could counteract the errors and national bias expressed in the American memoirs. As Churchill's six volumes of *The Second World War* appeared, Brooke felt compelled to speak for the British Chiefs and the work they did toward winning the war. According to Brooke, while the British guided strategy up to the time of the Teheran Conference in November 1943, the Allies made no strategic mistakes. After that time, Washington and Eisenhower made several that proved costly in blood and treasure, prolonged the war, and discarded the fruits of victory. Sir Arthur advised his readers that while the diary was an incomparable source as to decision making at the highest level, as biography it was a distorted mirror. Constantly critical, Brooke's diaries reflected the depths of frustration, anxiety, and overwork of the soldier who was in charge and could not complain out loud without being seen as disloyal to the British government or the Allied cause.[50]

The Turn of the Tide, Bryant's 1957 first volume in his edition of the Brooke diaries, was highly controversial in Britain because of its criticisms of Churchill as prime minister and minister of defense. *Triumph in the West* would be no different in 1959, for it was cut from the same cloth. Lord Ismay, Churchill's chief of staff and the one man who could attest to the tribulations of working with Churchill just as much as Brooke could, took both Bryant and Alanbrooke to task over publication of the diaries. In a letter to General Albert M. Gruenther, Eisenhower's chief of staff at SHAPE, Ismay wrote:

I have let off steam by telling Brookie what a bad turn Arthur Bryant has done him: and I have told Bryant that to quote verbatim extracts from the diary of a man immersed in problems on [a] world wide scale, and with events moving at break neck speed, is most unfair on the diarist. I know for sure that if I had indulged in a nocturnal commentary like that, I should have frequently bleated that Winston was impossible and intolerable . . . whereas when I had a little sleep, and regained my composure next morning I'd have written: "How could I have been such an ass. Thank God for him, warts and all."[51]

Brooke felt he had been dealt "a crushing blow" when the command of the invasion of France that Churchill had promised him went to an American.[52] The CIGS believed Eisenhower's career as a staff officer left him poorly prepared to command operations. On 15 May 1944 following the final briefing on the invasion, Brooke wrote:

The main impression I gathered was that Eisenhower was no real director of thought, plans, energy or direction. Just a co-ordinator, a good mixer, a champion of inter-Allied cooperation, and in those respects few can hold a candle to him. But is that enough? Or can we not find all qualities of a commander in one man? May be I am getting too hard to please, but I doubt it.[53]

On 28 August 1944, the British Chiefs considered Eisenhower's announced intentions to take command of the ground forces as of 1 September. Bryant's published version quoted Brooke's contention that Eisenhower's "plan is likely to add another three to six months on to the war." Equally worrisome to Brooke was Eisenhower's intention to split his forces, directing the Americans on Nancy and the British up the Channel coast. The CIGS thought, "If the Germans were not as beat as they are this would be a fatal move; as it is, it may not do too much harm."[54] Bryant omitted Brooke's conclusion about the national politics of Eisenhower's decision, which he rightly attributed to the effects of the American press:

Up to now he had been a Supreme Commander with separate commanders for naval, land, and air forces. Now he proposes to assume the dual role of Supreme Commander and commander of land forces. This change was brought about mainly by the American press resenting the fact that Monty was commanding all the land forces. Personally I consider it wrong for a Supreme Commander to attempt the role of the supreme task on one level and one of the services on the next level.[55]

Brooke attended the 5 October 1944 conference at SHAEF where Eisenhower explained his future strategy to all his army group commanders, including Montgomery. Brooke's diary noted that the need to open Antwerp to ship traffic dominated every issue on the agenda. Bryant quoted Brooke's conclusion regarding Montgomery's recent performance:

I feel that Monty's strategy for once is at fault. Instead of carrying out the advance on Arnhem he ought to have made certain of Antwerp in the first place. Ramsay brought this out well in the discussion and criticized Monty freely. Ike nobly took all the blame on himself as he had approved Monty's suggestion to operate on Arnhem. The atmosphere was good and friendly in spite of some candid criticisms of the administrative situation.[56]

The stalemate on the western front in November 1944 convinced Brooke and Montgomery that Eisenhower had to be relieved of the ground command. For a time Brooke thought Bradley might make a suitable replacement for Eisenhower as ground forces commander, but the documents make clear that Montgomery never gave up hope that he would regain that position. Meeting with the prime minister and Bedell Smith on 2 November for a review of SHAEF's strategy, Brooke was distressed by Eisenhower's intentions to attack "all along the front." Brooke confided to his diary, "I fear that the November attack will consequently get no farther than the Rhine at the most." A week later Brooke was less sanguine, predicting that the November offensive would not reach the Rhine; moreover, he doubted the Allies would cross the river in 1944. On 9 November, Montgomery came by Brooke's office before returning to the continent, and Brooke observed that Montgomery could not stop "harping over" how the command system in the European theater was prolonging the war. "I agree that the setup is bad," Brooke wrote, "but it is not one which can be easily altered, as the Americans naturally consider they should have a major say."[57]

During 10-14 November 1944, Brooke accompanied Churchill to France, and the trip convinced him to act on Montgomery's complaints. From Paris the British traveled to the French forces along the Doubs River. After a briefing by General Jean de Lattre de Tassigny, the First French Army commander, Brooke made up his mind about Eisenhower's ability to run a land battle and Eisenhower's strategy of attacking all along the line. Noting that the American army north of de Lattre was attacking through the Vosges Mountains, Brooke wrote that Eisenhower should have concentrated on the Belfort gap and established a defensive position to front the Vosges. Any successful offensive through the Belfort gap would turn the Vosges and obviate the costly frontal attack through the mountains. On 14 November, Churchill and Brooke had lunch at Eisenhower's forward headquarters overlooking the Rheims golf course. Bryant's footnote on the visit stated: "Accustomed to the more rigid hierarchy of the British Army, Brooke, during his visit, was surprised to find Mrs. Summersby presiding over the head of the luncheon table, with the Prime Minister on her right!"[58] When the prime minister's party returned to England that afternoon, Brooke was concerned by Eisenhower's rather vague idea of dispositions and "what was really going on."

Three days later Montgomery confirmed Brooke's recent impression. Writing on 17 November 1944, Montgomery pointed out that he had only seen Eisenhower four times since Normandy and he had not seen or spoken to him on the telephone since 18 October. Furthermore, Montgomery believed he could not implement his latest orders. The problem as Montgomery saw it was that "[Eisenhower] has never commanded anything before in his whole career; now, for the first time, he has elected to take direct command of very large-scale operations and he does not know how to do it." Brooke had already come to the same conclusion, noting the agenda in the Chiefs of Staff meeting on 20 November included "a discussion as to the unsatisfactory state of affairs in France, where Eisenhower completely fails as Commander. Bedell Smith lives back in Paris quite out of touch; as a result the war is drifting in a rudderless condition."[59]

Responding to Montgomery on 20 November 1944, the CIGS wrote, "We shall within the next week or fortnight have ample proof of the insufficiency of the present set-up and this will justify our making the strongest representations to Washington." Brooke's first draft had been even stronger, and the deleted phrase is a better indication of Brooke's thinking on the issue: "and this will justify a strong attack on our behalf insisting on the necessary changes being carried out without delay." Neither field marshal had any confidence in Eisenhower as ground commander, but Brooke realized that the preponderance of American strength meant that the British could not resist the American claim on the position, and Brooke wanted to know if Montgomery believed that Bradley could do the job.[60]

Informed by the CIGS that he could never expect to be renamed ground forces commander, Montgomery tried another tack. Bryant published Montgomery's letter of 22 November 1944 suggesting the division of the front at the Ardennes with Montgomery commanding north of it and Bradley commanding to the south. Then Eisenhower could come forward and form a suitable tactical headquarters with his air commander along with him, "who must be Tedder."

Brooke's letter of 24 November pointed out that Montgomery's latest alternative still required Eisenhower to plan and to allot supplies, two functions that Brooke doubted Eisenhower was capable of performing. Brooke said there would be no difference between Eisenhower's trying to command on a two-group basis opposed to a three-group basis. Furthermore, Brooke pointed out that Montgomery was seeking to command the group that would play the major role in the upcoming campaign. The CIGS asked, "Have you considered whether you are likely to be very acceptable in American eyes for this Command?"[61] As far as Brooke was concerned, Montgomery's only chance to have command of a northern group in a two-group theater would occur if Bradley should be named land forces commander and Patton should command the southern group of armies.

Meanwhile, the grim war of attrition continued. Bryant edited Brooke's diary entry of 24 November, and the edited material appears in italics:

At the end of this morning's COS meeting I showed the secretaries out and retained only "Pug." I then put before the Committee my views on the very unsatisfactory state of affairs in France, with no one running the land battle. Eisenhower, though supposed to be doing so, is *detached and by himself with his lady chauffeur* on the golf links at Rheims--entirely detached and taking practically no part in running the war. Matters got so bad lately that a deputation of Whiteley, Bedell Smith and a few others went up to tell him he must get down to it and RUN the war, which he said he would. *Personally, I think he is incapable of running the war even if he tries.*[62]

The fact that he excused the secretaries would lead to the conclusion that Brooke mentioned his fears very much as he recorded them here. Ten days earlier, Brooke had noted Summersby's position relative to the prime minister at lunch and had written that in promoting Summersby "one step up the ladder" Eisenhower "produced a lot of undesirable gossip which did him no good."[63]

On 26 November Montgomery flew to England for the second time that month to meet Brooke to discuss replacing Eisenhower as the ground forces commander. Bryant published their three essentials as described in Brooke's diary:

(a) to counter the pernicious American strategy of attacking all along the line.

(b) to obviate splitting an Army Group with the Ardennes in the middle of it, by forming two Groups (a Northern and a Southern) instead of three as at present.

(c) to appoint a Commander for the Land Forces. The problem is how to get this carried out! What we want is Bradley as a Commander of Land Forces, Montgomery Northern Group of Armies, with Patton's Army in his Group--by substituting Third Army for Ninth Army--and Devers commanding Southern Group.[64]

In London the field marshals agreed that Montgomery would not mention these proposals during his scheduled 28 November meeting with Eisenhower *unless* Eisenhower brought up the issue of command. Meanwhile, Brooke was to suggest to Churchill that General Marshall should be asked to come to Britain to discuss the matter.[65]

As *Triumph in the West* made clear, Eisenhower's strategy and command setup had earned a resounding vote of no confidence from Brooke and Montgomery. On 28 November, Brooke met with Churchill to discuss Eisenhower's strategy and command. Regarding strategy, Brooke pointed out that in Eisenhower's November offensive six armies had taken part in the attack and that SHAEF had no reserves. Brooke called it "sheer madness." Then the CIGS brought up his plan to name Bradley the ground forces commander and to establish two army groups on the western front with the Ardennes as a boundary, and to place Montgomery in command in the north and Devers in the south. "I think I succeeded in pointing out that we must take the control out of Eisenhower's hands, and the best plan was to repeat what we did in Tunisia when we brought in Alex as a Deputy to Eisenhower to command the Land Forces for him."[66] Churchill shared his field marshals' concern about the lack of concentration on the western front, but he did not concur in the necessity of establishing a land forces commander. Brooke and the prime minister agreed to wait a few days before attempting to get Marshall to come over to reexamine the command setup.

At this point, Montgomery sent his strategic reverse message to Whitehall on 28 November, which he followed immediately upon Eisenhower's departure from his headquarters on 29 November, with his allegation that Eisenhower had appeared worried and admitted: "Bradley had failed him as an architect of land operations." Thanks to *Triumph in the West*, what Montgomery's *Memoirs* omitted was available to the reading public by November 1959. Montgomery informed Brooke that there was no doubt that Eisenhower wanted to return to the Normandy command setup where Bradley was under Montgomery's operational control. Bryant printed most of Montgomery's message: "In fact, he now definitely wants me to handle main business but wants Bradley to be in on it and, therefore, he will put him under me." Montgomery recognized that Eisenhower would insist on retaining the ground command but added, "If he reverts to the system we had in NORMANDY it means that I shall in reality be in operational charge and be able to influence the whole land battle by direct approach to IKE myself."[67] Brooke was led by Montgomery's cables of 28 and 29 November to believe that Eisenhower had agreed to a single line of attack, and on 3 December was led to believe by

Montgomery that Eisenhower had changed his mind since seeing Bradley.[68] In Eisenhower's defense, this was clearly a case of influence by the last man who cabled his superior about him rather than influence being exerted by the last man who talked with him.

Following the Maastricht Conference of 7 December 1944 among Eisenhower and his army group commanders, Montgomery admitted to Brooke that he had failed to get Eisenhower to listen to sound strategy, and that from then on it would be up to Brooke. The truth of the matter was that Eisenhower had not agreed with Montgomery's interpretations of events expressed in his messages M-351 and M-352 to Brooke of 28 and 29 November, but based solely on Montgomery's interpretation of events, Brooke concluded that Eisenhower was waffling. Therefore, Eisenhower was invited to London to discuss on 12 December his plans for invading Germany. Accompanied by Tedder, Eisenhower met with Churchill and the British Chiefs in Churchill's map room and then had dinner at 10 Downing Street. Bryant quoted the Brooke diary:

Ike explained his plan which contemplates a double advance into Germany, north of the Ruhr and by Frankfurt. I disagreed flatly with it, accused Ike of violating principles of concentration of force, which had resulted in his present failures. I criticized his future plans and pointed out the impossibility of double invasion with the limited forces he has got. I stressed the importance of concentrating on one thrust. I drew attention to the fact that with his limited forces any thought of attack on both fronts could only lead to dispersal of effort.[69]

Owing to Eisenhower's dinner remark that he did not expect to cross the Rhine until May 1945, Brooke was so depressed that he considered resigning. On 13 December Brooke learned that his arguments had impressed the prime minister, whose silence at dinner was simply in deference to his guest. Moreover, Churchill asked the CIGS to repeat his presentation to the War Cabinet and to prepare a paper on the issue.

Brooke was the second man in less than a week to address the War Cabinet concerning the state of the western front. On 11 December 1944, Minister of Labor and National Service Ernest Bevin, M.P., commented that in trade union circles the impression existed that for "the last month or so" the situation on the western front had not been "properly gripped." Bevin feared that the stalemate "might have serious effects on the Coalition Government," and he hoped for a report to the War Cabinet soon on "the present situation and future strategy." On 13 December, the CIGS repeated his critique of Eisenhower's plans to the War Cabinet. Operations had demonstrated a tendency to launch thrusts of equal weight, but the CIGS stipulated that one of the thrusts had to have sufficient force concentrated behind it "to ensure the conclusion." According to Brooke's published diary, Eisenhower's May date for the Rhine crossing "had a profound effect on the Cabinet," which the CIGS regarded as a good thing because it countered the false optimism of the newspapers.[70]

Bryant paraphrased the paper prepared by Brooke's staff for submission by the Chiefs of Staff on 18 December 1944; it was not yet declassified in 1959. Prepared at Churchill's direction following Bevin's request, the report recalled the Combined Chiefs of Staff directive to Eisenhower from the Quebec Conference in September 1944, stressing that the northern line of attack was to be the main thrust. Despite those instructions, Eisenhower had allowed the two thrusts to take place against the Ruhr and the Saar, and both had failed. The British Chiefs estimated that Eisenhower would have between eighty and eighty-five divisions by the spring, but that twenty would be necessary to hold the front while sixty attacked. The Chiefs warned that with only sixty divisions attacking, the Allies would not be strong enough to complete Eisenhower's contemplated double envelopment of the Ruhr. On 28 December the prime minister noted agreement with the paper and its suggestion that the British Chiefs request that the Combined Chiefs of Staff require both a progress report and detailed appreciation of future plans from the supreme commander. However, owing to the German Ardennes offensive, Churchill wanted the telegram to the Combined Chiefs held for dispatch at a later date.[71]

On 20 December 1944, Eisenhower placed Montgomery in control of the northern half of the Bulge and two American armies, the First and the Ninth. Bryant printed Brooke's warning of 20 December, which was sent to Montgomery prior to learning of his increased command, cautioning him to "be careful about what you say to Eisenhower" about command because it would likely do more harm than good.[72] The next day the CIGS felt compelled to warn Montgomery:

Events and enemy action have forced on Eisenhower the setting up of a more satisfactory system of command. I feel that it is most important that you should not even in the slightest degree appear to rub this undoubted fact in to anyone at SHAEF or elsewhere. Any remarks you may make are bound to come to Eisenhower's ears sooner or later and that may make it more difficult to ensure that this new set-up for Command remains even after the present emergency has passed.[73]

Bryant's narrative revealed that Montgomery could not resist telling Bradley on Christmas Day that the Germans had given the Allies "a real bloody nose," and blaming the Eisenhower-Bradley double-thrust strategy for the defeat. Three days later, Montgomery informed Brooke that he had carried the point with Eisenhower that he should have operational control in the upcoming attack on the Ruhr. Bryant quoted Brooke's doubts of 28 December: "Monty has had another interview with Ike. I do not like the account of it. It looks to me as if Monty, with his usual lack of tact, has been rubbing into Ike the results of not having listened to Monty's advice!"[74] Brooke again received an impression from Montgomery that cannot be verified by any American archives: "According to Monty, Ike agrees that the front should now be divided in two and that only one major offensive is possible. But I expect that whoever meets Ike next may swing him to another point of view. *He is a hopeless commander.*"[75]

With the Battle of the Bulge virtually over on 15 January 1945, Brooke took a page out of Eisenhower's and Bradley's book and cautioned Montgomery that his plan for the Rhine campaign was too cautious, too concentrated. The CIGS pointed out that the narrow distance from Duesseldorf to Arnhem would not allow for the "necessary tactical surprise" for Montgomery's crossing. Brooke believed that Montgomery should close to the Rhine as far south as Bonn, widening the British frontage from 55 to over 100 miles, which would require more American troops, but the lesson of closing to the Rhine on a broad front was the same, and was what Eisenhower did.[76]

On 25 March 1945, Brooke and Eisenhower observed Montgomery's crossing of the Rhine at Rheinberg, which lay within the zone of the Ninth United States Army's XVI Corps. Eisenhower asked what Brooke thought of pushing for Frankfurt and Kassel in the south, and the CIGS replied that with the Germans collapsing there were no risks to the double envelopment now, whereas there had been when the Germans were still resisting.[77] The reader should recall that Eisenhower claimed that while watching the crossing of the Rhine, Brooke paid him a great compliment, saying, "'Thank God, Ike, you stuck by your plan. You were completely right.'"[78] Alanbrooke's published diary stated:

When this statement is considered in connection with what I wrote in my diary that evening, it will be clear that I was misquoted. To the best of my memory I congratulated him heartily on his success and said that, as matters had turned out, his policy was now the correct one; that, with the German in his defeated condition, no dangers now existed in a dispersal of effort. I am quite certain that I never said to him, "You were completely right," as I am still convinced that he was "completely wrong."[79]

Alanbrooke understood that as much as Eisenhower's faulty dispositions nearly led to disaster in the Ardennes, the Germans lost the battle. Subsequently, the Allies were justified in taking more risks, and he wrote, "The double attack soon became a double pursuit and as such was fully justified."[80]

Informed on 1 April 1945 of Eisenhower's decision not to go to Berlin, the CIGS saw Eisenhower as abandoning sound strategy to serve American military prestige. Brooke and his colleagues realized that the early liberation of Holland, the occupation of the north German naval bases, and the liberation of Denmark would be delayed by Eisenhower's shift of emphasis to central Germany. "Most of the changes," Brooke wrote, "are due to the national aspirations and to ensure that the U.S. effort will not be lost under British command."[81] On 3 April, Tedder attended the Chiefs of Staff meeting and, according to Brooke's diary, explained Eisenhower's message to Stalin and change in direction of the main effort as stemming from Montgomery's issuing a directive contrary to Eisenhower's concept. Brooke was incredulous, and he pointed out that the boundaries of the Ninth Army were the same in both Montgomery's and Eisenhower's directives. The only difference was that now the Ninth Army was under Bradley.[82]

The Kansas City Star, Thursday, 5 November 1959. Editorial page cartoon by S. J. Ray, entitled "How to Sell a Book." Reprinted courtesy of *The Kansas City Star*.

CONCLUSION

Throughout the battle for northwest Europe, Montgomery's behavior led Eisenhower, Smith, Bradley, Gale, and Marshall to conclude that the field marshal was concerned primarily with command.[83] However, in the postwar period the books dealt mainly with the strategic debate. Therefore, the general public and much of the historical community have been led to believe that the debate between Eisenhower and Montgomery was primarily over strategy, that is, broad front versus single thrust.

In 1958 Montgomery wrote the quotation that heads this chapter. In his letter to Eisenhower of 11 July 1957 in which he asked permission to quote from Eisenhower's letters, Montgomery included six paragraphs on Eisenhower, omitting the first two sentences of the quotation.[84] Montgomery's *Memoirs* undoubtedly brought about a rupture in his relationship with the president, but what made it irreconcilable was Montgomery's 28 April 1959 interview on CBS. Talking to Edward R. Murrow and Charles Collingwood, Montgomery updated his criticism of Eisenhower's command with criticisms of his presidency. Montgomery said that soldiers should stay out of politics: "The same man can't do both." Churchill was at the White House a week later and found Eisenhower still fuming. The president thought it hypocritical of Montgomery, who never hesitated to invite himself to the White House, to make a personal attack on him and several key members of his government.[85]

Alanbrooke's criticism of Eisenhower attracted the attention of the press. It inspired an editorial cartoon in the *Kansas City Star* entitled "How to Sell a Book," by S. J. Ray, which pictured Alanbrooke placing books in a display titled "Slaps at Ike," while Montgomery looked on carrying his own memoir. The *New York Times* ran a story on its front page on 31 October 1959 focusing on Eisenhower's headquarters being on the golf course at Rheims. Eisenhower's associates and even his biographer took literally what was meant figuratively. The point was not that Eisenhower was out of touch because he was playing golf or committing adultery at Rheims, but that he was vague about the conduct of ground operations.[86]

Eisenhower's reaction was instructive. He always thought of Alanbrooke in terms of what *Crusade in Europe* said about their meeting on the Rhine River in March 1945. Eisenhower wrote Ismay on 14 January 1959 describing his reaction to Montgomery's and Alanbrooke's books. The president judged that, while it may have been a mistake to publish a diary reflecting the frustrations of wartime, Brooke "was always honest, quick and generous."[87]

Both of the books under review in this chapter, along with Wilmot's earlier work, gave the reading public the notion that Eisenhower was most influenced by the last man with whom he spoke. That this reputation is not fully deserved has been pointed out; it was based on several cables and letters that remain uncorroborated. There is no evidence that Bradley ever agreed with a single thrust, nor can Montgomery's version of events be proven by Eisenhower's papers of November and December. This is not the first chapter in this study to point out Montgomery's peculiar attitude toward the truth. Even his own Intelligence officer remarked on it. It may be instructive to point out that a recent translation of Job, Chapter Five, Verse Seven reads: "But man himself begets mischief, as sparks fly upward."[88]

NOTES

1. *The Memoirs of Field-Marshal the Viscount Montgomery of Alamein* (London: Collins, 1958), 540.

2. Nigel Hamilton, *Monty: Final Years of the Field- Marshal, 1944-1976* (New York: McGraw-Hill, 1986), 863.

3. Nigel Hamilton, *Monty: The Making of a General, 1887-1942* (New York: McGraw-Hill, 1981), 3-5, for Montgomery's relationship with his mother; for the effect of his wife's death, see Montgomery, *The Memoirs,* 44.

4. For the British army in France, see Montgomery, *The Memoirs,* 49-66; see 77-78 for August 1942.

5. Ibid., 116-39, for El Alamein; for dual command, see 210-50; for the postwar era, see 504, 513.

6. Hamilton, *Monty: Final Years of the Field-Marshal,* 857; the Kemsley Group consisted of *The Daily Sketch* of London, *The Sunday Times,* and other allied Kemsley papers throughout the country, Robert W. Desmond, *Tides of War: World News Reporting, 1940-1945* (Iowa City: University of Iowa Press, 1984), 125, n.8.

7. Montgomery, *The Memoirs,* 15.

8. Bill Williams, "Gee One Eye-Sir," in T.E.B. Howarth, ed., *Monty at Close Quarters: Recollections of the Man* (London: Leo Cooper in Association with Martin Secker and Warburg; New York: Hippocrene Books, 1985), 29; Hamilton, *Monty: Final Years of the Field-Marshal,* 861.

9. Montgomery, *The Memoirs,* 265-82.

10. Ibid., 251.

11. Ibid., 216.

12. Ibid., 256.

13. M-508, Montgomery to CIGS, 7 July 1944, Papers of Field Marshal Viscount Montgomery of Alamein, Reel 11, BLM 126/9, IWM. Montgomery prefixed "M" to his messages, directives, and some letters. M-1 situation reports began 7 June 1944. He designated the M-500 series for important documents beginning on 9 June 1944, ending with M-602 on 8 May 1946. He began M-1000 on 22 February 1946 when his situation reports reached 499. See Mr. Stephen Brooks, The Papers of Field Marshal the Viscount Montgomery of Alamein, KG, GCB, DSO, DL, 1887-1976, IWM.

14. Martin Blumenson, *The Battle of the Generals: The Untold Story of the Falaise Pocket--The Campaign That Should Have Won World War II* (New York: William Morrow, 1993), 111, 244, 263-65.

15. Montgomery, *The Memoirs,* 262.

16. Carlo D'Este, *Decision in Normandy* (New York: E. P. Dutton, 1983), 263; for the connection between single thrust and cannibalization, see Nigel Hamilton, *Master of the Battlefield: Monty's War Years, 1942-1944* (New York: McGraw-Hill, 1983), 801-802.

17. Montgomery, *The Memoirs,* 266-67.

18. Ibid., 267-68.

19. Omar N. Bradley and Clay Blair, *A General's Life: An Autobiography by General of the Army Omar N. Bradley and Clay Blair* (New York: Simon and Schuster, 1983), 314; Montgomery, *The Memoirs,* 268.

20. Montgomery, *The Memoirs,* 268-69.

21. Ibid., 269.

22. Ibid., 270-71.

23. Ibid., 271-72.

24. Ibid., 271; D.K.R. Crosswell, *The Chief of Staff: The Military Career of General Walter Bedell Smith* (Westport, Conn.: Greenwood Press, 1991), 254-55.

25. Hamilton, *Monty: Final Years of the Field Marshal,* 209.

26. Montgomery, *The Memoirs,* 279, italics in the original.

27. Ibid., 277.

28. Montgomery to Bedell Smith, 21 September 1944, Papers of Field Marshal Viscount Montgomery of Alamein, Reel 10, BLM 109/34, IWM.

29. *First United States Army, Report of Operations, 1 August 1944-22 February 1945,* 4 vols. (Washington, D.C.: Government Printing Office, 1946), 1:10, for August 1944, and 54-55 for September 1944.

30. Hamilton, *Monty: Final Years of the Field-Marshal,* 87.

31. On the Canadians, see Montgomery, *The Memoirs,* 297; for Antwerp and the 10 September conference, see 289.

32. Hamilton, *Monty: Final Years of the Field-Marshal,* 49.

33. Gale Diary, 10 September 1944, BRUSSELS, II/22, Papers of Lieutenant General Sir Humphrey Myddleton Gale, LHCMA. Eisenhower's *Crusade in Europe* (Garden City, N. Y.: Doubleday, 1948), 306, states: "Air Chief Marshal Tedder and General Gale were also present." *With Prejudice: The War Memoirs of Marshal of the Royal Air Force Lord Tedder G.C.B.* (Boston: Little, Brown, 1966), 590, states: "On 10 September I went to Brussels with Eisenhower, in whose aircraft Montgomery joined us."

34. Gale Diary, 10 September 1944, BRUSSELS, II/22, Papers of Lieutenant General Sir Humphrey Myddleton Gale, LHCMA.

35. Montgomery, *The Memoirs,* 316.

36. "Notes on Command in Western Europe," 10 October 1944, Papers of Field Marshal Viscount Montgomery of Alamein, Reel 7, BLM 76/9, IWM; Hamilton, *Monty: Final Years of the Field-Marshal,* 110-11, prints a partial version.

37. For Brooke and Marshal on Antwerp, see Eisenhower to Montgomery, 13 October 1944, in Alfred D. Chandler, Jr., ed., Stephen E. Ambrose, assoc. ed., *The Papers of Dwight David Eisenhower: The War Years,* 5 vols. (Baltimore and London: Johns Hopkins University Press, 1970), 4:2221-25; for Montgomery's pledge concerning command, see Montgomery, *The Memoirs,* 317. Marshall thought Montgomery's comments concerning command and strategy were "overwhelming egotism"; see Forrest C. Pogue, *George C. Marshall: Organizer of Victory, 1943-1945* (New York: Viking Press, 1973), 475.

38. Memorandum for Chief of Staff, "Command Organization," 22 August 1944, NA, RG 331, Box 77, SHAEF, Post-OVERLORD Planning, vol. 1:2-3.

39. Ibid.

40. Montgomery, *The Memoirs,* 299-300.

41. Arthur Bryant, *Triumph in the West: A History of the War Years Based on the Diaries of Field-Marshal Lord Alanbrooke, Chief of the Imperial General Staff* (Garden City, N. Y.: Doubleday, 1959), 258.

42. "Inside Monty's Headquarters," by Lt. Colonel C. P. Dawnay, in T.E.B. Howarth, ed., *Monty at Close Quarters,* 16.

43. Montgomery, *The Memoirs,* 318.

44. Ibid., 311-14.

45. Ibid., 314-15. The best discussion of this press conference and American generals is in Brian Montgomery's *A Field Marshal in the Family* (London: Constable, 1973), 293-96.

46. Montgomery, *The Memoirs,* 331.

47. David Fraser, *Alanbrooke* (New York: Atheneum, 1982), 512. Throughout this chapter anything written after September 1945 will be attributed to Alanbrooke, and anything written or said prior to that date will be credited to Brooke.

48. Arthur Bryant, epilogue to *Alanbrooke,* "The Making of *The Turn of the Tide,*" 540-57. During the war, "Buster" Long worked in the office of the Minister of Defense, Chiefs of Staff Secretariat; see John Colville, *The Fringes of Power: 10 Downing Street Diaries, 1939-1945* (New York and London: W. W. Norton, 1985), 513n.

49. Fraser, *Alanbrooke,* 514-15; for the sale of his house and directorships; see 545-57 for the writing process.

50. Bryant, *Triumph in the West,* 3-12.

51. Ismay to Gruenther, 31 March 1957, Papers of General Hastings Lionel Baron Ismay, IV/GRU/80, LHCMA.

52. Arthur Bryant, *The Turn of the Tide: A History of the War Years Based on the Diaries of Field-Marshal Lord Alanbrooke, Chief of the Imperial General Staff* (Garden City, N. Y.: Doubleday, 1957), 579.

53. Bryant, *Triumph in the West,* 139.

54. Ibid., 195-96.

55. "Notes on My Life," vol. 13, 28 August 1944, 1004, Papers of Field Marshal Viscount Alanbrooke, LHCMA.

56. Bryant, *Triumph in the West,* 219.

57. Ibid.; the November offensive is on 241; for the command setup, see 244.

58. Ibid., the Belfort gap, 248. Bryant noted that a few days later this is what happened; for Eisenhower's headquarters, see 250; for Summersby, see 250, n.7.

59. Ibid., 252.

60. Bryant, *Triumph in the West,* 253; Draft of Message to Montgomery, 17 November 1944, Papers of Field Marshal Viscount Alanbrooke, 14/1/17, LHCMA.

61. Bryant, *Triumph in the West,* 255.

62. "Notes on My Life," vol. 14, 24 November 1944, 1075, Papers of Field Marshal Viscount Alanbrooke, LHCMA; for the published version see Bryant, *Triumph in the West,* 255.

63. "Notes on My Life," vol. 14, 14 November 1944, 1069, Papers of Field Marshal Viscount Alanbrooke, LHCMA.

64. Bryant, *Triumph in the West,* 256.

65. Ibid.

66. Ibid., 257.

67. Ibid., 259.

68. Ibid., 261.

69. Ibid., 266.

70. Bevin's concern over command is in PRO: CAB 65/44/163, War Cabinet Conclusions, 11 December 1944, 136; Brooke's remarks to the War Cabinet are in PRO: CAB, 65/44/167, War Cabinet Conclusions, 13 December 1944, 145; Bryant, *Triumph in the West,* 266-67.

71. Not strong enough for the double envelopment is in Bryant, *Triumph in the West,* 267; for the COS paper, see PRO: CAB 79/84, War Cabinet COS COM, 18 December 1944,

220; for Churchill's advice to delay the request, see PRO: PREM 3 341/3, General Ismay for COS COM, 28 December 1944, 218.

72. Bryant, *Triumph in the West,* 272.

73. Ibid., 278.

74. Ibid., 278-79.

75. Ibid., 279; for the italicized addition, see "Notes on My Life," vol. 14, 14 November 1944, 1094, Papers of Field Marshal Viscount Alanbrooke, LHCMA.

76. For Brooke's advice, see Bryant, *Triumph in the West,* 292; for distance, see Vincent J. Esposito, ed., *The West Point Atlas of American Wars:* vol. 2, *1900-1953* (New York: Frederick A. Praeger, 1959), Map 66b.

77. Bryant, *Triumph in the West,* 332.

78. Dwight D. Eisenhower, *Crusade in Europe* (Garden City, N. Y.: Doubleday, 1948), 372.

79. Bryant, *Triumph in the West,* 332-33; Pogue quoted Eisenhower's letter to Marshall of 26 March stating: "Yesterday I saw him on the banks of the Rhine and he was gracious enough to say that I was right, and that my current plans and operations are well calculated to meet the current situation." See Forrest C. Pogue, *The Supreme Command (United States Army in World War II: The European Theater of Operations,* Washington, D.C.: Office of the Chief of Military History, Department of the Army, 1954), 433; in 1971 Sir James Gault, Eisenhower's military assistant, wrote to E.K.G. Sixsmith basically confirming Eisenhower's letter to Marshall; see E.K.G. Sixsmith, *Eisenhower as Military Commander* (New York: Stein and Day, a Da Capo Paperback, 1973), 199.

80. Bryant, *Triumph in the West,* 302.

81. Ibid., 339.

82. Ibid., 340.

83. Speaking about Montgomery's planned Rhine crossing, Marshall said, "It was quite evident that what was wanted was complete command." See Larry I. Bland, ed., *George C. Marshall: Interviews and Reminiscences for Forrest C. Pogue* (Lexington, Vir.: George C. Marshall Research Foundation, 1991), 400.

84. Montgomery to Eisenhower, 11 July 1957, Dwight D. Eisenhower, Presidential Papers, Ann Whitman File, Name Series, Box 22, Field Marshal Montgomery (2), EL.

85. Montgomery said: "My observations would be that the leaders, your leaders over there, are people who are not awfully well. Foster Dulles . . . he's in hospital with cancer. Your President has had three very serious illnesses--very serious. A heart attack, this ileitis, and a stroke. The head of your State Department, today, walks about on two crutches." See Hamilton, *Monty: Final Years of the Field Marshal,* 901; for the effects of Montgomery's CBS interview on Eisenhower, see Martin Gilbert, *Winston S. Churchill,* vol. 8, *Never Despair, 1945-1965* (Boston: Houghton Mifflin; Cambridge, Mass.: Riverside Press, 1988), 1294, n.4.

86. For example, see Stephen E. Ambrose, *Eisenhower,* vol. 1, *Soldier, General of the Army, President-Elect, 1890-1952,* (New York: Simon and Schuster, 1983), 359n.

87. Eisenhower to Ismay, 14 January 1959, Dwight D. Eisenhower, Presidential Papers, Ann Whitman File, Name Series, Box 19, Lord Ismay (2), EL.

88. *The New American Bible* (New York: Catholic Book Publishing, 1970), 574.

7

The Official Historians Weigh In with Ismay and Tedder

The failure to open Antwerp is jeopardizing the administrative soundness of our entire winter campaign. . . . The present lack of support of [the] US 3rd and 9th Armies and minimum support of the 1st Army cannot be rectified until Antwerp is opened. Fifteen divisions are held impotent for lack of success in this relatively small operation, and this weakness may involve us in winter weather to such an extent that our advance into Germany may be delayed until spring.

--Colonel William Whipple
SHAEF Logistical Plans Branch, 8 October 1944[1]

This chapter focuses on logistics, the sinews of war, as the final logistics volume in the American official history appeared in 1959. The official Canadian volume pertinent to this controversy appeared in 1960, and the final volume in the British official history appeared in 1968. The final memoirs of eyewitnesses to these events were those of Ismay in 1960 and Tedder in 1966, and both associated with the Eisenhower camp. The reader of these volumes was led to the conclusion that the search for victory in the West in September 1944 was chimerical.

On the western front, Alexander Clifford of London's *Daily Mail* spent the first day of the fifth year of the war with British mechanized units trying to catch the Germans. In the first week of September, traveling over country where their fathers had fought for four years in World War I, and where they had retreated four years before, General Dempsey's Second Army, not Patton's Third, was setting the pace. "This mad chase is getting crazier hour by hour," Clifford wrote, "you cannot keep up with it all. You can't digest it in the least as you go along. It is so big and so swift that you almost feel it is out of control." Clifford said that there was no front, simply a space between the British and the Germans, and it was all the British could do to keep up with them. "Our columns just press on and on and on behind an army whose only strength is that of desperation. The idea of what we are doing is deliriously exciting. The atmosphere is heady and intoxicating."[2]

Within forty-eight hours, the 11th British Armored Division rolled up to the docks of Antwerp, seizing the fourth largest port in the world before the Germans could damage it. Two days later, 6 September 1944, Christopher Buckley told his readers in the *Daily Telegraph* how the seventy-three mile movement of British troops in one day had ended by chasing the Germans into and out of Brussels. Buckley proclaimed that, "It was an achievement which has scarcely a parallel in the whole realm of military history."[3]

But why did September 1944 seem to represent the great unrealized moment in the campaign? The answer lies in the history of both world wars. To British officers who had fought the Kaiser's armies, history seemed to be repeating itself. The Third Reich appeared about to collapse as the Second Reich had in October and November 1918. Everywhere in Europe the Nazis seemed to be on their last legs. In Germany Hitler was recovering from a botched assassination attempt. In Romania the pro-Axis dictatorship had been overthrown, and the new government sued for peace. The Bulgarians were also asking for peace terms. The Russians had reached the oil fields of Ploesti at the end of August, denying that essential source of oil to the Germans. Fifty German divisions were cut off in the Balkans, and another fifty-five were tied up in the Mediterranean rim from Greece and Yugoslavia into Hungary. The Danube Valley lay wide open to Russian assault.

A strategic victory in September 1944 depended on the ability of the Allies to supply their forces with enough of the tools of war to be able to prevent the Germans from catching their breath at the West Wall, known to Americans as the Siegfried Line. If the Allies could crack the Siegfried Line, cross the Rhine, and take the Ruhr, then perhaps the Germans' ability to resist would be so diminished that a race to Berlin would have ended it. The Allied problem stemmed from the fact that in the pursuit of the Germans, the distance between the front and the Allied base of operations grew until it was hundreds of miles in length. Meanwhile, the Anglo-American pursuit forced the Germans back on their base of operations. In military parlance the Allies were operating on exterior lines, and the Germans began to make the most out of operating on interior lines.

RUPPENTHAL'S *LOGISTICAL SUPPORT OF THE ARMIES*

In 1959 the student of broad front versus single thrust had available perhaps the most appropriate explanation as to why the campaign in Europe lasted eleven months rather than six. Roland G. Ruppenthal, an American official historian with his Ph.D. from the University of Wisconsin, produced his second volume on logistics. Ruppenthal, like Forrest Pogue, had been a combat historian in the European theater.[4] An earlier volume covered the period from 1941 to the logistical crisis in August 1944, and together Ruppenthal's *Logistical Support* volumes still represent the most thorough study of the impact of logistics on the campaign in northwest Europe. Ruppenthal's reader could now follow the impact of logistics on the campaign throughout the fall of 1944.

It is highly likely that the inherent defects in the Americans' organization of supply along with the personalities of the men involved in it doomed any effort to gain the Rhine or crack the Siegfried Line in 1944. As the senior American officer, General Eisenhower wore two hats: He was SCAEF as well as commanding general European theater of operations United States Army (ETOUSA). Under a reorganization completed on 17 January 1944, Lieutenant General John C. H. Lee became deputy theater commander. Lee had previously been commanding general ETOUSA-SOS (Service of Supply), which was now Communications Zone (COMZ); during the campaign in Europe COMZ would transport supplies from the Normandy base section to the forward units. Known to his friends as "Cliff" and to troops as "Jesus Christ Himself," Lee had a reputation as a hard-working martinet who delegated considerable authority to subordinates.[5]

On 17 July 1944, Eisenhower eliminated Lee's position as deputy theater commander, but Lee continued to regard his headquarters as a theater headquarters. While Eisenhower downgraded COMZ to equality with the ground and air forces commands, he cautioned SHAEF staff officers not to interfere with Lee's subordinates or methods. Ruppenthal concluded that SHAEF actually performed the functions of a theater staff, while COMZ performed the G-4 supply function. Eisenhower's use of a special staff to do the work normally assigned to a general staff perforce left the separation of responsibilities indistinct. Far from the ideal arrangement, it led to continuous hostility between SHAEF and COMZ on the one hand and the field commanders and COMZ on the other. Ruppenthal noted that personalities affected the operations of any organization and conceivably ETOUSA-COMZ "might have worked better in other hands"--in other words, Lee should have been relieved.[6]

Montgomery's unpublished "Notes on the Campaign in North-Western Europe" contained a perceptive comment on the American logistical setup. The 21st Army Group commander pointed out that in the American army, unlike the British army, an army group commander or corps commander had no determination in the distribution of material. The field marshal also doubted that the American system could be made to work given that Lee was also a commanding general rather than a staff officer. Too often the American solution to any problem was simply to relieve officers, but in this case, Montgomery was certain that the fundamental problem--the faulty organization--would remain.

Lieutenant General Sir Humphrey Myddleton Gale, Eisenhower's chief Administrative officer, kept a diary during the war, which is now in the Liddell Hart Center for Military Archives, King's College, London. The Gale diary shows how poorly SHAEF grasped the logistical handle on the campaign in the fall of 1944. Never impressed by SHAEF's logistical setup from the outset, Montgomery must have been floored when Gale admitted to him on 21 September 1944, concerning SHAEF: "In actual fact we have no means of knowing the exact logistical situation of the American Armies as their system dictates that this information is in the hands of Communications Zone and even their Army Group does not know the details."[7]

The field marshal believed that the American problem stemmed from not having any "Q" control as the British system enjoyed. The British divided their staff officers into "A" Staff and "A" Services that handled personnel, judge advocate, certain military police functions, and medical and religious services. The "Q" Maintenance services controlled and ran the line of communication, set up field maintenance centers, ran divisional administration, and estimated the scale of reserves and the priority of movement. "Q" Movements handled ports and rail, inland waterway, air, and truck transportation. In the British system every headquarters echelon had both "Q" and "A" officers as well as "O" officers, who handled the operational aspects of the profession. Montgomery's chief Administrative officer, General Graham, was not only a staff officer but also a commander who controlled his own line of communications.[8]

As Ruppenthal pointed out, the OVERLORD planners assumed that the Germans would hold up the Allied advance to the Seine for three months. The planners assumed that the Allies would pause for a logistical buildup at the Seine, allowing them to resume their offensive after about a month.[9] The strategic assumptions bore little relation to what took place, however, and on 19 August 1944 the supreme commander decided to pursue the Germans at the maximum rate allowed by Allied logistical capabilities.[10] As a result of Eisenhower's decision, COMZ was unable to perform its second mission of building up a system of depots while supplying troops.

The problem in August and September 1944, as pointed out in the American official history, was never a shortage of gasoline. Rather, it was a shortage of trucks with which to get the gasoline to the front. Ruppenthal described how ETOUSA rejected the 1943 recommendation of the Transportation Corps that COMZ would need 240 truck companies to meet its three hauling needs: port clearance, interdepot operations, and long-haul line-of-communication. ETOUSA recommended 100 companies and eventually compromised on 160.[11] Given that the number of truck companies in the European theater was two-thirds what the Transportation Corps had recommended, the difficulties in supplying rations, gasoline, ammunition, spare parts, replacements, and hundreds of other items come into sharper focus. On top of that, Eisenhower's almost inevitable decision to pursue the Germans without pause accentuated the theater's critical truck shortage.

Supply officers resorted to expediency. For example, they commandeered trucks from newly arrived divisions to create additional truck companies. They cut back on the number of support troops engaged in clearing ports and used these troops to deliver supplies to the front, thus causing delays and backlogs at the ports. The emergency forced supply officers to cut back or ignore shipping replacement engines and spare parts to the front. Ruppenthal concluded:

These were obviously makeshift arrangements which could not be continued indefinitely and later exacted a big price. They were expedients, moreover, which were attended by such practices as hijacking supplies and "diverting" entire truck companies, and involved many other irregular practices which prevented an orderly and business like organization of the

Communications Zone. They left deep scars and had a prolonged effect on its ability to serve the armies.[12]

The most famous of the expedients was the Red Ball Express, which began operation on 25 August 1944. Operating twenty-four hours a day and with headlights at night, the spur-of-the-moment truck convoys were supposed to enjoy one-way traffic from the beaches and the Channel ports to the armies. Out of an average of 5,400 trucks in total, about 1,542 trucks per day delivered a daily average of 8,209 tons over an average round trip of 714 miles. The Red Ball had an offshoot known as Red Lion that delivered supplies to Montgomery during the Arnhem operation. During Red Ball's eighty-one day history, which ended on 16 November 1944 when the Normandy beaches ceased off-loading, it had delivered 412,193 tons of supplies. The frantic pace took its toll on the drivers and trucks, which suffered from excessive use, speed, and weight, not to mention a lack of scheduled maintenance. Overworked drivers had numerous accidents, but passing and other violations accounted for one-third of all accidents requiring vehicle replacement. By the end of September, the average number of repairs ran to 1,500 a day.[13]

It was amazing that the Allies moved as far and as fast as they did. Traffic jams behind the lines in Normandy had been so extensive that only the absence of a German aerial threat prevented two possible disasters: one, the breakdown of the logistical system in July; and two, the strafing of columns that were miles long.[14] The Allies had jumped the Seine, junked the buildup, hijacked supplies, failed to clear important ports, and wasted time clearing others in Brittany, all the while wearing out critical engines, tanks, gun tubes, tracks, and tires. Not to mention that in the middle of September, the weather in Europe changed as ground troops entered Germany.

Postwar and even contemporary opinion had held that with a little more gasoline delivered to the right commander in September the war would have been over by Christmas, but Ruppenthal argued that this view ignored the requirements of modern warfare. Due to six weeks of pursuit, 25 July to 4 September 1944, ordnance equipment, especially trucks and tanks, were badly worn. "The whirlwind advances of August and September," the official historian noted, "left Communications Zone in the condition of an immature athlete who has overextended himself in his first test of endurance."[15] Whether a single axis of advance as proposed by Patton or Montgomery would have taxed equipment and personnel sufficiently less to have resulted in a strategic victory is open to question.

When Eisenhower approved Montgomery's MARKET-GARDEN plan, the British had all their transport on the road as well; there were no reserves of trucks anywhere in the theater. Wilmot's *The Struggle for Europe* pointed out that the British discovered in early September 1944 that 1,400 of their three-ton trucks along with their entire pool of replacement engines had defective piston rings. These trucks represented the daily maintenance demands of two British divisions, and only by rigging substitutes was Dempsey's Second Army able to get as far as Brussels and Antwerp.[16]

By SHAEF's calculations in early September 1944, it could form 181 truck companies, and in addition it could airlift the equivalent of another 60, giving SHAEF the recommended capacity of 240 truck companies put forward by the Transportation Corps. SHAEF believed that this capacity could support five corps: three driving on Berlin; or one British army driving on Bremen-Hamburg and another American army driving toward Frankfurt-Magdeburg. This meant the grounding of ten American divisions and leaving twelve more in secondary roles, virtually half of the Allied Expeditionary Force. Logistically, the plan was based on the assumption of reaching the Rhine and using Antwerp by 15 September 1944. The official historian concluded that, "Logistical limitations at the beginning of September thus made it inadvisable to attempt either of the two schemes outlined above."[17]

Logistical considerations came to dominate operational plans by mid-September. With a perverse logic every extension of the front eastward toward the Rhine brought about its inverse. That is, fewer divisions could be supported at the front owing to the additional distance required to haul fuel. Because the trucks hauled fuel to the front at the expense of clearing the ports, ports developed chronic backlogs, and supplies built up faster than they could be discharged. While the port-discharge problem remained unsolved, over 100 Liberty ships waited in England because there was not enough dock space in Allied-occupied Europe to unload them. Ruppenthal quoted one experienced staff officer who remarked with tongue in cheek, "The general principle is that the number of divisions required to capture the number of ports required to maintain those divisions is always greater than the number of divisions those ports can maintain."[18]

In the midst of this supply fiasco, one of General Lee's deputies, Brigadier General Royal B. Lord, moved COMZ headquarters 200 miles from Valognes to Paris on 1 September 1944, without his superior's knowledge or prior approval. Lee himself had just had the engineers complete a Nissan cantonment for over 11,000 officers and men, containing over a half-million square feet of space. The rats' rush was on for the hotel suites of Paris that Eisenhower wanted reserved for resting the combat troops but had failed to order it to happen. Forrest Pogue cited the French governor of Paris, General Pierre Joseph Koenig, who told Eisenhower that the Americans demanded more hotel space than Paris possessed; some Parisians thought that the Americans exceeded the Germans in this regard. In fact, COMZ wanted even more space, but none was available. Even though Eisenhower "sharply reproved" Lee for moving to Paris and commandeering over 300 hotels, the supreme commander realized he could not afford the trucks and the gasoline required to undo the *fait accompli*.[19]

Worse still, COMZ provided Eisenhower's communications at Granville, and when it took off, SHAEF's telegraphic signaling capacity was affected. For example, Eisenhower's two-part message to Montgomery of 5 September arrived in reverse order at Montgomery's headquarters on 7 September and 9 September 1944. Commenting to Forrest Pogue on the affair, SHAEF's Signals officer, Major General C.H.H. Vulliamy, called it a "shocking business." In his defense after the war, Lee told Pogue, "We took no hotel in Paris which had not been held by the

Germans." Furthermore, as the head of COMZ put it, "The rear echelon people have their morale problems too."[20]

The COMZ move into Paris could not have occurred at a more inopportune time. When a mechanized army is in pursuit, it needs more gasoline than ammunition, and when it is in a defensive battle, the opposite holds true. An important question in the logistical shortage was how much was enough. Eisenhower in 1948 and Wilmot in 1952 pointed out that an American division had a maintenance requirement of 600 to 700 tons per day. The Allies discovered that 500 tons per day kept a division adequately maintained, however. Wilmot noted that Montgomery's planned advance beyond the Ruhr was based on supplying his divisions 400 tons per day. After all, Patton kept eight divisions in the attack on the Moselle with a daily delivery of 3,500 tons to his army, or about 438 tons per division.[21]

The only answer to SHAEF's logistical problems was the capture and early use of the port of Antwerp, which ranked alongside New York, Rotterdam, and Hamburg as one of the world's great ports. Antwerp's potential dwarfed all the other Channel ports and expedients, such as artificial harbors and off-loading on the invasion beaches, which could not last beyond the onset of winter weather. On 4 September the British took the place. North and south of the city on both banks of the Scheldt lay almost thirty miles of quays and over 600 cranes, 900 warehouses, and almost 500 storage tanks for 124 million gallons of petroleum, oil, and lubricants. Furthermore, Antwerp had 500 miles of railroad tracks that integrated it into the Belgian railway system, which consisted of over 3,250 miles of tracks and was supplemented by over 1,370 miles of navigable waterways, including the Albert Canal. Unlike many other inland ports, Antwerp was reached by an estuary that was twenty-seven feet deep, making it usable around the clock.[22]

On 3 September 1944, Admiral Ramsay, the Allied naval commander, warned SHAEF and the 21st Army Group that both Antwerp and Rotterdam were vulnerable to blocking and mining, and if the Germans did either, no one could guess when the ports might be opened. One month later, following the battle for Arnhem, SHAEF's head of Logistical Plans Branch, Colonel William Whipple, issued the warning quoted at the beginning of this chapter. The first ship unloaded in Antwerp was the *James Weaver* on 28 November, but COMZ procedures prevented the opening of the port from immediately solving the crisis in transporting supplies to the front. Instead of establishing depots to store previously unloaded goods awaiting shipment, COMZ used railroad boxcars as storage containers. When the boxcars were full, after several days or weeks, they would be shipped, violating all known tenets of transport.[23]

American logistics planners estimated that Antwerp would discharge 15,000 tons a day in December, 21,500 in January, and 22,500 tons by March 1945. After the first week, Antwerp was up to 10,000 tons per day, and it discharged an average of 19,000 tons per day in its second week. At the end of January 1945, Antwerp discharged an average of 18,000 tons per day, while by contrast the far smaller ports of Le Havre and Rouen did 12,000 and 13,000, respectively. Thanks to

Antwerp, however, the American intake for the month of January 1945 was double October's figures.[24]

Ruppenthal pointed out that the opening of Antwerp alleviated the problem of insufficient port capacity.[25] It was also a relief to Montgomery, whose "Notes on the Campaign in North-Western Europe" recorded the following:

The elimination of the ANTWERP commitment was a great relief to the Field-Marshal, as American opinion would now have no cause for complaint. From a purely British point of view ANTWERP had never been a vital necessity; the PAS DE CALAIS ports provided all that we required. But to the Americans it had become vital; and for the British Armies it would be very convenient and would save a long haul over bad roads.[26]

By the time the Canadians took Walcheren Island and cleared the banks of the Scheldt Estuary, it was too late to end the war in 1944. Putting the operational cart before the logistical horse from August through September limited the Allies to the positions they held when gasoline could not reach their advanced units but the Germans could.

STACEY'S *THE VICTORY CAMPAIGN*

In 1960 the third volume in the Canadian official history *The Victory Campaign*, by Colonel Charles P. Stacey, appeared. Stacey pointed out that Eisenhower's 10 September decision to back Montgomery's attack through Holland represented enough of a change from the previous plan outlined to General Marshall that he sent a detailed explanation to the chief of staff. Implied in Eisenhower's tone was a fear of criticism that he might be going too far to appease the British.[27]

The Canadian historian offered what was arguably the most insightful discussion of the issue in print to that time. Stacey noted that the force Montgomery was advocating for a single thrust in early September was about twenty divisions: The Second British Army had eight, the First Canadian Army had six, there were three airborne divisions in England, and the First United States Army had nine, for a total of twenty-six. Twenty divisions represented more than half of the Allied divisions in the European theater. The Canadian official historian wrote, "The fate of the entire enterprise would have depended upon this relatively small group, for the rest of the Allied Expeditionary Force would have been immobilized, or largely immobilized, by the diversion of administrative resources, particularly gasoline, to support the thrust."[28]

German strength estimated by SHAEF's intelligence summary for the week ending 9 September totaled forty-eight divisions, including fourteen panzer or panzer grenadier, and thirty-four infantry. SHAEF concluded that their effective strength was more like four panzer and twenty infantry divisions, and four of those were isolated in French coastal garrisons. By 15 September 1944, the German commander in the West, Field Marshal Gerd von Rundstedt, informed Colonel General Alfred Jodl, chief of operations *Oberkommando der Wehrmacht* (OKW),

High Command of the Armed Forces, that Army Group B had eighty-four tanks, assault guns, and antitank guns in twelve divisions to hold a front of 250 miles.[29]

Stacey believed that 4 September 1944 was the critical moment for Germans and Allies alike. The Germans had virtually no armor and were badly unbalanced. If at this point the British had cut off the escape of the German Fifteenth Army by blocking the South Beveland isthmus, less than one and one-half miles wide at its narrowest point, and struck another heavy blow in the north, then, Stacey believed, it would have been too much for the Germans. However, this moment coincided with the height of the Allied supply crisis. The 21st Army Group's supplies were coming from the beachhead with the addition of the small port of Dieppe. Therefore, to do what Montgomery was asking would have meant immobilizing all other Allied formations. Furthermore, Stacey concluded that Montgomery's logistical planning was unsound. The field marshal made his Ruhr plans on the assumption that he would have "'one good Pas de Calais port.'" Yet, Boulogne would not be opened to shipping until 12 October, owing to the thoroughness of the German demolitions.[30]

By the time of Arnhem, the Germans had collected enough armor to repulse the 1st British Airborne Division and to intervene effectively north of Nijmegen. Given the German reaction during MARKET-GARDEN, a very difficult fight would have taken place east of the Rhine. Stacey speculated on what might have happened to an Allied single thrust as recommended by Montgomery:

Finally, it may be assumed that Hitler would not have accepted defeat in the West without withdrawing troops from the Eastern Front in an attempt to stave it off. It would not have been easy to find the troops; but two or three panzer divisions from the East, if they arrived in time, might well have turned the scale against an ill maintained and tired Allied army group in an autumn battle on the North German Plain. The available records suggest that two panzer divisions might possibly have been found on the Eastern Front from the 3rd Panzer Corps of the Fourth Panzer Army.[31]

Nevertheless, Stacey considered it possible that Montgomery's daring Operation MARKET-GARDEN might have gained the Rhine in 1944, pointing out the considerable changes Eisenhower made to his original plan to support Montgomery's single thrust. Based on the bureaucratic success of getting Eisenhower's backing for his offensive on Arnhem, Montgomery wrote at the time that it was "a great victory." "I feel somewhat overcome by it all but hope we shall now win the war reasonably quickly."[32]

ISMAY'S *MEMOIRS*

In 1960 General Hastings Lionel Lord Ismay published *The Memoirs of General Lord Ismay*. Most recently, Ismay had been secretary-general of the North Atlantic Treaty Organization and before that Lord Mountbatten's chief of staff in the last days of the Raj in India. During World War II, Ismay, known as "Pug" to his friends, was chief of staff to the minister of defense and Churchill's representative to the British Chiefs of Staff Committee. Ismay was the channel for communication between the Chiefs and the minister of defense, but he did not sign documents put out by the Chiefs; he was there to confer. Basically, he was the head of the Chiefs of Staff Secretariat.[33] Ismay's *Memoirs* are the best written of the works under consideration in this study.

With many years of staff jobs and colonial assignments behind him, Ismay was sensitive to the Montgomery-Brooke criticism of Eisenhower that he had no combat or command experience. Sounding remarkably like revisionist historians on the Eisenhower presidency, Ismay pronounced unfair the criticism of Eisenhower as a mere chairman. Neither was Eisenhower an amateur commander or strategist; Ismay believed that it was a ridiculous charge to level at a man who had spent all his adult life in the practice of the military profession. Oliver Cromwell and Stonewall Jackson, Ismay said, had managed well enough with no prior battlefield experience. After all as Ismay noted, Frederick the Great's mules had been through many campaigns, but they were still mules.[34]

Ismay wondered why after Eisenhower had commanded one of the most successful campaigns in military history there were still so many critics belittling his accomplishments. To the charges that Eisenhower's interference had prolonged the war by six months, Ismay answered, "Since the conduct of war is an art, and not a science, these dogmatic calculations must be accepted with reserve. What might have happened is in the realm of speculation. What did happen was singular and precise--overwhelming victory."[35]

In January 1945, the prime minister requested a Combined Chiefs of Staff conference in Malta before the February meeting of the Big Three at Yalta. On the agenda was a discussion of Eisenhower's progress report and his plans for the upcoming campaign, which had been requested by the British Chiefs of Staff. In 1947 Ismay told Forrest Pogue that he had warned the British Chiefs that General Marshall would take their request as a vote of no confidence in Eisenhower, as was pointed out in Chapter 6.[36] Eisenhower did not attend the meeting, instead, he sent General Smith, his chief of staff, General Bull, his G-3 Operations, and Air Marshal Robb, his deputy chief of staff for air.

The British Chiefs arrived at Malta with a plan that they wanted adopted as Eisenhower's directive from the Combined Chiefs of Staff. Sir Arthur Bryant published both the draft and final versions in *Triumph in the West*. The British plan was a blueprint for both single thrust and a land forces commander; it was a vote of no confidence and read as follows:

(a) All the resources which can be made available for offensive operations should be concentrated on one main thrust. This thrust should be made in the maximum possible strength with sufficient fresh formations held available to keep up the momentum of the advance. Only such forces as cannot be employed to support this main thrust should be used for subsidiary operations. Only if the main thrust is held and the subsidiary operations prosper should the latter be exploited.
(b) If tactical considerations allow, this main thrust should be made in the north, in view of the overriding importance to the enemy of the Ruhr area.

(c) The best result will be achieved if one Land Force Commander directly responsible to you, is given power of operational control and coordination of all ground forces in the main thrust.[37]

The American Joint Chiefs of Staff were convinced that Eisenhower fully intended to make the main thrust in the north. General Smith in discussion on 30 January 1945 pointed out to the Combined Chiefs that the 21st Army Group estimated that it could maintain twenty to twenty-one divisions in the north. Eisenhower deemed that insufficient for the main thrust, and he directed that every logistical effort be made to support thirty divisions in the main effort; later, this was upped to thirty-six divisions. Smith pointed out that the roadnet in the north limited the attack to twenty-five divisions; there would be a reserve of about ten divisions. Thus, under Eisenhower's plan twelve divisions would take part in the secondary offensive. General Bull pointed out the importance of flexibility in Eisenhower's plan. The relatively short length of the Rhine necessitated alternative crossings so as to draw off Germans from the scene of the major effort. Bull said that Eisenhower wanted secondary crossings as far south as Mainz-Mannheim and an advance on the line Frankfurt-Kassel. Speaking to Bull's point, General Smith said a secondary effort in the Cologne area was too close to Montgomery's crossing in the north to compel the Germans to disperse their forces, and too little diversion value would be gained by threatening a crossing so near Cologne.[38]

The British Chiefs liked what they heard, and it was agreed that Smith would redraft the original Eisenhower plan to conform to Smith's explanation of it. Smith telegraphed the second draft to Eisenhower, who accepted it but added, "I will advance across the Rhine in the North with maximum strength and complete determination as soon as the situation in the South allows me to collect the necessary forces and do this without incurring unnecessary risks."[39] The British Chiefs balked at this sentence. On the night of 31 January, Brooke and Smith had a long talk. When Brooke doubted Eisenhower's ability to command and referred to him as a "good chairman of the board," Smith responded that Brooke should ask the Combined Chiefs of Staff to replace Eisenhower. Brooke feared Eisenhower's readiness to compromise would lead to another September fiasco where the main assault faltered through failure to concentrate. The CIGS admitted, however, that there was no one who could perform the supreme commander's job as well as Eisenhower.

During their 1 February 1945 meeting, the political struggle for command was settled by the Chief of Staff of the United States Army in favor of Eisenhower. Marshall wanted Eisenhower's plan approved, and he opposed issuing a directive to the supreme commander. Brooke refused to approve Eisenhower's appreciation; instead, he would only "take note" of it. Months of debate culminated when General Marshall asked the secretaries to leave. At that point, according to Brooke's published diary, Marshall expressed his "dislike and antipathy for Montgomery." As Ismay described it, "the altercation which ensued was vehement and at times acrimonious," but the British had no choice but to go along. Brooke's unpublished diary stated that, "Marshall clearly understood nothing of strategy and could not even argue out the relative merits of various alternatives. Being unable to judge for himself he trusted and backed Ike, and felt it was his duty to guard him from interference."[40]

At this point in the campaign, Brooke and Montgomery guessed that Eisenhower would close to the entire length of the river before crossing in the north, the site of the scheduled main effort under Montgomery. The field marshals also thought that Eisenhower and Bradley would prolong the war by doing so. Their expectations proved correct, their fears exaggerated. Eisenhower's strategy worked in this instance. Despite his assurances to the Combined Chiefs of Staff, Eisenhower did close to the line of the Rhine, and in the process two American armies jumped the river without pause. Third Army's Oppenheim crossing was midway between Mainz and Mannheim in the area Smith described to the Combined Chiefs at Malta.

Following publication of Ismay's *Memoirs*, on 3 December 1960 President Eisenhower sent him a twelve-page letter, commenting on his book and the broad front. Eisenhower related how he had taken Tedder and Gale to his meeting in Brussels with Montgomery on 10 September 1944. Eisenhower wrote, "That was the time when the so-called 'pencil thrust' really came into our vocabulary. We were unanimous in our convictions that his scheme was impractical--in fact, slightly harebrained." Eisenhower concluded that Montgomery's subsequent Arnhem operation proved the impracticality of a long thrust to Berlin. By the time the Allies got to the Rhine in 1945, Eisenhower wrote, they had far too many divisions to be supported on any one line of communications. Not to have used all the forces available or to have employed them in column, as Montgomery proposed doing, would have been an "unwarranted *dispersion in depth*." The British proposal in the spring of 1945 would have idled American forces rather than employing them to destroy the German army.[41]

Eisenhower explained that his decision to remove the Ninth Army from Montgomery's command and give it to Bradley resulted from his staff's conclusion that the coastal areas of Germany provided the worst route into the interior of the country in early April 1945. Furthermore, Eisenhower was criticized by Brooke because the CIGS believed Eisenhower's main advance, now under Bradley, was too narrow. Brooke wanted the Ninth Army reassigned to Montgomery--in other words, to broaden the 21st Army Group's front. In conclusion, Eisenhower wrote, "The terms broad front and narrow front mean now and meant then nothing, unless they were applied to specific cases and specific circumstances."[42]

TEDDER'S *WITH PREJUDICE*

The deputy supreme commander of the Allied Expeditionary Force was Air Chief Marshal Sir Arthur Tedder, RAF. During World War I, Tedder turned from infantry to flying in 1915. Always more of an administrator than a pilot, he made a name for himself in North Africa, where he commanded the Middle East Air Force. Tedder waited until 1966, following Churchill's death, to publish his memoir *With Prejudice: The War Memoirs of Marshal of the Royal Air Force Lord Tedder*. Tedder's memoir was the last of the high command and as such could reflect on much that had been written. A personal animus existed between Montgomery and Tedder, which originated in North Africa and festered in Normandy, during the battle for Caen. Butcher's unpublished diary noted that Tedder wanted Montgomery sacked for his failure to promptly take Caen and its surrounding airfields. Tedder and Montgomery worked together after the war when Montgomery was CIGS and Tedder, by then marshal of the Royal Air Force and a lord, was chief of air staff, but neither could stand the other.[43]

Tedder was afraid that what he perceived as Montgomery's and Churchill's distortions of history would be allowed to stand if left unchallenged. Writing to Eisenhower on 22 January 1960, Tedder thanked the president for hosting a dinner of World War II associates at Regents Park in September 1959. The dinner was a memorable occasion, "happily free from any sparks despite the presence of two modest 'authors,'" that is, Alanbrooke and Montgomery. It was in fact the last time that Eisenhower and Montgomery were in the other's company. A large part of the letter explained Tedder's conflicting emotions concerning writing on the war. Tedder and Marshal of the Royal Air Force Lord Portal had been silent up to 1960, and he recognized that silence was the more dignified course. On the other hand, many people had pressed Tedder to "'come into the open'" and "correct the perversions and debunk the myths."[44] In 1963 Tedder wrote to British military historian Basil H. Liddell Hart:

I wonder if it has struck you that there is a remarkable likeness between Monty and Winston in their respective attitudes toward history. In other words, each of them determined, so far as lay within his own power, to make sure that his story should record his own version of events rather than history. . . . Indeed, while it is evident that Winston's story will in due course be disentangled, on the other hand as regards Monty the record was so skillfully adjusted at the time that I see little, if any, prospects of the truth being disentangled from the story.[45]

As a witness to the 10 September 1944 Brussels meeting between Eisenhower and Montgomery, Tedder shed new light on the strategic discussion. Eisenhower told Montgomery that without railway bridges over the Rhine and plentiful supplies, there could be no talk of going to Berlin. Tedder cabled Portal that "the advance to Berlin was not discussed as a serious issue, nor do I believe it was so intended. The real issue is the degree of priority given to the American Corps operating on Montgomery's right flank, and the extent to which Montgomery controls operations."[46] Because the British left hook was largely dependent on the beachhead for its supplies, no consideration was given to Montgomery's Berlin objective.

With Prejudice squared the circle when it came to the command views of the British Chiefs of Staff, relating Tedder's 2 December 1944 meeting with Chief of the Air Staff Marshal Portal. Portal had just come from talking with Montgomery and was convinced of the need for a ground forces commander; there had been too much dispersal of effort and not enough concentration. According to Portal, one man needed to be in charge of the ground battle. Tedder disagreed. The larger point to be considered was that the British Chiefs were of one mind well before the German Ardennes counteroffensive. Neither Admiral Cunningham nor Brooke believed the supreme commander ought to attempt to exercise ground command as well.[47]

Clearly, by the first week of December 1944, Eisenhower's stock as a ground commander had fallen to a very low point at Whitehall. On 8 January 1945, the British War Cabinet heard the next line of attack on Eisenhower's conduct of ground operations: "The Prime Minister also expressed doubts as to whether in present circumstances it would not be better to have an Army Officer as Second-in-Command to General Eisenhower instead of Air Marshal Tedder, who had been placed in that post in view of the extreme importance of the air weapon at the time of the original assault."[48]

According to Tedder's account, while he was traveling to Moscow attempting to pin down the date of the upcoming Soviet offensive, Churchill on 4 January 1945 talked to Eisenhower about bringing in Alexander from Italy. The talk at that time was that Tedder was headed to the Air Ministry to became Portal's deputy.[49] When Tedder returned from Moscow on 29 January, Eisenhower informed him that he had already asked for Alexander. *With Prejudice* mentioned that Admiral William D. Leahy, President Roosevelt's chief of staff, stated in his memoir that Churchill brought up at Yalta the idea of substituting Alexander for Tedder as deputy supreme commander.[50]

"Montgomery," Tedder wrote, "apparently forgetting that he had been consulted about, and had welcomed, my proposed replacement, records in his *Memoirs* his amazement that the question of a ground force commander was reopened in February 1945 by the Prime Minister."[51] Brooke's published diary mentioned that the CIGS broached the idea with Montgomery on 5 January 1945.[52] Concerning Tedder's replacement by Alexander, Montgomery knew from de Guingand that Marshall would not countenance a ground forces commander, and Eisenhower had made it clear that he would tolerate nothing more from Montgomery concerning the command setup. Much had changed in northwest Europe while Tedder was in Moscow. Montgomery wrote in 1958 that to bring in Alexander would have created a storm of protest from the press and the American generals.

Montgomery's *Memoirs* detailed Eisenhower's visit to Montgomery's headquarters on 14 February. The supreme commander said that Churchill had told either the president or Marshall at Malta that Eisenhower did not visit Montgomery often enough. The implication was that the British were being ignored. Eisenhower was in an invidious position. When he was solicitous of the British, then he was the "best general the British have got." If he favored an American plan, then his national prejudice was criticized. Eisenhower wanted to know what Montgomery thought of the command setup at the present. The field marshal said that he understood that Eisenhower did not want anyone between himself and his army group commanders, and added that the command setup at present was satisfactory.[53]

Judging that any contretemps over command began with Montgomery, Eisenhower was relieved to find that the senior British officer in the European theater was finally satisfied. *With Prejudice* stated that on 15 February Eisenhower told Tedder that he would take Alexander as his deputy only in a political-cum-economic function, not in a military role. Eisenhower told Tedder, "I will have nobody standing between me and my Group Commanders."[54] Tedder was highlighting what Pogue's *The Supreme Command* had already pointed out about command. On 16 February, Eisenhower wrote his strongest letter of the war to the CIGS. The supreme commander stated that he would not have any ground forces headquarters, official or otherwise, between himself and his army group commanders. As Pogue pointed out, the supreme commander warned Brooke that if the British press should trumpet Alexander's proposed appointment as the establishment of a ground headquarters, he would state publicly that it was not. Such an announcement would hurt Alexander's feelings unnecessarily and might jeopardize the goodwill built up within the alliance.[55] On 5 March 1945, the prime minister in a meeting with Eisenhower and Tedder accepted the command arrangements as they were. Brooke's nightly entry for the next day said that "to insert Alex now is only likely to lead to immediate trouble for all I gather. . . . Therefore, I feel it is best to leave Alex where he is."[56]

ELLIS' AND WARHURST'S *VICTORY IN THE WEST*

This chapter concludes with a discussion of the 1968 British official history by Major Lionel F. Ellis with Lieutenant Colonel Arthur Warhurst, *Victory in the West,* vol. 2, *The Defeat of Germany (History of the Second World War: United Kingdom Military Series).* By the time the second volume of *Victory in the West* appeared, the British official historians were able to use all the principal postwar memoirs. Ellis pinpointed the origin of broad front to the May 1944 policy paper, which argued for a broad front and against a narrow thrust. Eisenhower approved his planners' strategy and utilized his army group commanders to modify it and to carry it out. He presented the plan to his naval and air commanders in May 1944 and asked for their concurrence. Ellis could find no evidence, however, that Montgomery ever saw the planning document.[57]

Concerning Montgomery's claim that the single northern thrust could have ended the war in 1944 if Eisenhower had given it more support, Ellis said that Montgomery's contention "is open to question." There could have been no marked improvement in operations without similar improvement in administration. *Victory in the West* also took issue with Montgomery's assertion that Eisenhower did not stress Antwerp until 9 October 1944, pointing out that Montgomery himself had been the first to mention the importance of taking Antwerp in August. Furthermore, Eisenhower's directive of 4 September stated, "The mission of the Northern Group of Armies . . . is to secure Antwerp, breach the Siegfried Line covering the Ruhr and seize the Ruhr." As Ellis told it, there was enough blame over Arnhem and Antwerp to attach to both Eisenhower and Montgomery. Eisenhower knew when he approved the Arnhem operation that it would delay the opening of the Scheldt. Montgomery liked to say that Eisenhower's directive of 15 September contained four objectives, but he knew the difference between a long- and short-term objective. Eisenhower left it to his army group commanders how they would accomplish their missions, and even though Montgomery's long-term mission was the Ruhr, he knew his short-term objective was opening Antwerp to ship traffic. Commenting on Montgomery's *Memoirs*, the British official historian said that its charge that Eisenhower failed to give Antwerp first priority until 9 October "is hardly justified."[58]

Ellis devoted as much attention to Montgomery's views on command as his strategic conceptions. For example, the official history reprinted Montgomery's "Notes on Command in Western Europe" of 10 October 1944. Ellis followed that document with the Eisenhower rebuke of 13 October. *Victory in the West* also contained the fullest discussion of Eisenhower's ultimatum to Montgomery over the issue of command at the end of December 1944. Ellis made use of the Montgomery *Memoirs* as well as Pogue's *The Supreme Command* and included de Guingand's most recent account contained in his 1964 *Generals at War*.[59]

Ellis did not let Eisenhower escape criticism for the Antwerp fiasco. The British official historian believed that Eisenhower should not have waited until 9 October before announcing his dissatisfaction with the rate of progress in clearing the Scheldt. Even more remarkable was the Admiralty's silence over the port's clearance, with the single exception of Admiral Ramsay's 3 September warning. Unfortunately, besides the Germans and Ramsay, few others were paying attention to Antwerp's approaches. Before Antwerp was open, the Allies lived from hand to mouth; after it was open, they kept eighty-four divisions supplied and had excess port capacity.[60] SHAEF, Ellis pointed out, immediately adopted this logistical improvement into its thinking about the next campaigning season. From December 1944 on, SHAEF concluded that there would be no great problems in supply and therefore units could continue to fight in the winter and expect to thrust deep into Germany by next spring.[61] Neither Brooke nor Montgomery seemed to have made a similar mental adjustment to the changed supply setting.

The British official historian also took issue with Brooke's and Montgomery's insistence on the principle of concentration in light of the improved supply situation. As a general rule, concentration was better to follow than to ignore, but to insist on it in March 1945 when there were eighty-five divisions in the European theater made considerably less sense than it did in September 1944 when there were about forty.[62]

Ellis concluded that Eisenhower made a serious mistake in undertaking the Arnhem operation before Antwerp was open to ships. Ellis wrote, "It is difficult to avoid the conclusion that General Eisenhower should have said on the 10th of September that not another day should be lost before Twenty-First Army Group freed Antwerp port."[63] Hastening to point out that this was not simply hindsight, Ellis added that Eisenhower realized at the time that a bridge over the Rhine was not going to solve the supply problem behind it. According to the official historian, Montgomery allowed himself to become distracted by the singular notion that

Eisenhower's direction of the battle was likely to prolong the war. For a time in the fall of 1944, Ellis believed Montgomery lost his feel for operations, that is, at Arnhem.[64]

CONCLUSION

Ruppenthal, Stacey, and Ellis taken together raised the question as to whether anything other than stalemate could have resulted from the strategic decisions and the logistical realities of August and September 1944. None of the official historians believed that a single thrust under Montgomery or Patton would have ended the war in northwest Europe in 1944. These books also raised the question of whether or not Eisenhower ever gave serious consideration to Montgomery's single thrust on or toward Berlin. The evidence cited by the official histories and by Tedder's *With Prejudice* suggests that Eisenhower never took the Berlin proposal seriously. Tedder also concluded that even Montgomery did not really propose to go to Berlin in September 1944.

Tedder's memoir taken together with that of Admiral Lord Cunningham and Field Marshal Lord Alanbrooke's published diaries proved that *all* of the British Chiefs of Staff favored a land forces commander. Therefore, the only reason why there was no ground forces commander in the European theater was that the Americans, particularly Marshall, did not want one; they certainly did not want the one they had in Normandy. A full-scale British effort was made from November 1944 to January 1945 to change the command structure in northwest Europe, but the American embarrassment over the German Ardennes counteroffensive made it politically impossible to alter the command in the ETO. Had there been no embarrassing German counterattack in December 1944 and no subsequent press crisis over command, Field Marshal Alexander might have become deputy supreme commander for ground forces.

NOTES

1. Roland G. Ruppenthal, *Logistical Support of the Armies,* vol. 2, *September 1944-May 1945 (United States Army in World War II: The European Theater of Operations,* Washington, D.C.: Office of the Chief of Military History, Department of the Army, 1959), 107.

2. "Clifford Says: This Is Victory, Not War," by Alexander Clifford, *Daily Mail* (London), 2 September 1944, p. 1.

3. Christopher Buckley, "British Chased Nazis in and out of Brussels, 73-Mile Drive in a Day Was Greatest in History," *Daily Telegraph* (London), 6 September 1944, p. 1.

4. Ruppenthal, *Logistical Support of the Armies,* vol. 2.

5. Roland G. Ruppenthal, *Logistical Support of the Armies,* vol. 1, *May 1941-September 1944 (United States Army in World War II: The European Theater of Operations,* Washington, D.C.: Office of the Chief of Military History, Department of the Army, 1953), 267-68 for Lee's personality; for Lee's nickname, see Russell F. Weigley, *Eisenhower's*

Lieutenants: The Campaign of France and Germany, 1944-1945 (Bloomington: Indiana University Press, 1981), 84.

6. For continuous hostility, see Ruppenthal, *Logistical Support of the Armies*, 1: 437-38; for personalities, see Ruppenthal, *Logistical Support of the Armies*, 2:506.

7. "Notes on the Campaign in North-Western Europe," Part V, "The Choice of the Thrust Line," 7, Papers of the Field-Marshal the Viscount Montgomery of Alamein, Reel 7, BLM 77, IWM; Gale Diary, 21 September 1944, II/22, Papers of Lieutenant General Sir Humphrey Myddleton Gale, LHCMA; Dominick Graham and Shelford Bidwell, *Coalitions, Politicians and Generals: Some Aspects of Command in Two World Wars* (London and New York: Brassey's, 1993), 271.

8. *The Administrative History of Operations of 21 Army Group on the Continent of Europe, 6 June 1944-May 1945* (Germany: November, 1945), 134, 142, 150, Center for Military History, Washington, D.C. The American general staff setup was: G-1, Personnel; G-2, Intelligence; G-3, Operations; G-4, Supply; G-5, Civil Affairs. The special staff consisted of ordnance, signal, chemical, chaplains, medical, and other support and operational services; Graham and Bidwell, *Coalitions, Politicians and Generals*, 271.

9. Ruppenthal, *Logistical Support of the Armies*, 2:6-7.

10. Ruppenthal, *Logistical Support of the Armies*, 1:479.

11. Ibid., 509; for no shortage of gasoline; for the estimate and actual number of truck companies, 315 and 553.

12. Ruppenthal, *Logistical Support of the Armies*, 2:8.

13. Ibid., for the average round trip, see 135; for tonnage delivered, 137; for accidents, 144-45.

14. Ruppenthal, *Logistical Support of the Armies*, 1:432.

15. Ruppenthal, *Logistical Support of the Armies*, 2:8.

16. Chester Wilmot, *The Struggle for Europe* (London: Collins; New York: Harper and Brothers, 1952), 472.

17. Ruppenthal, *Logistical Support of the Armies*, 2:10-11.

18. Ibid., for the port discharge problem, 12-13; for the number of divisions, 46.

19. Ruppenthal, *Logistical Support of the Armies*, 2:31; for Koenig's reaction, see Forrest C. Pogue, *The Supreme Command (United States Army in World War II: The European Theater of Operations,* Washington, D.C.: Office of the Chief of Military History, Department of the Army, 1954), 322-23.

20. For the signal of 5 September, see *The Memoirs of the Field-Marshal Viscount Montgomery of Alamein* (London: Collins, 1958), 272-73; for Vulliamy on the COMZ move, see Interview with Major General C.H.H. Vulliamy, 27 January 1947; for Lee's comments, see Interview with Lieutenant General J.C.H. Lee, 21 March 1947, OCMH Collection, *Supreme Command,* Pogue Interviews, USAMHI.

21. See Dwight D. Eisenhower, *Crusade in Europe* (Garden City, N. Y.: Doubleday, 1948), 290; Wilmot, *The Struggle for Europe*, 529-30.

22. Ruppenthal, *Logistical Support of the Armies*, 2:104-105.

23. For Ramsay's warning, see Ruppenthal, *Logistical Support of the Armies*, 2: 50; for COMZ's holding railroad cars under storage, see the Gale Diary, 1-7 December 1944, II/22, Papers of Lieutenant General Sir Humphrey Myddleton Gale, LHCMA.

24. For Antwerp, see Ruppenthal, *Logistical Support of the Armies*, 2:110; for comparison with Le Havre and Rouen, see 116.

25. Ibid., 116.

26. "Notes on the Campaign in North-Western Europe," Part V, Papers of Field Marshal the Viscount Montgomery of Alamein, Reel 7, BLM 77/8, IWM.

27. Charles P. Staccy, *The Victory Campaign, Official History of the Canadian Army in the Second World War,* vol. 3, *The Operations in North-West Europe, 1944-1945* (Ottawa: Queen's Printer and Controller of Stationery, 1960), 308.

28. Ibid., 3: 319n.; for the fate of the enterprise, ibid.

29. Ibid., 319-20.

30. Ibid., 320-21.

31. Ibid., 321.

32. Stacey, *The Victory Campaign,* 3:321-22; for Montgomery's remarks, see Montgomery to VCIGS, M-196, 13 September 1944, Papers of the Field Marshal the Viscount Montgomery of Alamein, Reel 11, BLM 128/8, IWM.

33. *The Memoirs of General Lord Ismay* (New York: Viking Press, 1960), 171-72.

34. Ibid., 313.

35. Ibid., 313-14.

36. For Ismay on the British Chiefs action as a vote of no confidence, see Interview with General Sir Hastings L. Ismay, 20 December 1946, OCMH Collection, *Supreme Command,* Pogue Interviews, USAMHI.

37. Arthur Bryant, *Triumph in the West: A History of the War Years Based on the Diaries of Field-Marshal Lord Alanbrooke, Chief of the Imperial General Staff* (Garden City, N. Y.: Doubleday, 1959), 298.

38. Bryant, *Triumph in the West,* 298-99; *The Memoirs of General Lord Ismay,* 385; Combined Chiefs of Staff, Argonaut Conference, 30 January 1945, 182d Meeting, NA, RG 218, Joint Chiefs of Staff, Box 196.

39. Bryant, *Triumph in the West,* 299.

40. For the published version, see Bryant, *Triumph in the West,* 301-302; *The Memoirs of General Lord Ismay,* 385; for Brooke on Marshall, see "Notes on My Life," vol. 14, 1 February 1945, 1121, Papers of Field Marshal Viscount Alanbrooke, LHCMA.

41. Eisenhower to Ismay, 3 December 1960, Dwight D. Eisenhower, Presidential Papers, Ann Whitman File, Name Series, Box 19, Lord Ismay (1), EL. Italics in the original.

42. Ibid.

43. Arthur Tedder, *With Prejudice: The War Memoirs of Marshal of the Royal Air Force Lord Tedder* (Boston: Little, Brown, 1966). For Harry Butcher on Tedder concerning Montgomery, see Nigel Hamilton, *Master of the Battlefield: Monty's War Years, 1942-1944* (New York: McGraw-Hill, 1983), 737-38.

44. Tedder to Eisenhower, 22 January 1960, Dwight D. Eisenhower, Presidential Papers, Ann Whitman File, Name Series, Box 53, Arthur Tedder (3), EL.

45. Carlo D'Este, *Decision in Normandy* (New York: E. P. Dutton, 1983), 494, n.3. D'Este points out that Tedder was referring to North Africa, but that his comments apply equally to the campaign in northwest Europe.

46. Tedder, *With Prejudice,* 590-91.

47. Ibid., 619.

48. PRO: CAB 65/49 War Cabinet Conclusions, 10, 8 January 1945.

49. Tedder, *With Prejudice,* 661; Tedder's source is Bryant, *Triumph in the West,* 284. Tedder dates Churchill's discussion with Eisenhower as 4 January, but Alanbrooke's printed diary dates it a day earlier.

50. Tedder, *With Prejudice,* 662; the reference to Admiral Leahy's memoirs is in William D. Leahy, *I Was There: The Personal Story of the Chief of Staff to Presidents Roosevelt and Truman Based on His Notes and Diaries Made at the Time* (New York: Whittlesey House, McGraw-Hill, 1950), 295.

51. Tedder, *With Prejudice,* 662.

52. Bryant, *Triumph in the West,* 285.

53. *The Memoirs of Field-Marshal the Viscount Montgomery* (London: Collins, 1958), 324-25.

54. Tedder, *With Prejudice,* 663.

55. Pogue, *The Supreme Command,* 390.

56. Bryant, *Triumph in the West,* 324.

57. Major Lionel F. Ellis with Lieutenant Colonel Arthur Warhurst, *Victory in the West,* vol. 2, *The Defeat of Germany (History of the Second World War: United Kingdom Military Series,* London: Her Majesty's Stationery Office, 1968), 93.

58. For "open to question," see Ellis, *Victory in the West,* 2:94; for the mission to seize Antwerp, see 94-95; for Montgomery on change of priority, see 95.

59. For "Notes on Command," see Ellis, *Victory in the West,* 2:85-88; for Eisenhower's rebuke of 13 October, see 88-91; for the December imbroglio, see 199-203; for de Guingand's account, see Francis de Guingand, *Generals at War* (London: Hodder and Stoughton, 1964), Chapter 6, "Europe 1944--A Signal that Saved the Team," 99-117.

60. Ellis, *Victory in the West,* 2:95-97, 138.

61. Ibid., 140.

62. Ibid., 347-48.

63. Ibid., 350-51.

64. Ibid., 354.

8

The Continuing Debate

Almost everyone who argues that a strategic decision in Allied strategy during World War II was wrong assumes that if we had done something different the enemy would still have done the same thing that he actually did. That, in most cases, is a major fallacy; for, if we had done something different, the enemy would have altered his strategy to counteract it.

--Samuel Eliot Morison,
Strategy and Compromise[1]

Military history promotes speculation, and the postwar memoirs contained much speculation concerning Eisenhower's strategy and command, especially his alleged failure to end the war in September 1944. Eisenhower's broad-front strategy was based on the political and military needs of the predominant member of the Anglo-American coalition, and its criticism came primarily from the subordinate member, which was never convinced of its applicability to circumstances. The myth of September 1944 stated that Eisenhower and SHAEF failed to grasp the chance to win a strategic victory in the West, and critics blamed the supreme commander for prolonging not only the war in the West but also the entire anti-Nazi war effort, as well as losing what Wilmot called "the struggle for Europe" with the Soviets.

Broad front was a political inevitability, while single thrust was an operational necessity, and political necessity triumphed. Eisenhower commanded coalition forces, primarily American, British, Canadian, and French, and each nation's forces had to play a role in Germany's defeat. Out of political necessity, Eisenhower broadened the Anglo-American approach to the Ruhr to include the United States 12th Army Group as well as the British 21st Army Group. Crossing the Rhine in the north on the line of the Ruhr became a political necessity because it promised to reward the coalition both politically and militarily. When Devers' 6th Army Group pushed patrols across the Rhine in late November 1944, Eisenhower put his foot down--the Rhine crossing would take place in the north.[2] A crossing so far south made little military sense, the roadnet was terrible, but it made even less sense from a political standpoint. The British government would not have accepted a tertiary role for 21st Army Group behind the Americans and the French.

Broad front was also a pursuit strategy, not an attack strategy. As a pursuit strategy, broad front made a great deal of sense because it forced the Germans to cover multiple avenues of approach while retreating, and it sought to use the entire roadnet of northwest Europe. Broad front made less sense, however, when the Germans won the race to their West Wall and advances were limited, much like the pre-breakout fighting in the hedgerows of Normandy. After the pursuit phase ended, Eisenhower's strategy entailed insufficiently concentrated frontal assaults through forests, like the Hürtgen debacle, in October and November.

Again on the defensive, fighting in prepared positions, defending their homeland, while the weather negated the great Allied advantage, tactical airpower, the Germans put on what has been called "the Miracle of the West." Once the Germans occupied the bunkers of the Siegfried Line, the quality of their troops was no longer as crucial as it might have been in open country. The Operations officer of the 110th Infantry Regiment, 28th Infantry Division, Major James C. Ford, said, "It doesn't much matter what training a man may have when he is placed inside such protection as was afforded by the pillboxes. Even if he merely stuck his weapons through the aperture and fired occasionally, it kept our men from moving ahead freely."[3]

Any strategy rests on assumptions, and both Eisenhower and Bradley believed that superior Allied mobility would allow them to advance on exterior lines, that is, an advance on multiple avenues of approach that would force the Germans to defend simultaneously more than one invasion route into Germany. Sooner or later Eisenhower and Bradley assumed the German line would break from the strain. The Allies had control of the air, railroads, and highways and had the advantage of trucks over the Germans' horses. However, the Germans still proved capable of reinforcing the most threatened areas of the front and forming a strategic reserve, and the Anglo-American attacks were of insufficient mass to accomplish much more than attrition of forces.

While the Allies were advancing on exterior lines along a so-called broad front without a strategic reserve, the Germans created a strategic reserve of over thirty divisions, which they used in their Ardennes counteroffensive. SHAEF's failure to coordinate Bradley's November offensive with Montgomery's operations allowed the Germans to reinforce units fighting Bradley's army group with troops taken from Montgomery's front, or to refit for the Ardennes counterattack. For example, the 10th SS Panzer Division from Holland replaced the 9th SS Panzer Division, which was refitting for the upcoming Ardennes counteroffensive. The 363rd *Volksgrenadier* Division from Holland went into position behind the Roer River and into the line, relieving the 340th Division, and two other German divisions, the 353rd Infantry from Luxembourg and the 85th Infantry from Holland, blocked the approaches to Dueren, east of Aachen.[4] In September the Germans threw hastily assembled units against Patton, who was resupplied much to Montgomery's chagrin and managed to draw off the Germans along the Meuse before they could concentrate for their planned massive, single blow against him. Eisenhower and Bradley resupplied Patton in spite of Montgomery's objections because fears raised by ULTRA made it vital to do so. Yet Eisenhower and Bradley could not defend themselves from Montgomery's criticism in the postwar period without divulging the ULTRA secret.[5]

Technology had altered the transmission of orders, and Bradley's *A Soldier's Story* predicted the historians' difficulty in attempting to assess responsibility for the conduct of operations in the campaign in northwest Europe. Equipped with scrambler telephones after October 1944, Eisenhower and Bradley could talk with little concern for security. Pointing out that he and Eisenhower often altered plans on the telephone or during late-night conversations, Bradley said that Eisenhower contributed as much or more to their tactical discussions than Montgomery did.[6] Air Marshal Robb, SHAEF's deputy chief of staff for air, noticed that the two West Point classmates were in almost daily contact, but that Eisenhower hardly ever spoke on the phone to Montgomery. At one point during the Battle of the Bulge, Eisenhower asked if there were a "scrambler" phone link to Montgomery's headquarters.[7] It was the sixth month of the campaign, and the supreme commander was unaware whether or not he had spoken on a scrambler phone to Britain's ranking officer in the European theater.

Robb's story was significant. It pointed to the asymmetrical communications between SHAEF and its army groups, especially the 21st Army Group, but it could also have been said of Devers' 6th Army Group, the poor relation of the ETO. Either Eisenhower or his British Deputy G-3, General Whiteley, would talk to de Guingand, Montgomery's chief of staff, or Whiteley would visit Montgomery if SHAEF sought a resolution to an issue. Significant to this study, the lack of personal contact between Eisenhower and Montgomery and Eisenhower's rather vague managerial style have skewed interpretation of the campaign.

Advances in air and ground transportation since the First World War also made it possible for commanders to meet face to face on a regular basis, and the Eisenhower-Bradley conversations must have refined operations well beyond the original. The fifth volume of *The Papers of Dwight David Eisenhower: The War Years* detailed the supreme commander's daily schedule. Examination of Eisenhower's calendar between 17 August 1944 and the end of the war shows that Bradley visited SHAEF headquarters twenty-one times and stayed overnight nine times. Montgomery visited SHAEF once, on 5 October 1944, and never stayed overnight. Eisenhower traveled to see Montgomery fifteen times and once stayed overnight at 21st Army Group, on 28 November 1944. The supreme commander met with Bradley at 12th Army Group or a third location twenty-six times and stayed overnight with Bradley nineteen times. Including their vacation in Cannes over 20-22 March 1945, Eisenhower and Bradley had the potential of thirty late-night conversations. The West Point classmates met forty-seven times compared to sixteen encounters between Eisenhower and Montgomery. Eisenhower met with Devers, the 6th Army Group commander, a total of thirteen times and stayed overnight at 6th Army Group headquarters three times. To see Eisenhower, Devers traveled once to Bradley's headquarters and seven times to SHAEF headquarters.[8]

At the Yalta Conference in mid-February 1945, according to Montgomery, Churchill mentioned to either Roosevelt or Marshall that Eisenhower did not see Montgomery enough, which simply stated the obvious.[9] This lack of contact and difference in outlook between Eisenhower and Montgomery led to the field marshal's 1958 comment that "We did not advance to the Rhine on a *broad* front; we advanced to the Rhine on *several* fronts, which were un-coordinated."[10] No matter where one stands on Montgomery's refusal to travel to see the supreme commander, the necessary job of coordination was being left to chance. Both men share the blame, but the responsibility for coordination belonged to the supreme commander.

The historical record of the campaign and the arguments in the memoirs assumed their shape largely as a result of Eisenhower's dealings with his army group commanders. Eisenhower and Montgomery avoided seeing one another; they communicated in writing. Furthermore, both Eisenhower and Montgomery explained their differences with each other to their respective superiors at the Pentagon and Whitehall, further defining the historical record. There was no equivalent correspondence between Eisenhower and Bradley for obvious reasons; they met on average once a week. Subsequently, there was far less of a written record of the Eisenhower-Bradley collaboration than there is of the arguments between Eisenhower and Montgomery.

Yet the strategy of northwest Europe was clearly an Eisenhower-Bradley strategy; witness the double thrust upon crossing the Seine, the attrition of November, the "calculated risk" of December, the closing to the Rhine in March, and the final offensive away from Berlin in April. Clearly, the cooperation between Eisenhower and Bradley had just as much, if not more, to do with the shape of operations on the western front than did Eisenhower's uneasy dealings with Montgomery. Bradley's prediction that historians would experience difficulty attributing credit for operations proved correct, the result of a documentation gap. Subsequently, the postwar memoirs take on added importance for both readers and scholars alike, filling the void, albeit imperfectly, when it came to operational decision making.

Following the war, Montgomery's papers provided grist for the mill of a generation of Eisenhower's critics, beginning with *The Sunday Times* in November 1948, Chester Wilmot, and recently Nigel Hamilton. Two questions the historian should ask are whether Montgomery's correspondence accurately reflected meetings with Bradley and Eisenhower, and whether the field marshal's papers contained a realistic political and military alternative worthy of two generations of books. Montgomery's recounting of meetings with Eisenhower sent to Brooke on 28 and 29 November and 31 December 1944 cannot be verified by American archives, and in the former instance have been contradicted by Montgomery's own military assistant.[11] Similarly, General Bradley denied that he ever agreed to Montgomery's single-thrust proposal of 17 August 1944.[12]

What were the historiographical effects of Montgomery's avoidance of SHAEF conferences? The field marshal's absences generated ever more written evidence, which tended to support single-thrust hypotheses. Montgomery's absences necessitated Eisenhower, or more commonly third parties, traveling to the 21st Army Group, which voided SHAEF headquarters diaries. Two SHAEF headquarters diaries lent themselves to publishers, one by Butcher and one by Summersby, but Butcher was in Paris serving in PRD for most of the campaign, and Summersby was excluded from 21st Army Group by Montgomery's prohibition against women. Because Montgomery refused to travel to Eisenhower's headquarters, Summersby's diary contained descriptions of meetings held at third locations where she had accompanied Eisenhower, such as Bradley's Namur headquarters on 5 February 1945.

Montgomery's inclination to speak to Eisenhower in private also created problems for researchers. For example, at their 23 August 1944 meeting, the field marshal excluded Eisenhower's chief of staff. On 28 December 1944, aboard Eisenhower's train at Hasselt, Montgomery insisted on speaking to Eisenhower in private without staff officers. In late November 1944, Montgomery had called for a meeting at Maastricht, Holland, in which their chiefs of staff would not be permitted to speak. Owing to the fact that de Guingand often spoke for Montgomery at meetings, this must have been aimed at Smith, who had a reputation for being a tougher negotiator than Eisenhower. In mid-December, Montgomery complained to Major General Frank E. W. Simpson, DMO (Director Military Operations), that "Ike floats about by himself with no senior staff officer with him."[13] Even when staff officers were present, such as the Brussels meeting of 10 September, Montgomery would claim that they were not participants.

Because of the field marshal's insistence that Eisenhower visit him at 21st Army Group, Montgomery's perspective on such meetings dominates the historical record. Moreover, the field marshal maintained three separate back channels of correspondence: one with the CIGS, Field Marshal Brooke; the second with the DMO, Major General Simpson; and a third with the VCIGS, the Vice Chief of the Imperial General Staff, Lieutenant General Sir Archibald Nye. Montgomery also had his headquarters diary kept by Lieutenant Colonel Dawnay, which was known as "Notes on the Campaign in North-Western Europe." Eisenhower's comments concerning Montgomery were made to his personal staff or to SHAEF staff officers and were mild in comparison. Nothing like Montgomery's reference to Eisenhower as "useless" exists in the Eisenhower papers concerning Montgomery.

Historians of the campaign in northwest Europe have had to face yet another documentation hazard, which has caused them to rely overly on the memoirs of participants--that is, SHAEF's failure to make a stenographic record of all high-level conferences. For example, the best source for the one SHAEF conference that Montgomery attended during the war was the diary kept by Ramsay. Two months later, after the conference at Maastricht, Holland, on 7 December, Tedder kept the notes for a SHAEF report and sent an account to the chief of air staff, Marshal Portal.[14]

The lack of standardized documentation of important conferences increased the importance of those postwar memoirs that reproduced documents. Montgomery's *Memoirs* and Alanbrooke's published diaries reprinted a large number of documents, continuing the style of Churchill's memoirs. Brooke kept a nightly record of his thoughts and opinions to which Sir Arthur Bryant inserted relevant documents. Montgomery's *Memoirs* benefited from his almost daily reports sent to Brooke and his diary kept by Dawnay. The British memoirs with their mixture of prose and documents provided a sense of verisimilitude, and became valuable for the reprinting of many otherwise classified British documents.

Few readers could guess at the British documents that remained unprintable because they were judged too controversial. Air Marshal Coningham, commander of the Second Tactical Air Force, published a paper on the campaign in northwest Europe that was so controversial it was withdrawn by the Air Ministry. After the war, Coningham told Forrest Pogue that the Air Ministry believed that his criticism of Montgomery "had out Ingersolled Ingersoll." For the good of the services, Coningham's report was buried because the Air Ministry did not want a war with the War Ministry.[15] Coningham believed that the Allies could have reached the Rhine in September 1944 by backing Patton rather than Montgomery.

Coningham told Pogue that Montgomery was a "little man" who twisted history to build up his own image, and that Montgomery had even managed to get the supreme commander to alter his original description of the Caen operation in his official report. Obviously, had Coningham lived it was highly likely that a British publisher would have sought out his story. Unfortunately for the students of the debate over strategy and command, Coningham died in a plane crash off Bermuda on 30 January 1948.[16]

Airplane crashes also took the lives of Admiral Sir Bertram Ramsay and Air Chief Marshal Sir Trafford Leigh-Mallory. Both of these men were Montgomery's equals, respectively commanding the naval and air components of the invasion forces. Ramsay had warned SHAEF and the 21st Army Group that Antwerp and Rotterdam were susceptible to mining and blocking, but to no avail. Subsequently, when Ramsay attended the 5 October commanders' conference at SHAEF, and Montgomery hinted that operations beyond the Rhine were possible without opening Antwerp, Ramsay attacked the field marshal's failure to take good advice. This is not to say that had Ramsay lived to write his memoirs he would have been uncritical of Eisenhower. During the Battle of the Bulge, Ramsay was appalled at the state of command at SHAEF. "It is most disturbing that Supreme HQ should be without information later than about 36-48 hours," Ramsay wrote the day before Christmas. "It is only too clear that there is no Supreme Operational Command in existence. No master mind and therefore no staff of one."[17] Ramsay was killed near Paris on 2 January 1945 when his plane stalled on takeoff.

Leigh-Mallory died in a plane crash near Grenoble in November 1944. A controversial figure in Britain owing to his replacement of Air Chief Marshal Sir Hugh Dowding as head of Fighter Command immediately following the Battle of Britain, Leigh-Mallory got along with Montgomery during the Normandy campaign. Regarding Allied strategy in the advance to the Rhine, however, Leigh-Mallory believed (like Coningham) that Montgomery's Arnhem operation had cost Patton an almost certain chance to crack through the Siegfried Line.[18] Had Ramsay, Coningham, and Leigh-Mallory lived, it is highly likely that their memoirs would have focused on Patton's hypothetical single thrust because all three believed that

Arnhem had been a mistake and Eisenhower ought to have backed Patton instead of Montgomery. There can be no doubt that memoirs from these three plane crash victims would have altered the conventional account of the campaign of northwest Europe.

The viability of Patton's single thrust was first put forward in 1946 by Ralph Ingersoll's *Top Secret*. In his final memoir written along with Clay Blair, Bradley addressed the contention that by crossing the Rhine via a single thrust Patton could have ended the war in September. "I am not aware," Blair quoted Bradley as saying, "that anyone other than Patton has taken this seriously." Bradley told Chester Hansen after the war that a double thrust was not the same thing as a broad front. In fact, the Bradley Commentaries show that Bradley was not a proponent of the broad front per se. Indeed, he felt that the term was a misnomer: "My philosophy did not envision an advance on a broad front. I think you [would] be more accurate to describe me as a two-thrust man; Montgomery as a one-thrust man."[19] Bradley favored two concentrated thrusts on the Ruhr, one north and one south of the Ardennes, and, as far as Patton was concerned, Bradley doubted that the Third Army could have gotten beyond the Siegfried Line in September 1944.

War As I Knew It made a case for a single thrust without ever calling it that, but Patton did not argue the point with Eisenhower in the manner of his contemporaries. As an army commander it was not Patton's place to push SHAEF for strategic consideration, but Bradley could do so as an army group commander. Eisenhower tolerated Patton's behind-the-scenes insults because Patton's obvious tactical skills compensated.[20] Just as plane crashes probably spared Montgomery from the criticism of two air marshals and one admiral, a traffic accident spared Eisenhower from a more vitriolic Patton memoir. For a Russophobe such as Patton to have avoided jumping on the Vienna, Prague, Berlin bandwagon would have been difficult indeed. Ladislas Farago, one of Patton's biographers, contended that in November 1945 Patton told General Joseph T. McNarney, acting theater commander, that the Americans should fight the Russians with German prisoners of war. Supposedly Patton said, "In ten days I can have enough incidents happen to have us at war with those sons of bitches and make it look like their fault."[21] Immediately following his conversation with McNarney, Patton told one of his staff officers, "I really believe that we are going to fight them, and if this country does not do it now, it will be taking them on years later when the Russians are ready for it and we will have an awful time whipping them."[22]

Given the size and scope of Patton's wartime files, the depth of his anti-communism, and his flair for writing, it would have been difficult for him not to have criticized Eisenhower's decision that prevented the Third Army from liberating Prague ahead of the Russians, especially since Patton had beaten the Red Army to Prague. Following his relief from command of the Third Army, Patton wrote in his diary that Eisenhower had acted in a "most pusillanimous" fashion. Patton attributed his relief and Eisenhower's decreasing moral fortitude to his being "bitten with the presidential bee."[23]

In 1948 Eisenhower responded to the so-called crackpot theories of Ingersoll, Allen, and Patton that blamed SHAEF for not ending the war in September 1944.

Eisenhower's criticism of single-thrust options chose not to mention Patton by name and infuriated Montgomery, who interpreted *Crusade in Europe* as both a personal attack and an attack on the British army and its wartime CIGS.

Since Eisenhower's *Crusade in Europe* followed up on the criticism of Montgomery's single-thrust proposal contained in Francis de Guingand's 1947 *Operation Victory*, Montgomery was likely feeling a bit gun shy by 1948. Eisenhower had called his strategy "pencillike" and his proposals "fantastic." To a modern reader five decades since its publication, Eisenhower's comments seem so mild that it is hard to imagine them upsetting anyone as important as a British field marshal. That misses the point, however. Montgomery's irritation with *Crusade in Europe* was understandable measured against the even blander staff-college narrative, *Normandy to the Baltic*.

For the historiography of the debate over strategy and command, *Crusade in Europe* and Montgomery's reaction to it marked a watershed. Montgomery shifted from the limited support that he had provided Alan Moorehead to providing scathing commentary for Sir Denis Hamilton's review in *The Sunday Times*. Sir Denis Hamilton was the editor of *The Sunday Times* when it serialized Montgomery's *Memoirs*, and, as noted earlier, he would select his son, Nigel, to write Montgomery's authorized biography. Both Hamiltons enjoyed longstanding personal relationships with the field marshal.[24]

Montgomery developed a professional relationship with Chester Wilmot, who enjoyed access to the field marshal's papers and interviewed him for *The Struggle for Europe*. Wilmot's criticism of the American-dominated war effort in Europe caught a rising revisionist tide that was evolving in Great Britain. More than any other work, *The Struggle for Europe* elevated Montgomery's proposed single thrust to the importance that it enjoys today. Wilmot wrote about what Montgomery had shown him, and the field marshal had not shown him his cables concerning command. As a result, Wilmot gave the debate over strategy and command an ethereal quality that it did not enjoy during the war when American generals believed that Montgomery was motivated primarily by his desire to command additional American armies.

In his chapter "The Great Argument," Wilmot quoted Montgomery's call for "a solid mass of forty divisions, which would be so strong that it need fear nothing."[25] However, Wilmot failed to point out that when Montgomery wrote that paper on 17 August 1944, Eisenhower's entire command did not contain forty divisions. Neither did the journalist print Montgomery's conclusion on Operation MARKET-GARDEN from their interview in 1949, when he told Wilmot that he had hoped to get a bridgehead over the Rhine before the winter set in and be set to break out in 1945.[26]

Wilmot's arguments in 1952 were more applicable to Eisenhower's 1948 "pencillike" reference than to the strategic and command debate as it existed in August and September 1944. If Wilmot's point was to prove that Montgomery's single-thrust plan had not been "pencillike," then only Montgomery's plans to employ forty divisions need be cited. If, however, the point was to prove a negative, that is, that broad front prevented a September single thrust from ending the war, then the field marshal's 1949 comments about the tactical significance of MARKET-GARDEN were better omitted in 1952. In either case Wilmot protected a myth.

The forty divisions Montgomery mentioned in his *Memoirs* were more like thirty-five in mid-August. In fact, Churchill put them at "more than thirty-seven" at the time of the liberation of Paris on 25 August. When Montgomery first mentioned a forty-division attack in mid-August 1944, a literal interpretation meant that he was demanding *all* of the Allied divisions in France, including those in southern France under the command of the Mediterranean theater, while a figurative interpretation meant he was demanding a strong force. Fifty years later, "A solid mass of forty divisions . . . so strong that it need fear nothing" serves as a symbol for the single thrust. It is now part of the history of the war, in spite of the mythical, almost biblical, quality of the forty metaphor. It was not until mid-September that Eisenhower's order of battle included over forty divisions.[27]

British and American speculation on what forty Allied divisions might have accomplished in September 1944 engages in a perverse ethnocentric military conceit. Not only was it politically impossible that Eisenhower would have turned over the entire expeditionary force to an Englishman in the late summer of 1944, but also it was and is perverse to assert that these forty divisions could have ended the anti-Nazi war in 1944. According to John Ellis in *Brute Force: Allied Strategy and Tactics in the Second World War*, the Russians accounted for almost 90 percent of the Germans killed in the war and they never fought less than 66 percent of the German army.[28] The single-thrust school would have its readers believe that Eisenhower prevented Germany from losing the war to one-third of the anti-Nazi ground forces before it could lose to the other two-thirds, or the entirety of its adversaries.

At the time Wilmot's book appeared, Eisenhower was running for the presidency, and Wilmot's book was unlikely to damage him politically. Eisenhower was president when Prime Minister Churchill's final volume of his war memoirs appeared in 1953, and a frank recounting of British wartime opinion would have been impolitic to say the least. The prime minister spared the president the embarrassment that would have attended publication of the Churchillian reservations about General Eisenhower's control of the land battle.

When the official history of the United States Army, *The Supreme Command*, was published in 1954, good relations with the British were vital. By 1949, when Forrest Pogue had completed most of his research, China had gone communist and the Russians had developed the atomic bomb, and within a year war broke out in Korea, involving American and British troops. While Pogue's book was in draft form in 1951, the former commander of the British Second Army, General Dempsey, read it as undue criticism of the British war effort. Field Marshal Montgomery, then Eisenhower's deputy at SHAPE, wrote to Eisenhower asking him to see that Pogue's book was not printed as written. The publication date may have been delayed somewhat, but not one word was changed for censorship reasons.[29]

And there was no reason why it should have been censored. Indicative of the lack of written documentation concerning high-level strategic decision making,

Pogue interviewed the men who worked at SHAEF and as many of the commanders and staff officers as he needed to get the story of Allied headquarters. Pogue bent over backward to be fair to Montgomery's single-thrust scheme, omitting the scathing opinion of Bedell Smith, who called it "the most fantastic bit of balderdash ever proposed by a competent general."[30] Owing to Pogue's standards of scholarship and decorum, Montgomery's single-thrust proposals received lenient treatment because it was Pogue's belief that the success of the alliance was the story, not the controversies stirred up along the way to victory.

Pulled punches were the order of the day. In his *Memoirs* Montgomery was nowhere near as critical as he had been during the war in his correspondence with Brooke, Simpson, and Nye. However, the field marshal had told several different stories regarding the September circumstances, and his *Memoirs* added to the variations on the theme. For example, in early September 1944, Montgomery had written to the DMO, Major General Simpson, saying that with the right decision "we could be in Berlin in three weeks and the German war would be over."[31] On 13 September, he wrote the VCIGS, Lieutenant General Nye, that he had won a "great victory," and Eisenhower was going to give him what he needed for his Arnhem offensive.[32] As a result of his "great victory," Montgomery was reasonably certain that he would win the war relatively quickly. Yet Montgomery's reader had no way of knowing that the field marshal considered Arnhem a tactical operation by the time Eisenhower got around to approving it and not a strategic operation, and that by 17 September 1944 he had hoped to go only as far as the Ruhr.[33] *Normandy to the Baltic* said that the war would have petered out within six months of the Ruhr's seizure.[34]

Montgomery's case against Eisenhower's twin decision to take over the ground forces command and to locate his headquarters at Granville, overlooking the Bay of Brittany and Mont St. Michel, was far more convincing. The field marshal's criticism of Eisenhower as a ground forces commander was clearly motivated by personal ambition, but that does not invalidate his criticism of the timing of the change in ground forces command and the location of Eisenhower's headquarters. On the other hand, the validity of Montgomery's criticism of Eisenhower as ground forces commander does not prove the merits of Montgomery's single-thrust strategy. There were simply not enough Anglo-American divisions in late August 1944, or even early September, for that matter, to do what Montgomery's *Memoirs* suggested was possible, that is, win the campaign through concentration along one axis of advance. Going to Berlin in 1944 was a myth. Following the Brussels meeting of 10 September 1944, General Gale confided to his diary, "My own view is that MONTGOMERY never intended to go to BERLIN and that it was merely a manoeuvre 'off the record' to show that he had been prevented from ending the war in a few days by the Supreme Commander himself."[35]

By the 1950s, motivating much of the criticism of Eisenhower's broad-front strategy was the influential political criticism by Grigg, Wilmot, Churchill, Montgomery, and Alanbrooke that if the Anglo-Americans had taken Berlin, the cold war with the Soviets, indeed contemporary Europe, would somehow have been different. Berlin developed a grail-like quality after 1948. The problem with the memoirs as a genre was that they grew ever more prescient and ever more present oriented as the cold war intensified. Revisionist criticism of broad front was nearly always accompanied by the stated or implied inference that a successful single thrust would have both shortened the war and saved lives, thus guaranteeing the Anglo-Americans a better position relative to the Russians in the postwar period. No one ever really said what that better position entailed, but the terminus of the tale was always Berlin. According to this version of the past, nothing the Western Allies might have done could possibly have worsened relations with the Soviets more than they already were by the early 1950s.

In October 1948 an out-of-power Winston Churchill pointed to the Allied failure to take Berlin and argued for a harder line over the current Berlin crisis. Churchill was totally consistent in assuming that his recommended courses of action contained *no* risks to the Western Allies in either 1945 or 1948. The reader, however, should not confuse Churchill's campaign speeches of 1948, which called for "a general confrontation" with the Soviets in 1945, with his thoughts of late March and April 1945. The British official historian John Ehrman pointed out in his 1956 volume, *Grand Strategy,* Volume VI, *October 1944-August 1945,* that attitudes should not be confused with policy. Neither Churchill nor his foreign secretary, Anthony Eden, proposed in 1945 that the Anglo-Americans take action on the basis that the Russians were their future enemies.[36]

By the 1950s many Americans sympathized with the British argument that the Anglo-Americans would have been better situated in cold war Europe if the Western Allies had gone on to Berlin at the end of the hot war. Few Americans would have approved the Montgomery corollary, however: That had Montgomery been the ground forces commander everything would have worked out better for the alliance and that he was the man to enter Berlin representing the Anglo-American coalition. For Americans the issue was simple and clear cut: American soldiers should be commanded by American officers. "Remembering General Pershing's troubles in World War I," Omar Bradley wrote, "I was determined to fight any proposal for the assignment of American troops to British field command."[37]

Given the relative weight of ground forces involved and the politics of war, it was inevitable that an American command the ground forces in northwest Europe. Neither President Roosevelt nor Secretary of War Stimson would have stood for a British ground forces commander. Eisenhower might have allowed Montgomery to remain in command of the ground forces beyond 1 September 1944 but not after being pressured by General Marshall and Stimson to assume command of the American contingent. During the Battle of the Bulge, President Roosevelt held an on-the-record press conference, with Marshall by his side, insisting that the recent command shift in the Ardennes was temporary. On 6 January 1945, the *New York Times*, covering the Roosevelt-Marshall press conference, summed up official Washington: "There was reassertion that any British effort to lessen General Eisenhower's command would meet strong opposition."[38] Clearly, the president had signaled the British that the American government would not tolerate a British ground forces commander.

As long as Marshall was chief of staff of the United States Army, there would never have been a British ground forces commander. Marshall told Eisenhower that he would have resigned first. Marshall was suspicious of British motives, and when Churchill suggested replacing Tedder with Alexander as Eisenhower's deputy, Marshall judged the Alexander for Tedder swap as an attempt to regain control of ground operations beyond the level warranted by the size of the British army.[39]

If Montgomery believed that victory would have mollified public opinion in the United States, then the question needs to be asked: What about opinion in the Soviet Union? Perhaps, the only pertinent question is: What about Stalin's opinion? After pleading for a Second Front since 1941 and having been disappointed in 1942 and 1943, what would have been Stalin's reaction to an Operation OVERLORD less than three months old that announced that its own logistical failure necessitated an all-out attempt to end the war in September 1944?

All of Montgomery's single-thrust schemes, except for the original "forty divisions so strong that they need fear nothing," were predicated on immobilizing part of the Allied Expeditionary Force. The forty-division option was politically and militarily impossible. General Smith's Malta Conference comments on the relationship between divisions and roadnet put an end to such single-thrust talk from the British. The roadnet and bridges of northwest Europe would have severely taxed a single thrust of forty divisions on Montgomery's line of advance, if indeed that had ever been the plan. Divisions would have had to drop off for purposes of flank protection. This is not to argue that single-thrust schemes were impossible. For example, Patton's own narrow advance stood a chance of piercing the West Wall and getting to the Rhine had it received unqualified support. However, Patton's avenue of advance vis-à-vis the Ruhr limited him to a secondary role. Furthermore, it raises the question of how Montgomery could have advanced beyond the Ruhr without opening Antwerp. When General Marshall raised the proposition of an all-out offensive in the west to end the war in late October 1944, the British Joint Planning Staff concluded that it was impossible without Antwerp being open to ship traffic.[40]

Either way, a single thrust in northwest Europe had the potential to infuriate Stalin. If twenty-five Allied divisions could have ended the anti-Nazi war in September 1944, 120 days after invading the continent, then it stands to reason that Stalin would have wondered what the Allies were doing in 1943 when Churchill protested that the time was not right for invasion, that is, that the Germans were too strong. On the other hand, if the single thrust resulted in a German victory west of the Rhine, the Anglo-Americans would have required a respite of several months, which would have allowed the Germans to transfer troops to their eastern front while holding the line of the Rhine. The original OVERLORD plan called for just such a halt to build up logistical depots on the Rhine; imagine the postwar criticism of that hypothetical case. It is difficult to avoid the conclusion that Eisenhower's broad-front strategy was far less risky given the likelihood of a cold war with the Soviet Union then anything Montgomery or Patton ever recommended. Given the possibility of a German defeat of any Allied single thrust in September, what would Chester Wilmot have said about forfeiting central

Europe to the Soviets? Defeat of an Anglo-American single thrust had the potential to cede even more of Europe to Stalin than Eisenhower's actual strategy.

Only Colonel Stacey, the Canadian official historian, enlarged upon the fundamental fallacy of the single thrust, which was that Hitler would have done nothing different while the Western Allies were hypothetically winning the war in September by crossing the Rhine and enveloping the Ruhr. Stacey argued that the Germans had troops available on the eastern front to move against a crossing of the Rhine River in 1944. After the Russian summer offensive came to a halt on the Vistula in August, the Germans could have redeployed units to stop a hypothetical attack on the Ruhr by Montgomery.[41]

None of the proponents of single thrust mentioned that Allied fighter-bombers would have required forward bases in order to provide the air cover necessary to make up for the Anglo-American shortage of ground troops. Without air cover the British and American armies would have been in an operational situation similar to that brought on by the meteorological conditions during the German Ardennes counteroffensive in December, when fog grounded Allied planes for a week. Major General J. Lawton Collins, VII Corps commander within the First United States Army, summed up September 1944 by stating, "We ran out of gas . . . we ran out of ammunition; and we ran out of weather. The loss of our close tactical air support because of weather was a real blow."[42]

An attack across the Rhine in September 1944 would have occurred while the Germans still had the means to move troops across Germany by railroad and before their shortage of fuel was critical. With half the Allied forces stopped for lack of transport and gasoline, the Germans could have counterattacked in Lorraine against Patton. Montgomery and Churchill had been opposed to ANVIL/DRAGOON, yet all the American divisions as well as the French divisions in General Devers' 6th Army Group were supplied through the ports of southern France, gained as a result of Eisenhower's insistence on the invasion of southern France. Without Marseilles it is highly likely that a large part of the United States forces would have been immobilized in the winter of 1944-1945. Yet British field marshals at the time, and many critics since, assume that there had been no synergistic logistical gains from southern France during the Battle of the Bulge when its tonnage surpassed Antwerp's.[43]

As important as it was, Marseilles and the Mediterranean ports were merely substitutes for Antwerp. The American official historian, Roland G. Ruppenthal, pointed out that there were too few truck companies in the European theater to transport supplies to the front. If the port of Antwerp had been opened earlier, there would have been a proportionate savings in the number of trucks needed because Antwerp was so much closer to the front. The war in Europe ended within six months of the opening of Antwerp to ship traffic rather than the six months after the seizure of the Ruhr mentioned in Montgomery's *Normandy to the Baltic*. If the approaches to Antwerp had been taken in late September, by this hypothetical calculus the European war would have been over sometime in late March 1945.

The greatest tactical irony of Operation MARKET-GARDEN, the closest thing to an Eisenhower-Montgomery single thrust, was the delay imposed on the ground offensive by troops of the German Fifteenth Army, attacking Montgomery's left flank from the west. By not paying more attention to his western flank, Montgomery allowed more than 86,000 Germans of the Fifteenth Army to escape capture by crossing to the far side of the Scheldt. Montgomery's criticism of Eisenhower as a ground forces commander was apt--a better ground commander would have ordered Montgomery to prevent the escape of the German Fifteenth Army. However, the German Fifteenth Army had been allowed to escape, and the British paratroopers at Arnhem paid the price.

Proponents of the September single-thrust school overemphasized German weakness and dangerously underestimated the hold of a police state on its citizens and soldiers. Following the attempted assassination of 20 July 1944, Hitler replaced the military salute with the Nazi salute and demanded that every German General Staff officer become a National Socialist officer-leader.[44] At the same time that the British were disbanding their 59th Infantry Division, Hitler forced the German army to accept the *Reichsführer* of the SS, Heinrich Himmler, as the new commander of the Replacement Army, which was turning out *Volksgrenadier* divisions of about 8,000 men armed with the newest automatic and heavy weapons for service in prepared defenses. Over the months of August, September, and October, the Germans transferred hundreds of thousands of men from factory jobs to the front; their places were taken by slave laborers and, for the first time, German women. By combing out naval and air force ground personnel, equipping training units, garrison commands, and rear echelon types, the Germans raised over thirty-five divisions.[45] In late September 1944 the Germans formed a home guard called the *Volkssturm*, calling all males from sixteen to sixty, and by October teenaged girls joined the boys of the *Flakhelfer*, the antiaircraft auxiliaries.[46] Hitler stated in September and November 1939 and again in November 1942 that Germany would never surrender as it had in November 1918 and that he would never survive the defeat of his people.[47]

The Anglo-Americans possessed no magic bullet that would have ended both their campaign and the Russo-German War in September 1944. When a single thrust might have been a strategic option in the second half of August, there were neither enough Allied divisions nor trucks on the continent. Furthermore, there were not enough dead Germans by September 1944 for Nazi Germany to give up the ghost, whereas by May 1945 there were. The campaign in northwest Europe would have to be won by attrition no matter the Allied avenues of advance. World War II demonstrated that in wars between doctrinal and numerical equals, modern warfare reverts to stalemate and stalemate reverts to attrition. By the time of the campaign in northwest Europe, 1944-1945, the belligerents were numerically and doctrinally equivalent with no side holding a pronounced advantage over the other once September's change in weather limited the Allies' tactical air support as the front reached the West Wall.

Considering all the potential problems facing an attack across the Rhine in September 1944 on a single-thrust line, de Guingand's 1947 conclusion bears repeating: "It took a Russian offensive using about 160 divisions, massive offensives on our part, as well as eight months of devastating air attack, to force the Germans to capitulate. And even then Hitler and his gang never gave up."[48] The American naval historian Samuel Eliot Morison wrote the words at the beginning of this chapter in 1958 as an extended review of Sir Arthur Bryant's first volume of Alanbrooke's published diaries, *The Turn of the Tide*. To the critics of broad front, it appeared that moving on Berlin in the spring of 1945 posed no risks, only benefits. The same seemingly applied to the situation of September 1944 when single thrust allegedly would have won the war without risk.

The error made by the single-thrust school in thinking that success in September would have ended the war is that it posits a rational opponent in Berlin, who, having seen the inevitable would have surrendered. Nothing of the sort existed in Germany in 1944-1945. The most perverse ethnocentric fallacy connected to the optimistic assumptions behind single thrust did not involve anything that Eisenhower either controlled or prevented from happening. It had little to do with what Stalin hoped to gain from another winter of war. Rather, the greatest error that the proponents of single thrust made was to assume that anything the Allies did short of killing Adolf Hitler would have ended the German war. Hitler did not kill himself until 30 April 1945, by which time his army was annihilated, his country lay in ruins, and the Russians were three blocks from his bunker.

NOTES

1. Samuel Eliot Morison, *Strategy and Compromise* (Boston: Little, Brown, an Atlantic Monthly Press Book, 1958), 9.

2. Jeffrey J. Clarke and Robert Ross Smith, *Riviera to the Rhine (United States Army in World War II: The European Theater of Operations,* Washington, D.C.: Center of Military History, United States Army, 1993), 439-40; William K. Wyant, *Sandy Patch: A Biography of Lt. Gen. Alexander M. Patch* (Westport, Conn.: Praeger, 1991), 6.

3. Charles B. MacDonald, *The Siegfried Line Campaign (United States Army in World War II: The European Theater of Operations,* Washington, D.C.: Office of the Chief of Military History, United States Army, 1963), 46.

4. Ibid.; see 567 for the 10th SS Panzer Division; the 363rd *Volksgrenadier* Division is on 573; for the two divisions from Holland and Luxembourg, see 583.

5. Russell F. Weigley, *Eisenhower's Lieutenants: The Campaign of France and Germany, 1944-1945* (Bloomington: Indiana University Press, 1981), 344.

6. Omar N. Bradley, *A Soldier's Story* (New York: Holt, 1951), 354-55.

7. Diary of Air Marshal Robb, Meeting in Supreme Commander's Office, 12 January 1946, Papers of Air Chief Marshal Sir James Robb, AC 71/9/26, RAFM.

8. Alfred D. Chandler, Jr., ed., and Stephen E. Ambrose, assoc. ed., *The Papers of Dwight David Eisenhower: The War Years,* 5 vols. (Baltimore and London: Johns Hopkins University Press, 1970), 5: 164-89.

9. On the matter of visitation, see *The Memoirs of Field-Marshal the Viscount Montgomery* (London: Collins, 1958), 324-25; Richard Lamb, *Montgomery in Europe, 1943-1945: Success or Failure?* (London: Buchan and Enright, paperback edition, 1984), 348-49.

10. Montgomery, *The Memoirs,* 286.

11. For Montgomery to Brooke, 28 November 1944, see Arthur Bryant, *Triumph in the West: A History of the War Years Based on the Diaries of Field-Marshal Lord Alanbrooke, Chief of the Imperial General Staff* (Garden City, N. Y.: Doubleday, 1959), 258; Brooke's impression of Montgomery's 28 December 1944 meeting with Eisenhower came from a letter from the DMO, Major-General Frank E. W. Simpson, to the CIGS, 31 December 1945, Papers of Field Marshal Viscount Alanbrooke, LHCMA.

12. Omar N. Bradley and Clay Blair, *A General's Life: An Autobiography by General of the Army Omar N. Bradley and Clay Blair* (New York: Simon and Schuster, 1983), 314.

13. Montgomery to Simpson, 17 December 1944, Papers of Field Marshal the Viscount Montgomery of Alamein, Reel 8, BLM 94/11, IWM.

14. Tedder's notes were issued as a report by SHAEF; see Major Lionel F. Ellis with Lieutenant Colonel Anthony E. Warhurst, *Victory in the West: The Defeat of Germany,* vol. 2, *(History of the Second World War: United Kingdom Military Series,* London: Her Majesty's Stationery Office, 1968), 167-68; PRO: CAB 106/1106, "The 'Broad Front' versus 'Narrow Front' Controversy," Documents of Importance, No. 17; CAB 80/46, COS COM Memorandum 1944, 16 October-30 December; M-537, Montgomery to CIGS, 7 December 1944, Papers of Field Marshal the Viscount Montgomery of Alamein, BLM 78/3, IWM.

15. Vincent Orange, *Coningham: A Biography of Air Marshal Sir Arthur Coningham* (London: Methuen, 1990), 243-45.

16. For Coningham's comments on Montgomery, see Interview with Air Marshal Sir Arthur Coningham, 14 February 1947, OCMH Collection, *Supreme Command,* Pogue Interviews, USAMHI; for Coningham's disappearance, see Orange, *Coningham,* 249-53.

17. PRO: CAB 116/1124, Diary of Admiral Sir Bertram Ramsay, 24 December 1944.

18. PRO: CAB 116/1124, Diary of Admiral Sir Bertram Ramsay, 30 September 1944.

19. The Bradley Commentaries, 38-A, S-13, USAMHI.

20. Colonel S.L.A. Marshall, Interview with General Dwight D. Eisenhower, 7 June 1946, OCMH Collection, *Supreme Command,* Pogue Interviews, USAMHI.

21. Ladislas Farago, *Patton: Ordeal and Triumph* (New York: Ivan Obolensky, 1964), 806.

22. Ibid., 807.

23. Martin Blumenson, ed., *The Patton Papers,* 2 vols. (Boston: Houghton Mifflin Company, 1972-1974), 2:799.

24. Interview with Dr. Forrest C. Pogue, 17 March 1991.

25. Chester Wilmot, *The Struggle for Europe* (London: Collins; New York: Harper and Brothers, 1952), 460.

26. Wilmot-Montgomery Interview, 23 March 1949, "Allied Strategy after the Fall of Paris," 5, 15/15/127, Montgomery, Chester Wilmot Papers, Liddell Hart Collection, LHCMA.

27. Winston S. Churchill, *The Second World War,* vol. 6, *Triumph and Tragedy,* (Boston: Houghton Mifflin; Cambridge, Mass.: Riverside Press, 1953), 190; G. E. Patrick Murray, "Eisenhower and Montgomery: The Biblical Forty Divisions," The Colonel Tom Elam Symposium, University of Tennessee, Martin, 9 March 1994.

28. John Ellis, *Brute Force: Allied Strategy and Tactics in the Second World War* (New York: Viking Press, 1990), 129-30.

29. Pogue said that "we just waited them out." Interview with Dr. Forrest C. Pogue, 17 March 1991.

30. Interview with Lieutenant General Walter Bedell Smith, 13 May 1947, OCMH Collection, *Supreme Command,* Pogue Interviews, USAMHI.

31. Montgomery to Simpson, 5 September 1944, Papers of the Field Marshal the Viscount Montgomery of Alamein, BLM 94/9, IWM.

32. M-196, 13 September 1944, Montgomery to Nye, Papers of the Field Marshal the Viscount Montgomery of Alamein, Reel 11, BLM 128/8, IWM.

33. Wilmot-Montgomery Interviews, 23 March 1949, "Allied Strategy After the Fall of Paris," 5, 15/15/127, Montgomery, and "Notes on Conversation with Monty," 18 May 1946, 4, Chester Wilmot Papers, Liddell Hart Collection, LHCMA.

34. Field Marshal the Viscount Montgomery of Alamein, *Normandy to the Baltic* (London: Hutchinson and Company, 1947), 120.

35. Gale Diary, "Forward Headquarters," 10 September 1944, II/22, Papers of Lieutenant General Sir Humphrey Myddleton Gale, LHCMA.

36. John Ehrman, *Grand Strategy: October 1944-August 1945,* vol. 6 *(History of the Second World War, United Kingdom Military Series,* London: Her Majesty's Stationery Office, 1956), 150.

37. Omar N. Bradley, *A Soldier's Story* (New York: Holt, 1951), 327.

38. "Roosevelt Explains Shift," by Sidney Shalett, *New York Times,* 6 January 1945, p. 3.

39. Marshall to Eisenhower, 11 January 1945, BD, Dwight D. Eisenhower, Pre-Presidential Papers, 1916-1952, Principal File, Harry C. Butcher, Box 169, (1 January-28 January) (2), EL.

40. Forrest C. Pogue, *The Supreme Command (United States Army in World War II: The European Theater of Operations,* Washington, D.C.: Office of the Chief of Military History, Department of the Army, 1954), 308.

41. Charles P. Stacey, *The Victory Campaign (Official History of the Canadian Army in the Second World War,* 3, *The Operations in North-West Europe, 1944-1945,* Ottawa: Queen's Printer and Controller of Stationery, 1960), 321.

42. MacDonald, *The Siegfried Line Campaign,* 95.

43. Clarke and Smith, *Riviera to the Rhine,* 575-76.

44. Sir John Wheeler-Bennett, *The Nemesis of Power: The German Army in Politics, 1918-1945* (New York: St. Martin's Press, 1964), 678.

45. Hugh M. Cole, *The Lorraine Campaign (United States Army in World War II: The European Theater of Operations,* Washington, D.C.: Historical Divisions, United States Army, 1950), 33-34.

46. Gerhard L. Weinberg, *A World at Arms: A Global History of World War II* (Cambridge: Cambridge University Press, 1994), 755-56.

47. Alan Bullock, *Hitler: A Study in Tyranny.* Revised ed. (New York: Harper and Row, 1964), 551, 569, 688.

48. Francis de Guingand, *Operation Victory* (London: Hodder and Stoughton, 1947), 412.

Abbreviations and Acronyms

BBC	British Broadcasting Corporation
BD	Butcher Diary
CBHP	Chester B. Hansen Papers
CBS	Columbia Broadcasting System
CCS	Combined Chiefs of Staff
CIGS	Chief Imperial General Staff
CMH	Center of Military History, Washington, D.C.
COMZ	Communications Zone
COS	Chiefs of Staff
DMO	Director Military Operations
EL	Eisenhower Library, Abilene, Kansas
ETO	European Theater of Operations
ETOUSA	European Theater of Operations, United States Army
ETOUSA-SOS	European Theater of Operations, United States Army--Service of Supply
FUSAG	First United States Army Group
HD	Hansen Diary
IWM	Imperial War Museum, Lambeth, London
JCS	Joint Chiefs of Staff
JPS	Joint Planning Staff
LHCMA	Liddell Hart Center for Military Archives, King's College, London
NA	National Archives, College Park, Maryland
OCMH	Office of the Chief of Military History
OKW	*Oberkommando der Wehrmacht*
PRD	Public Relations Division, SHAEF
PRO	Public Record Office, Kew, London

RAFM	Royal Air Force Museum, Hendon, London
RG	Record Group
SCAEF	Supreme Commander Allied Expeditionary Force
SD	Summersby Diary
SGS	Secretariat General Staff
SHAEF	Supreme Headquarters Allied Expeditionary Force
SHAPE	Supreme Headquarters Allied Powers Europe
SOOP	Senior Officer Oral History Project
TAC	Tactical
USAMHI	United States Army Military History Institute, Carlisle Barracks, Pennsylvania
USNR	United States Naval Reserve
VCIGS	Vice Chief Imperial General Staff

Selected Bibliography

ARCHIVAL SOURCES

The Eisenhower Library, Abilene, Kansas.
  Dwight D. Eisenhower, Pre-Presidential Papers, 1916-1952, Principal File:
    General Omar Bradley
    The Butcher Diary
    Harry C. Butcher, Correspondence
    Crusade in Europe, Correspondence
    Major General Sir Francis de Guingand
    General of the Army George C. Marshall
    Field Marshal Viscount Bernard Law Montgomery
    Dr. Forrest C. Pogue
    The Kay Summersby Diary
    Chester Wilmot
  Dwight D. Eisenhower, Presidential Papers, Ann Whitman File, Name Series:
    Emmet John Hughes
    Field Marshal Viscount Bernard Law Montgomery
    Lord Ismay
    Harry C. Butcher Papers, Correspondence File

The National Archives and Records Service, Archives II, College Park, Maryland
  Record Group 165, War Department General and Special Staff, Operations Division
  1942-1945, 384 ETO, Box 1312, Case 46.
  Record Group 331, Box 74, SHAEF, General Staff, Post-OVERLORD Planning, Volume
  I.
  Record Group 331, Box 77, SHAEF, Secretariat General Staff, Post-OVERLORD
  Planning, Volume I.

The United States Army Military History Institute, Carlisle Barracks, Pennsylvania.
  The Papers of General of the Army Omar N. Bradley

The Bradley Commentaries
The Chester B. Hansen Papers
   The Hansen Diary
   Office of the Chief of Military History Collection, *Supreme Command*
   The Pogue Interviews
   Senior Officers Oral History Program
      James E. Moore, General, United States Army (Retired), Oral History Interview,
      Project 84-19, Interview by Lieutenant Colonel Larry F. Paul, USA.

The Imperial War Museum, Lambeth, London.
   The Papers of Field Marshal Viscount Montgomery of Alamein
      Mr. Stephen Brooks, Introduction to The Papers of Field Marshal Viscount
      Montgomery of Alamein KG, GCE, DSO, DL, 1887-1976.
   The Papers of Major General Sir Francis de Guingand

The Liddell Hart Center for Military Archives, King's College, London.
   The Papers of Field Marshal Viscount Alanbrooke
   The Papers of Lieutenant General Sir Humphrey Myddleton Gale
   The Papers of General Hastings Lionel Baron Ismay
   The Liddell Hart Collection
      The Chester Wilmot Papers

The Public Record Office, Kew, London.
   CAB 65/44, War Cabinet Conclusions, December 1944.
   CAB 65/49, War Cabinet Conclusions, January 1945.
   CAB 65/51, War Cabinet, Confidential Annex, 12 January 1945.
   CAB 79/84, War Cabinet, Chiefs of Staff Committee, December 1944.
   CAB 80/91 War Cabinet, Chiefs of Staff Committee, January 1945.
   CAB 106/1106, "The Broad Front versus Narrow Front Controversy," Appended Notes,
   Copies of Extracts of Important Documents Not Available Elsewhere from Churchill Pa-
   pers, File 341, "OVERLORD Operations Post D-Day."
   CAB 106/1124, Diary of Admiral Sir Bertram Ramsay.
   PREM 3/341 The Prime Minister's Papers, December 1944-January 1945.

The Royal Air Force Museum, Hendon, London.
   The Papers of Air Chief Marshal Sir James Robb

The British Newspaper Library, Colindale, London.
   The *Daily Express,* August 1944-May 1945.
   The *Daily Mail,* August 1944-May 1945.
   The *Daily Mirror,* August 1944-May 1945.
   The *Daily Telegraph,* August 1944-May 1945.
   The *News Chronicle,* August 1944-May 1945; April 1946.
   The Sunday Times, August 1944-May 1945; November 1948.

The Library of Congress, Washington, D.C.
   The *New York Times,* August 1944-May 1945; 1947-1959.
   San Francisco Chronicle, August 1944-May 1945.
   The Washington *Times-Herald,* 16 August 1944.

Interview: Dr. Forrest C. Pogue, 17 March 1991.

SIGNED ARTICLES

Andidora, Ronald. "The Autumn of 1944: Boldness is Not Enough." *Parameters* 17, No. 4 (December 1987): 71-80.

Ferrell, Robert H., and Francis H. Heller. "Plain Faking?" *American Heritage* 46, No. 3 (May/June 1995): 14-16.

Galambos, Louis, Duan van Ee, and Elizabeth Hughes. "Eisenhower's First Presidency." *Columbia: The Magazine of Columbia University* 10, No. 4 (February 1985): 11-18.

Loehr, Rodney C. Review of *Top Secret,* by Ralph Ingersoll. *The American Historical Review* 52, (October 1946): 105-107.

Marshall, S.L.A. "Military Memoirs," *The Yale Review* 37 (June 1948): 757-60.

Smith, Walter Bedell. "Eisenhower's Six Great Decisions: 3, The Battle of the Bulge." *The Saturday Evening Post* 218 (22 June 1946): 46.

Smith, Walter Bedell. "Eisenhower's Six Great Decisions: 4, Victory West of the Rhine." *The Saturday Evening Post* 218 (29 June 1946): 26.

Smith, Walter Bedell, "Eisenhower's Six Great Decisions: 5, Encirclement of the Ruhr," *The Saturday Evening Post* 219 (6 July 1946): 20, 68.

REFERENCES CITED

Allen, Robert S. *Lucky Forward: The History of General Patton's Third U. S. Army.* New York: Vanguard Press, 1947. Reprint, New York: MacFadden-Bartell, 1965.

Ambrose, Stephen E. *Eisenhower.* Vol. 1, *Soldier, General of the Army, President-Elect, 1890-1952.* New York: Simon and Schuster, 1983.

Ashley, Maurice. *Churchill as Historian.* New York: Charles Scribner's Sons, 1968.

Ben-Moshe, Tuvia. *Churchill: Strategy and History.* Boulder, Colo.: Lynne Rienner Publishers; Hertfordshire: Harvester Wheatsheaf, 1991.

Bland, Larry I., ed. *George C. Marshall: Interviews and Reminiscences for Forrest C. Pogue.* Lexington, Vir.: George C. Marshall Research Foundation, 1991.

Blumenson, Martin, ed. *The Patton Papers.* Vol. 2. Boston: Houghton Mifflin, 1974.

Blumenson, Martin. *Patton: The Man Behind the Legend, 1885-1945.* New York: William Morrow, 1985. Reprint, New York: Berkley Books, 1987.

Blumenson, Martin. *The Battle of the Generals: The Untold Story of the Falaise Pocket--The Campaign That Should Have Won World War II.* New York: William Morrow, 1993.

Bradley, Omar N. *A Soldier's Story.* New York: Holt, 1951.

Bradley, Omar N., and Clay Blair. *A General's Life: An Autobiography by General of the Army Omar N. Bradley and Clay Blair.* New York: Simon and Schuster, 1983.

Bryant, Arthur. *The Turn of the Tide: A History of the War Years Based on the Diaries of Field-Marshal Lord Alanbrooke, Chief of the Imperial General Staff.* Garden City, N. Y.: Doubleday, 1957.

Bryant, Arthur. *Triumph in the West: A History of the War Years Based on the Diaries of Field-Marshal Lord Alanbrooke, Chief of the Imperial General Staff.* Garden City, N. Y.: Doubleday, 1959.

Butcher, Harry C. *My Three Years with Eisenhower: The Personal Diary of Captain Harry C. Butcher, USNR, Naval Aide to General Eisenhower, 1942 to 1945.* New York: Simon and Schuster, 1946.

Cave Brown, Anthony. *Bodyguard of Lies.* New York: Harper & Row, 1975.

Chandler, Alfred D., Jr., ed., and Stephen E. Ambrose, assoc. ed., et al. *The Papers of Dwight David Eisenhower.* Vols. 3, 4, 5, *The War Years.* Baltimore and London: The Johns Hopkins University Press, 1970.

Chandler, Alfred D., Jr., and Louis Galambos, eds., et al. *The Papers of Dwight David Eisenhower.* Vol 6, *The Occupation.* Baltimore and London: The Johns Hopkins University Press, 1978.

Churchill, Winston S. *The Second World War.* Vol. 5, *Closing the Ring.* Boston: Houghton Mifflin; Cambridge, Mass.: Riverside Press, 1951.

Churchill, Winston S. *The Second World War.* Vol. 6, *Triumph and Tragedy.* Boston: Houghton Mifflin; Cambridge, Mass.: The Riverside Press, 1953.

Clarke, Jeffrey J., and Robert Ross Smith. *Riviera to the Rhine (United States Army in World War II: The European Theater of Operations.* Washington D.C.: Center of Military History, United States Army, 1993.

Cole, Hugh M. *The Lorraine Campaign: United States Army in World War II: The European Theater of Operations.* Washington, D.C.: Historical Divisions, United States Army, 1950.

Cole, Hugh M. *The Ardennes: Battle of the Bulge. United States Army in World War II: The European Theater of Operations.* Washington, D.C.: Center of Military History, United States Army, 1993.

Colville, John. *The Fringes of Power: 10 Downing Street Diaries, 1939-1955.* New York and London: W. W. Norton, 1985.

Corlett, Charles H. *Cowboy Pete: The Autobiography of Major General Charles H. Corlett.* Edited by Wm. Farrington. Santa Fe, N. M.: Sleeping Fox Enterprises, 1974.

Creveld, Martin van. *Supplying War: Logistics from Wallenstein to Patton.* Cambridge: Cambridge University Press, 1977.

Crosswell, D.K.R. *The Chief of Staff: The Military Career of General Walter Bedell Smith.* Westport, Conn.: Greenwood Press, 1991.

Cunningham, Andrew Browne. *A Sailor's Odyssey: The Autobiography of Admiral of the Fleet Viscount Cunningham of Hyndhope.* New York: E. P. Dutton, 1951.

David, Lester, and Irene David. *Ike and Mamie: The General and His Lady.* New York: G. P. Putnam's Sons, 1981.

de Guingand, Francis. *Operation Victory.* London: Hodder and Stoughton, 1947.

de Guingand, Francis. *Generals at War.* London: Hodder and Stoughton, 1964.

de Guingand, Francis. *From Brass Hat to Bowler Hat.* London: Hamish Hamilton, 1979.

Desmond, Robert W. *Tides of War: World News Reporting, 1940-1945.* Iowa City: University of Iowa Press, 1984.

D'Este, Carlo. *Decision in Normandy.* New York: E. P. Dutton, 1983.

Ehrman, John. *Grand Strategy: August 1943-September 1944.* Vol. 5, *History of the Second World War, United Kingdom Military Series.* London: Her Majesty's Stationery Office, 1956.

Ehrman, John. *Grand Strategy: October 1944-August 1945.* Vol. 6, *History of the Second World War, United Kingdom Military Series.* London: Her Majesty's Stationery Office, 1956.

Eisenhower, David. *Eisenhower: At War, 1943-1945.* New York: Random House, 1986.

Eisenhower, Dwight D. *Crusade in Europe.* Garden City, N. Y.: Doubleday, 1948.

Eisenhower, Dwight D. *At Ease: Stories I Tell to Friends.* Garden City, N. Y.: Doubleday, 1967. Reprint, New York: Avon Books, 1968.

Ellis, John. *Brute Force: Allied Strategy and Tactics in the Second World War.* New York: Viking Press, 1990.

Ellis, Lionel F., with Arthur Warhurst. *Victory in the West.* Vol. 2, *The Defeat of Germany. History of the Second World War: United Kingdom Military Series.* London: Her Majesty's Stationery Office, 1968.

Erickson, John. *The Road to Berlin: Continuing the History of Stalin's War with Germany.* Boulder, Colo.: Westview Press, 1983.

Esposito, Vincent J., ed. *The West Point Atlas of American Wars.* Vol. 2. *1900-1953.* New York: Frederick A. Praeger, 1959.

Farago, Ladislas. *Patton: Ordeal and Triumph.* New York: Ivan Obolensky, 1964.

First United States Army, Report of Operations. Vol. 1. *1 August 1944-22 February 1945.* Washington, D.C.: Government Printing Office, 1946.

Fraser, David. *Alanbrooke.* New York: Atheneum, 1982.

Gaddis, John Lewis. *The United States and the Origins of the Cold War, 1941-1947.* New York and London: Columbia University Press, 1972.

Galambos, Louis, ed., et al. *The Papers of Dwight David Eisenhower.* Vol. 7, *The Chief of Staff.* Baltimore and London: Johns Hopkins University Press, 1978.

Galambos, Louis, ed., et al. *The Papers of Dwight David Eisenhower.* Vols. 10-11, *Columbia University.* Baltimore and London: Johns Hopkins University Press, 1984.

Gilbert, Martin. *Winston S. Churchill.* Vol. 7, *Road to Victory, 1941-1945.* Boston: Houghton Mifflin; Cambridge, Mass.: Riverside Press, 1986.

Gilbert, Martin. *Winston S. Churchill.* Vol. 8, *Never Despair, 1945-1965.* Boston: Houghton Mifflin; Cambridge, Mass.: Riverside Press, 1988.

Glantz, David M. and Jonathan M. House. *When Titans Clashed: How the Red Army Stopped Hitler.* Lawrence, Kan.: University of Kansas Press, 1995.

Graebner, Walter. *My Dear Mr. Churchill.* Boston: Houghton Mifflin; Cambridge, Mass.: Riverside Press, 1965.

Graham, Dominick, and Shelford Bidwell. *Coalitions, Politicians and Generals: Some Aspects of Command in Two World Wars.* London and New York: Brassey's, 1993.

Grigg, P. J. *Prejudice and Judgment.* London: Jonathan Cape, 1948.

Hamilton, Nigel. *Monty: The Making of a General, 1887-1942.* New York: McGraw-Hill, 1981.

Hamilton, Nigel. *Master of the Battlefield: Monty's War Years, 1942-1944.* New York: McGraw-Hill, 1983.

Hamilton, Nigel. *Monty: Final Years of the Field-Marshal, 1944-1976.* New York: McGraw-Hill, 1986.

Hinsley, F. H., E. E. Thomas, C.A.G. Simkins, and C.F.G. Ransom. *British Intelligence in the Second World War.* Volume 3, Part 2, *Its Influence on Strategy and Operations.* London: Her Majesty's Stationery Office, 1988.

Hoopes, Roy. *Ralph Ingersoll: A Biography.* New York: Atheneum, 1985.

Howarth, T.E.B., ed. *Monty at Close Quarters: Recollections of the Man.* London: Leo Cooper in association with Martin Secker and Warburg; New York: Hippocrene Books, 1985.

Ingersoll, Ralph. *Top Secret.* New York: Harcourt, Brace, 1946.

Ismay, Hastings Lionel. *The Memoirs of General Lord Ismay.* New York: Viking Press, 1960.

Keegan, John. *The Second World War.* New York: Viking Press, 1989.

Knightley, Phillip. *The First Casualty: From the Crimea to Vietnam: The War Correspondent As Hero, Propagandist, and Myth Maker*. New York: Harcourt Brace Jovanovich, 1975.

Lamb, Richard. *Montgomery in Europe, 1943-1945: Success or Failure?* London: Buchan and Enright, 1984.

Leahy, William D. *I Was There: The Personal Story of the Chief of Staff to Presidents Roosevelt and Truman Based on His Notes and Diaries Made at the Time*. New York: Whittlesey House, McGraw-Hill, 1950.

MacDonald, Charles B. *The Siegfried Line Campaign: United States Army in World War II: The European Theater of Operations*. Washington, D.C.: Office of the Chief of Military History, United States Army, 1963.

Miller, Merle. *Plain Speaking: An Oral Biography of Harry S. Truman*. New York: Berkley Publishing, 1974.

Montgomery, Bernard Law. *Normandy to the Baltic*. London: Hutchinson, 1947.

Montgomery, Bernard Law. *The Memoirs of Field-Marshal the Viscount Montgomery of Alamein*. London: Collins, 1958.

Montgomery, Brian. *A Field Marshal in the Family*. London: Constable, 1973.

Moorehead, Alan. *Montgomery*. London: Hamish Hamilton, 1946; New York: Coward-McCann, 1947.

Moran, Lord [Sir Charles Wilson]. *Churchill Taken from the Diaries of Lord Moran: The Struggle for Survival, 1940-1965*. Boston: Houghton Mifflin; Cambridge, Mass.: Riverside Press, 1966.

Morison, Samuel Eliot. *Strategy and Compromise*. Boston: Little, Brown, an Atlantic Monthly Press Book, 1958.

Oldfield, Barney. *Never a Shot in Anger*. New York: Longmans, 1956. Reprint, Santa Barbara, Calif.: Capa Press, 1989, Battle of Normandy Museum Edition.

Orange, Vincent. *Coningham: A Biography of Air Marshal Sir Arthur Coningham*. London: Methuen, 1990.

Order of Battle of the United Sates Army: World War II (European Theater of Operations: Divisions). Paris: December 1945.

Patton, George S., Jr. *War As I Knew It*. Annotated by Colonel Paul D. Harkins. Boston: Houghton Mifflin, 1947.

Payne, Robert. *The Great Man: A Portrait of Winston Churchill*. New York: Coward, McCann and Geoghegan, 1974.

Pogue, Forrest C. *The Supreme Command: United States Army in World War II: The European Theater of Operations*. Washington, D.C.: Office of the Chief of Military History, Department of the Army, 1954.

Pogue, Forrest C. *George C. Marshall: Organizer of Victory, 1943-1945*. New York: Viking Press, 1973.

Report by the Supreme Commander to the Combined Chiefs of Staff on the Operations in Europe of the Allied Expeditionary Force, 6 June 1944 to 8 May 1945. Washington, D.C.: Government Printing Office, 1945. Reprint, New York: Arco Publishing, 1946.

Richardson, Charles. *Send for Freddie: The Story of Monty's Chief of Staff Major-General Sir Francis de Guingand*. London: William Kimber, 1987.

Ruppenthal, Roland G. *Logistical Support of the Armies, May 1941-September 1944*. Vol. 1, *United States Army in World War II: The European Theater of Operations*. Washington, D.C.: Office of the Chief of Military History, Department of the Army, 1953.

Ruppenthal, Roland G. *Logistical Support of the Armies, September 1944-May 1945.* Vol. 2, *United States Army in World War II: The European Theater of Operations.* Washington, D.C.: Office of the Chief of Military History, Department of the Army, 1959.

Ryan, Cornelius. *The Last Battle.* New York: Simon and Schuster, 1966. Reprint, New York: Pocket Books, 1967.

Sherwood, Robert E. *Roosevelt and Hopkins: An Intimate History.* New York: Harper and Brothers, 1948.

Sixsmith, E.K.G. *Eisenhower as Military Commander.* New York: Stein and Day, a Da Capo Paperback, 1973.

Smith, Walter Bedell. *Eisenhower's Six Great Decisions: Europe, 1944-1945.* New York and London: Longmans, Green, 1956.

Stacey, Charles P. *The Victory Campaign.* Vol. 3, *The Operations in North-West Europe, 1944-1945. Official History of the Canadian Army in the Second World War.* Ottawa: Queen's Printer and Controller of Stationery, 1960.

Summersby, Kay. *Eisenhower Was My Boss.* Edited by Michael Kearns. New York: Prentice-Hall, 1948.

Tedder, Arthur. *With Prejudice: The War Memoirs of Marshal of the Royal Air Force Lord Tedder.* Boston: Little, Brown, 1966.

Weigley, Russell F. *Eisenhower's Lieutenants: The Campaign of France and Germany, 1944-1945.* Bloomington: Indiana University Press, 1981.

Weinberg, Gerhard L. *A World at Arms: A Global History of World War II.* Cambridge: Cambridge University Press, 1994.

Wheeler-Bennett, Sir John. *The Nemesis of Power: The German Army in Politics, 1918-1945.* New York: St. Martin's Press, 1964.

Willmott, H. P. *The Great Crusade: A New Complete History of the Second World War.* New York: Free Press, 1991.

Wilmot, Chester. *The Struggle for Europe.* London: Collins; New York: Harper and Brothers, 1952.

Wyant, William K. *Sandy Patch: A Biography of Lt. Gen. Alexander M. Patch.* Westport, Conn.: Praeger, 1991.

Index

94; and Churchill, 99, 100; Eisenhower, and ground command, 19-20,
171; Yalta Conference, 108
Rotterdam, Germany, 105, 106
Ruhr, Germany, 1, 15, 17, 77, 83, 84,
108, 110, 142; Allied strategy, 5, 16,
74, 150, 172; and Antwerp, 110,
172; Bradley, 73, 167; Eisenhower,
131, 155; encirclement of, 32, 56,
73, 80, 173; German war effort, 38,
46, 150; Montgomery, 120-22, 124,
132, 156, 170; nationalistic considerations, 60, 161; Ramsay, 86;
Ruhr pocket, 73; and the Saar, 84,
97, 132
Rundstedt, Field Marshal Gerd von
(Commander in chief West), 17, 21,
22, 78, 148
Ruppenthal, Roland G., (Official
historian, U.S. Army), *Logistical
Support of the Armies,* 2 vols., 5,
142-48, 157, 173; COMZ, 143;
expedients, 144-45; ports, 146; Red
Ball and Red Lion Express, 145
Russians: and Allied victory, 6, 35, 56,
142, 169; and eastern Europe, 62, 83,
172-73; junction with, 108-9

Saar, Germany, 84, 97, 119, 120, 123;
Saar offensive, 75, 76
A Sailor's Odyssey. See Cunningham,
Admiral Sir Andrew B.: post-war
St. Vith, Belgium, 76
Saturday Evening Post, 4, 15, 32, 40,
52, 53, 56
Scheldt Estuary, Belgium, Holland, 77,
148; German Fifteenth Army and,
174; opening of, 73-74, 85, 86-87,
96, 156
Schimpf, Major General Richard (3rd
German Parachute Division), 42
Seine River, France, 32, 38, 144, 145,
164
September 1944, ending war in, 110;
assumptions, 84-85; Bradley on, 167;
Collins and, 173; ethnocentrism, 5,
65, 169; gasoline and, 145-46; myth
of, 161, 168-69; Patton and, 103,
166-67; possibilities, 5, 56, 84; truck

companies and, 146; weather, 145,
173, 174; World War I, comparison,
142
SHAEF (Supreme Headquarters Allied
Expeditionary Force), 2, 24, 36, 57,
60, 75, 103, 110, 117, 163; Bulge
command shift, 76-78; diaries, 3, 45,
165; meetings at, 73-74, 86-87, 127,
165, 166; OVERLORD plan, 144;
planning staff, and broad front, 33-
34, 104, 155; politics and, 123-24,
161; PRD, 10, 11, 77; "prolonged"
the war, 25, 31, 40, 42, 47, 58, 62,
63, 64, 65, 84, 167; Ramsay and, 86
SHAPE (Supreme Headquarters Allied
Powers Europe), 72, 116-17
Shepley, James (*Time*), 19
Sherwood, Robert E., (*Roosevelt and
Hopkins*), 94
Sibert, Brigadier General Edwin (Intelligence officer 12th Army Group), 80
Siegfried Line, Germany, 31, 38, 40,
56, 74, 142, 143, 155, 162, 166-67,
174
Simpson, Major General Frank E.
(DMO), 165, 170
Simpson, General William (Ninth U.S.
Army), 45, 74, 75, 76, 77, 99
single-thrust strategy, 1, 31, 38, 47, 62-
63, 83, 104, 119, 120, 148; British
Chiefs and, 150; documentation and,
164; fallacy, 173; immobilizing Patton, 15, 31, 35, 38, 41, 74, 75, 85-
86, 104, 120, 148, 149, 172; operational necessity, 161; Patton and, 40,
42, 47, 103, 105, 166; politics, 172;
risks to coalition, 35, 172, 175; postwar: Wilmot's influence on, 82-83,
168. *See also* Montgomery, Field
Marshal Sir Bernard Law; single-
thrust plan
Smith, General Walter Bedell Smith
(Chief of staff SHAEF), 4, 32, 34,
36, 52, 75, 76, 80, 87, 105, 107, 109,
118, 121, 123, 129, 135; Brooke, 18-
19, 48, 108; Montgomery, 128, 165,
104, 170; post-war: broad-front
strategy, 32-33; "Eisenhower's Six
Great Decisions," *Saturday Evening*

About the Author

G. E. PATRICK MURRAY is professor of history at Valley Forge Military College.

ISBN 0-275-94795-5

90000>

EAN

9 780275 947958

HARDCOVER BAR CODE